W9-DAQ-646

Nature and the Environment in Twentieth-Century American Life

**The Greenwood Press
"Daily Life Through History" Series**

The Age of Charlemagne
John J. Butt

The Age of Sail
Dorothy Denneen Volo and James M. Volo

The American Revolution
Dorothy Denneen Volo and James M. Volo

The Ancient Egyptians
Bob Brier and Hoyt Hobbs

The Ancient Greeks
Robert Garland

Ancient Mesopotamia
Karen Rhea Nemet–Nejat

The Ancient Romans
David Matz

The Aztecs: People of the Sun and Earth
David Carrasco with Scott Sessions

The Byzantine Empire
Marcus Rautman

Chaucer's England
Jeffrey L. Singman and Will McLean

Civil War America
Dorothy Denneen Volo and James M. Volo

Colonial New England
Claudia Durst Johnson

Early Modern Japan
Louis G. Perez

The Early American Republic, 1790–1820:
Creating a New Nation
David S. Heidler and Jeanne T. Heidler

18th-Century England
Kirstin Olsen

Elizabethan England
Jeffrey L. Singman

The Holocaust
Eve Nussbaum Soumerai and Carol D. Schulz

The Inca Empire
Michael A. Malpass

The Industrial United States, 1870–1900
Julie Husband and Jim O'Loughlin

Jews in the Middle Ages
Norman Roth

Maya Civilization
Robert J. Sharer

Medieval Europe
Jeffrey L. Singman

The Medieval Islamic World
James E. Lindsay

The Mongol Empire
George Lane

The Nineteenth Century American Frontier
Mary Ellen Jones

The Nubians
Robert S. Bianchi

The Old Colonial Frontier
James M. Volo and Dorothy Denneen Volo

Renaissance Italy
Elizabeth S. Cohen and Thomas V. Cohen

The Roman City: Rome, Pompeii, and Ostia
Gregory S. Aldrete

Science and Technology in Colonial America
William E. Burns

Science and Technology in the
Nineteenth-Century America
Todd Timmons

The Soviet Union
Katherine B. Eaton

The Spanish Inquisition
James M. Anderson

Traditional China: The Tang Dynasty
Charles Benn

The United States, 1920–1939: Decades of
Promise and Pain
David E. Kyvig

The United States, 1940–1959: Shifting
Worlds
Eugenia Kaledin

The United States, 1960–1990:
Decades of Discord
Myron A. Marty

Victorian England
Sally Mitchell

The Vikings
Kirsten Wolf

World War I
Neil M. Heyman

NATURE AND THE ENVIRONMENT IN TWENTIETH-CENTURY AMERICAN LIFE

BRIAN BLACK

The Greenwood Press "Daily Life Through History" Series
Nature and the Environment in Everyday Life

Greenwood Press
Westport, Connecticut • London

Library of Congress Cataloging-in-Publication Data

Black, Brian, 1966–
    Nature and the environment in twentieth-century American life / Brian Black.
        p. cm—(The Greenwood Press "Daily life through history" series, ISSN 1080–4749)
    Includes bibliographical references and index.
    ISBN 0–313–33200–2
    1. Human ecology—United States—History—20th century. 2. Nature—Social aspects—United States—History—20th century. 3. Green movement—United States. 4. United States—Social conditions—20th century.   I. Title.   II. Series.
    GF503.B54   2006
    304.20973'0904—dc22   2005036622

British Library Cataloguing in Publication Data is available.

Library of Congress Catalog Card Number: 2005036622
ISBN: 0–313–33200–2
ISSN: 1080–4749

First published in 2006

Greenwood Press, 88 Post Road West, Westport, CT 06881
An imprint of Greenwood Publishing Group, Inc.
www.greenwood.com   ,

Printed in the United States of America

The paper used in this book complies with the
Permanent Paper Standard issued by the National
Information Standards Organization (Z39.48–1984).

10 9 8 7 6 5 4 3 2 1

For Dick and Hazel who brought me to both the nature of marsh mud and the modernity of city life.

Contents

Preface

Nature in everyday life requires that we attach blinders to our view of history. We are not interested in each historical event; in fact, there are many essential events of twentieth-century American history that this volume will not discuss at all. Great characters of American history will likely be entirely overlooked. Our "historical blinders" help us to spotlight what is most important to our specific approach to historical information.

The perspective used to tell history in these pages accentuates the idea of nature. American definitions of terms such as "nature" or "environment" change a great deal over time. This book seeks to catalogue such changes in definition from radical environmentalists who believed God could be found in nature to scientists who tried to alter the nature of the human species.

The resources that compose the natural environment are a crucial part of this story. With each alteration to American ideas of nature, resources are used differently. Often, the use of resources functions as a weather vane to indicate shifts in national ideals. During one era, the Mississippi River may be seen as a tremendous foe to be tamed, while at another time it may be a great treasure to be preserved. A blade of turf grass in suburban California may at once appear as a leap forward for American society and in another moment as a blasphemous transgression of natural limitations. And a refinery for chemical or petroleum production might signal economic progress for one era and a toxic pollutant for later generations. Nature may at one moment seem to be Americans' great partner in building a solid future while in other moments—such as Hurricane Katrina in 2005—our nemesis. This volume seeks to tell some of those stories.

This approach to understanding the past is often contained within a branch of historical inquiry called "environmental history." Although the bibliography for this book will provide many useful sources in the field, readers who would like to know more about environmental history should contact: http://www.h-net.org/~environ/ASEH/welcome_NN6.html.

A portrait of American life from this perspective takes shape after quite a few years of teaching this material. My students in environmental history consistently offer me new ideas and the opportunity to better contextualize old ones. I would like to thank my students and colleagues at the New York University, University of Kansas, Gettysburg College, Skidmore College, and Penn State Altoona for their contributions over the years. Finally, Carole Bookhammer and Clyde Black provided me superior assistance in preparing this manuscript.

INTRODUCTION: DESIGNING THE HUMAN FUTURE

In 1893, the United States rallied as never before to direct its combined resources of finance and technology toward a single end. The outcome was not a new method of producing goods, a remedy for a common illness, or a weapon to defeat a desperate enemy. And yet, the outcomes that were related to this effort eventually included these and many other great accomplishments of the twentieth century. Like much of twentieth-century American life, these outcomes derive from the modern idea of using technology to solve problems of everyday, domestic life.

In 1893, as the world changed rapidly for citizens of any industrialized country, Americans concentrated their abilities and their aspirations to create a spectacle for the world in the World's Columbian Exposition in Chicago, Illinois. Visitors, it was hoped, would tour the Exposition and come away with an understanding of where the nation intended to go in the future. The designers hoped that by creating the site they would in some small way help create that future. To create this site, designers manipulated nature to create a park and fairground that could thrill and impress any visitor. In doing so, the creators of the Columbian Exposition created a symbol for an age when technology and the solutions of engineering were no longer relegated to factories and workplaces.

Historian Thomas Hughes calls technology the "effort to organize the world for problem solving so that goods and services can be invented, developed, produced, and used" (Hughes, *Genesis,* 6). The surge of American society toward technology grew out of European models. Hughes continues:

The Europeans held up a mirror in which the Americans could see themselves as the raw materials of modernity which the Europeans wanted to fashion into modern

World's Fair, Chicago, 1893. Lagoon looking east from Transportation Building.
Courtesy Library of Congress.

culture. European engineers, industrialists, artists, and architects came to America
to admire its "plumbing and its bridges" and made . . . the second discovery of
America—the great systems of production. . . . In so doing they were inventing the
forms and symbols for a modern technological culture. (Hughes, *Genesis*, 9)

This rethinking of the human condition, including its relationship to the
natural world, helps make the twentieth century one of dramatic change.
Historian Stephen Kern writes: "These old scaffoldings had supported
the way of life and culture of the Western world for so long that no one
could recall exactly how they all started or why they were still there, and
it took a generation of restless scientists, artists, and philosophers to dismantle them. . ." (Kern, 210). In Kern's argument, the modern sensibility
redefined essential human concepts, including those of time, space, and
self. In each of these relationships, technology now brokered an important
role. Such was also true with the American relationship with the natural
world. Although interest in nature grew rapidly in dynamic new fashions
during the twentieth century, it was most often seen through the ideas
of management, planning, and regulation that human technology placed
around all the resources that we needed to live.

VISIONS OF THE WHITE CITY

The "White City," as the spectacle was popularly called, spread out in front of the world in 1893 and demonstrated where the United States wanted to go in the future. Standing at the dawn of the twentieth century— what *Time* magazine founder Henry Luce would later dub the "American century"—the White City helped to define the way Americans did basic things, including leisure and planning. Through its use of technology and planning, in particular, the White City established a new instrumentalized role for the natural environment in the life of most Americans. The grand landscape of the Columbian Exposition was one of the first planned, multi-use sites in American history; despite this tremendous feat, however, it remained a landscape ripe with irony.

Intended as a celebration of Columbus's voyages 400 years prior, the Exposition attracted more than 27 million visitors in its single year of existence. That was the irony of the great spectacle—this great example of modern design was not intended to last. The material that held together the exterior of many buildings resembled papier-mâché and began disintegrating after one year. Designers and architects had made buildings that could be dismantled and moved elsewhere or whose infrastructure could be used for other purposes. Ironically, this aspect of modern planning became even more pronounced in the "disposable society" that followed World War II.

The symbol of a great American past and future, the White City also became a symbol of the nation's precarious present. The industrial, and increasingly electrical, revolutions were transforming America at a remarkable pace. Most Americans no longer earned their living on farms, but worked in factories and lived in urban centers. Historian Alan Trachtenberg calls this an era of the "incorporation of America," the shift of social control from the people and government to big business (Trachtenberg, 3–10). Overall, the United States was in the process of shifting from a producer society to one of consumers. This required a culture that accepted and even expected consumption. As strikes, economic depression, and social issues (such as unemployment and homelessness) marred the early 1890s, the nation collectively looked to a more positive future, a glimpse of which could be found in the "White City."

Many American historians have dubbed the World's Columbian Exposition the beginning of the consumer-based society that would go on to prosper in the twentieth century. While some of the designers and conceivers of the fair might have entertained such aspirations, the real success of the World's Columbian Exposition derived from its timing. Most important, the 1890s witnessed the emergence of revolutionary new technologies that radically altered everyday human life. The fair offered an opportunity for the unveiling of such innovations. In addition, modern thought was reconsidering a variety of ideas relating to social progress and the laissez-faire treatment of corporations. All together, the fair created symbols of American aspirations and ideals, even if some of these symbols were icons of consumption, including Juicy Fruit Gum, Pabst Blue Ribbon beer, ragtime music, and Quaker Oats.

Financially, the World's Columbian Exposition was an overwhelming success. The world—now equipped with modes of transportation that facilitated tourism—had never seen anything like it. Although August attracted 3.5 million visitors, the month of October nearly doubled this figure with more than 6.8 million paid visitors. The concession stands alone brought in over $4 million. The final calculations revealed in excess of a $1 million surplus for the fair's 30,000 stockholders. More important, though, in the stretch of Chicago known most for its worthless swampland, the United States had grasped a glimpse of its future (Columbian Exposition).

NEW IDEAS ABOUT NATURE

The White City, of course, was no city at all. It had no residences or utilities; however, it was a fully designed space. The greatest landscape planner of the era, Frederick Law Olmsted, who had designed New York's Central Park in 1862, gave the Columbian Exposition a unifying ground plan. In its unity, the landscape taught visitors about beauty and living among art while also possessing state-of-the-art amenities and technologies.

The scene's aesthetic beauty was a coordination of Olmsted's management of water, ornamental plants, and landscape art with the structures that had been organized by the director of works Daniel H. Burnham, one of the first great American architects. As an overall design, Burnham wanted a neoclassical style set in overwhelming whiteness. Seven hundred acres of swampy land had been dredged and filled to create artificial canals, plazas, promenades, lagoons, and even a forest preserve. This setting then held 400 buildings, each with an intricate design and specific purpose (i.e., Manufactures, Agriculture, Electricity, and Women's Progress). The idea of a landscape that both performed and functioned well while also appearing beautiful seemed a fantasy to visitors who resided in farms and cities thick with the grit and grime of life in 1893. Trachtenberg writes, "For a summer's moment, White City had seemed the fruition of a nation, a culture, a whole society: the celestial city of man set upon a hill for all the world to behold" (Trachtenberg, 230).

In laying out this new city form, Burnham relied on overall organization and symmetry. This was most obvious in the Court of Honor, where the elaborate buildings balanced one another around Olmsted's system of pools, trees, and bridges. To most visitors, Machinery Hall was the grandest attraction of all. It covered 17 acres and housed an elevated, moveable crane. Two dynamos powered a 2,000-horsepower engine and lit nearly 20,0000 lights. Although the structure was made of steel and iron, it was covered with the white plaster-like material called "staff" that covered most of the structures in the court. It was this plaster veneer that added a fantasy-like aura to the landscape, transforming the diverse structures into the spectacle known as the "White City." Trachtenberg observes that these buildings were "composed . . . as pictures of art, thus establishing the place of culture in relation to the activities of society embodied by the exhibitions within" (Trachtenberg, 215–16).

Although there were many significant speakers at the Exposition, the words of one have proven to have remarkable repercussions: the lecture given by Frederick Jackson Turner, which is now referred to as the "Frontier Thesis." Using demographic data from counties in the western territories, Turner proclaimed that the American West was populated and, therefore, "settled." He worried that Americans now had to live without the emotional and demographic "safety valve" of the empty western lands. Turner spoke of a spiritual frontier as well as a physical one, and he urged Americans to now seek out new challenges (Smith, *Virgin Land,* 15–20).

Historian Roderick Nash argued that Turner's formulation forced Americans to reconfigure the expansive spirit that had driven the nation's development thus far. Some energy would be channeled abroad, providing the United States with a new prominence in global affairs. In addition, the American effort to tame the wilderness would be channeled to a new effort to preserve remaining wild areas. The preservation impulse grew from panic concerning overdevelopment as well as a growing aesthetic appreciation for the beauty of raw nature. This impulse resulted in the movement for National Parks as well as in efforts to conserve natural resources. Turner's general theme about limits, however, could be found at the core of each (Nash, 24).

TECHNOLOGY AND THE MIDDLE GROUND

Behind the pastoral, park-like façade of the White City lurked the primary agent of change: new technological advances. The early 1900s involved such significant change that these years moved Karl Marx to describe them as follows:

All fixed, fast-frozen relations, with their train of ancient and venerable prejudices and opinions, are swept away, all new-formed ones become antiquated before they can ossify. All that is solid melts into air, all that is holy is profaned, and men at last are forced to face . . . the real conditions of their lives and their relations with their fellow men. (quoted in Berman, 21)

At the Exposition, technology was symbolically portrayed as the nation's successful future. But there was a cost to technological development. Trachtenberg observes the other side of this equation when he writes: "If the machine seemed the prime cause of the abundance of new products changing the character of daily life, it also seemed responsible for newly visible poverty, slums, and an unexpected wretchedness of industrial conditions" (Trachtenberg, 38). The realities of the vicious change wrought on society by the machine were most acute at the beginning of the century when factories concentrated labor into the cities that they polluted. Reform and regulation informed better urban planning and eventually helped create new understandings of environmental health.

The pace of growth stemming from the technology emerging at the start of the twentieth century cannot be overstated. Historian John R. McNeil estimates that during this century, the world's gross domestic product increased by more than 10 times. The world population also increased incredibly: demographic historians estimate that if one took all the years lived by the 80 billion hominids that have ever been born in the past four million years, 20 percent of those years took place during the twentieth century (McNeil, 8–9). The engine behind this century of rapid change was the United States, which became the international industrial leader by the end of World War I.

Technology came to permeate every aspect of American life. For instance, the literary scholar Leo Marx argues that American culture is defined by two alternating pulls: the machine toward technological advancement and the garden toward aesthetic and natural beauty (Marx, 2–10). In this formulation, however, Marx makes room for a middle ground between technology and nature. City planner and writer Lewis Mumford believed that the application of modernist design helped to construct such a middle ground in urban spaces (Mumford, 321–25). This was one of the primary tasks of planners and designers (such as Mumford) who emerged after 1900. Just as Burnham and Olmsted had created a new reality at the Exposition, urban planners rationalized human existence and planned its most suitable environment. Possibly, the most startling intellectual revolution of the twentieth century was the ability to entirely diminish the human's role in the natural world. In other words, just as humans mastered very unnatural forms such as the urban skyscraper, they alternatively realized what was being lost and initiated efforts to set aside other areas from development.

In the same general time period that Americans constructed the Empire State Building, Hoover Dam, and some of the early highways, a scholar in the Wisconsin marsh developed an ethic that would inspire environmentalists for generations. Referred to as the "Land Ethic," the words written by Aldo Leopold contained a new way of viewing the human's place within the natural environment. He wrote:

In short, a land ethic changes the role of Homo sapiens from conqueror of the land-community to plain member and citizen of it. It implies respect for his fellow-members, and also respect for the community as such. (Leopold, 240)

Although this perspective draws inspiration from romanticism of the nineteenth century, the Land Ethic is grounded in new scientific understandings of the mid-twentieth century. Therefore, just as engineers taught us new, innovative ways to solve everyday problems, scientists, writers, and naturalists took the opportunity to better explain and consider the complexity of the human condition, particularly as we relate to the natural world.

Armed with a modern sensibility such as that exhibited at the Columbian Exposition, Americans redefined many portions of their everyday lives. Cities took shape in difficult climates and locations suspended by only the contrivances of modern technology. During the twentieth century, nature brought momentary reminders of our tenuous relationship with nature in some of these locations. In 2005, for example, Hurricane Katrina wrought a reminder of nature's power that promises to last more than a moment.

Although the heavy manipulation of nature brought heightened impacts on the natural world, it also helped to usher in the beginning of an environmental sensibility. During the twentieth century, both

Water view from southwest of Wright's Fallingwater as seen from downstream. Courtesy Library of Congress.

perspectives—the use of technology and the appreciation of the natural environment—each gathered the interest of the American public. In this era of modernity, we can locate a few symbols of the compromise that became necessary.

Nestled in the White City, one could find a stunning Japanese cottage built by the unknown protégé of one of the greatest American architects, Louis Sullivan. In the Asian styling and the use of natural forms, one could make out the fusion of modernist sensibilities with an awareness of natural forms and materials. Four decades later, the organic architecture of the young architect reached its maturity in the Laurel Highlands of Pennsylvania. Frank Lloyd Wright's design in Pennsylvania was the renowned structure known as Fallingwater. Utilizing modern technology to cantilever the structure like a diving board from a hillside, Wright merged the building's form with the rushing water of the mountain stream (Smith, *Modern*, 142–45).

Today, Fallingwater remains the preeminent example of designing with nature as builders and landscape designers continue to try to infuse their forms with a similar ethic. In this effort for reconciliation, Fallingwater presents a suitable representation for Americans' relationship with nature during the entire twentieth century. As this volume traces the role of nature in everyday life during the twentieth century, though, it demonstrates the significant vacillations within this relationship.

Undoubtedly, during the twentieth century Americans became the most technologically advanced humans that the world had ever seen. Although the details of these technical feats are fascinating as well, the most remarkable point might be that massive technological development contributed to perpetuating and complicating Americans' relationship with nature. In short, during the twentieth century Americans' fascination with nature did not diminish; instead, Americans used new technologies and scientific understanding to define for themselves a new place in the natural world.

1

RESOURCE EXPANSION

EVERYDAY SETTING: SPINDLETOP, TEXAS

Without warning, the level plains of eastern Texas near Beaumont abruptly give way to a lone, rounded hill before returning to flatness. Geologists call these abrupt rises in the land "domes" because hollow caverns lie beneath. Over time, layers of rock rise to a common apex and create a spacious reservoir underneath. Often, salt forms in these empty, geological bubbles, creating a salt dome. Over millions of years, water or other material might fill the reservoir. At least, that was Patillo Higgins's idea in eastern Texas during the 1890s.

Higgins and others imagined such caverns as natural treasure-houses. Higgins's intrigue grew with one dome-shaped hill in southeast Texas. Known as Spindletop, this salt dome—with Higgins's help—would change human existence.

Texas had not yet been identified as an oil producer. Well-known oil country lay in the Eastern United States, particularly western Pennsylvania. Titusville, Pennsylvania introduced Americans to massive amounts of crude oil for the first time in 1859. By the 1890s, petroleum-derived kerosene had become the world's most popular fuel for lighting. Thomas Edison's experiments with electric lighting placed petroleum's future in doubt; however, petroleum still stimulated boom wherever it was found. But in Texas? Every geologist who inspected the "Big Hill" at Spindletop told Higgins that he was a fool.

With growing frustration, Higgins placed a magazine advertisement requesting someone to drill on the Big Hill. The only response came from Captain Anthony F. Lucas, who had prospected domes in Texas for salt and sulfur. On January 10, 1901, Lucas's drilling crew, known as "roughnecks" for the hard physical labor of drilling pipe deep into Earth, found mud bubbling in their drill hole. The sound of a cannon turned to a roar and suddenly oil spurted out of the hole. The Lucas geyser, found at a depth of 1,139 feet, blew a stream of oil over 100 feet high until it was capped nine days later. During this period, the well flowed an estimated 100,000 barrels a day—well beyond any flows previously witnessed. Lucas finally gained control of the geyser on January 19. By this point, a huge pool of oil surrounded it. Throngs of oilmen, speculators, and onlookers came and transformed the city of Beaumont into Texas's first oil boomtown.

The flow from this well, named Lucas 1, was unlike anything witnessed before in the petroleum industry: 75,000 barrels per day. As news of the gusher reached around the world, the Texas oil boom was on. Land sold for wildly erratic prices. After a few months over 200 wells had been sunk on the Big Hill. By the end of 1901, an estimated $235 million had been invested in oil in Texas. This was the new frontier of oil; however, the industry's scale had changed completely at Spindletop. Unimaginable amounts of petroleum—and the raw energy that it contained—were now available at a low enough price to become part of every American's life.

ENERGY FUTURES

Oil was just one example of the expansive culture of the early twentieth century. When the historian Frederick Jackson Turner stood at the Columbian Exposition in 1893 and offered his concern that the frontier had closed, he did not suggest what alternatives Americans might use to fill that void. With the help of massive supplies of raw energy, though, technology quickly became one of the clearest applications of the American expansionary spirit in the new century.

More than any human civilization before it, twentieth-century Americans tied their everyday life to the expenditure of energy. In the

Spindle Top oil field, Beaumont, Texas. Courtesy Library of Congress.

most conventional sense, energy is the capacity to do work. In 1850, the United States consumed 2.5 trillion BTUs of energy. By 1910 this had risen to 16.5 trillion BTUs, and it would more than double by 1950 and then again by 1970 to 72.5 trillion BTUs. Today, U.S. energy use exceeds 80 quadrillion BTUs, which breaks down to approximately 300 million BTUs per person. The change in energy use after the Civil War was an expression of a new culture of industry. In 1860 there were fewer than one and a half million factory workers in the country; by 1920 there were 8.5 million. In 1860 there were about 31,000 miles of railroad in the United States; by 1915, there were nearly 250,000 miles. Such infrastructure demanded energy to power it (Melosi, 34).

The most flexible source of energy was electricity. Thomas Edison, Nicholas Tesla, and other inventor/entrepreneurs were rapidly devising new technologies that allowed electricity to be moved from place to place and applied to a variety of tasks. With the expansion of electricity, the early 1900s saw a rapid redefinition of the basic physics of nature in everyday life. The scale and scope of human work expanded with the assistance of additional energy sources, called prime movers. Coal, a product of the nineteenth century, remained the primary source of heat to produce electricity. For other tasks, though, the more flexible liquid hydrocarbon, petroleum, became increasingly important in everyday American life. Indeed, the expansion of petroleum through Spindletop and beyond defined many social, political, and technological aspects of the twentieth century.

A GLOBAL COMMODITY

The commodification of petroleum, of course, preceded Patillo Higgins. In fact, by the late 1800s, John D. Rockefeller had exploited petroleum to redefine corporate business. Working within the South Improvement Company for much of the late 1860s, Rockefeller laid the groundwork for his effort to control the entire industry at each step in its process. Rockefeller's Standard Oil first demonstrated the possible domination available to those who controlled the flow of crude oil if it became a primary part of human life. Rockefeller's system of refineries grew so great that at the close of the nineteenth century he could demand lower rates and eventually even kickbacks from rail companies. One by one he put his competitors out of business, and his own corporation grew into what observers in the late 1800s called a trust (what, today, is called a monopoly). Standard's reach extended throughout the world and it became a symbol of the "Gilded Age," when businesses were allowed to grow too large and benefit only a few wealthy people. Reformers vowed things would change (Chernow, 438–40).

Before they changed, however, Rockefeller and Standard Oil exported petroleum technology and began exploiting supplies worldwide. The modern-day oil company became a version of the joint-stock companies that had been created by European royalty to explore the world during the period of mercantilism of the 1600s. Now, though, behemoth oil companies were transnational corporations, largely unregulated and seeking one thing: crude oil. Wherever "black gold" was found, oil tycoons set the wheels of development in motion. Boomtowns modeled after those in the Pennsylvania oil fields could suddenly pop up in Azerbaijan, Borneo, or Sumatra (Yergin, 117–19).

In the United States, the supply of oil was a far cry from the domestic supplies of a century later. As East Texas gushers created uncontrollable lakes of crude, no one considered the idea of shortage or conservation. Even the idea of importing oil was a foreign concept. California and Texas flooded the market with more than enough crude oil and then from nearly nowhere, Oklahoma emerged in 1905 to become the nation's greatest oil producer. Texas recaptured the top spot in 1928 and has been the nation's largest producer of petroleum ever since. Its image has been inextricably linked with oil in popular culture, thanks to films such as *Giant* (1960) and *Boomtown* (1949), television programs such as *Dallas,* and oil executives-turned-politicians such as George Bush, George W. Bush, and Dick Cheney. This image suggests the larger legacy of Spindletop.

THE MARRIAGE OF OIL AND THE AUTOMOBILE

How could a single resource become so intertwined with everyday American life? The single greatest development lay in the transportation sector. This sector of Americans' lives changed radically during the early twentieth century. A steady supply of cheap crude oil became the necessary resource to support everyday American life after 1900, particularly after Americans had begun their love affair with the automobile. However, this affair almost never began.

When Oliver Evans built the first motor vehicle in the United States in 1805, his prime mover of choice was steam. A combination dredge and flatboat, it operated on land and water. Richard Dudgeon's road engine of 1867, which resembled a farm tractor, could carry 10 passengers. By the late 1890s, nearly 100 manufacturers were marketing steam-driven automobiles. Twin brothers Francis E. and Freelan O. Stanley of the United States received the greatest fame of the steamer era with their 1897 creation of the "Stanley Steamer." Most of the models of steam cars burned kerosene to heat water in a tank that was contained on the car. The pressure of escaping steam activated the car's driving mechanism, which moved the vehicle. The popularity of the steam car declined at about the time of World War I and production came to an end in 1929. This was not, however, due to a decline in interest in automobility. Instead, powerful interests had swayed Americans toward a new model of vehicle construction.

Some Americans adopted electrically powered automobiles that were built in Europe by the 1880s. In the United States, William Morrison is credited with the first "electric" in 1891. Other manufacturers followed quickly though, and, between 1896-1915, 54 American manufacturers turned out almost 35,000 vehicles. Many people thought the great models of the era, including, the Columbia, the Baker, and the Riker were just the beginning; however, the first decade of the twentieth century turned out to be the high-point of the American manufacture of electrics. Most early electrics, however, did not run efficiently at speeds of more than 20 miles per hour. In addition, most were difficult to charge. Early electrics were assumed to be limited to city use. The true revolution in automobility would first require a new source of energy.

This moment of historical convergence brings together the timing of the strike at Spindletop with the public's growing interest in the speed and independence of the automobile. The massive quantities of petroleum drove its price downward. Edison's experiments with electric lighting forced those in the industry, particularly Rockefeller of Standard Oil, to search for new uses for petroleum. When Henry Ford and other entrepreneurs began manufacturing autos in the United States, they followed the urging of Rockefeller and others and opted for a design powered by an internal combustion engine that used gasoline, derived from petroleum. Patillo Higgins's dream at Spindletop helped to define human life and world power in the twentieth century by revolutionizing transportation in everyday American life (Yergin, 40–43).

HENRY FORD DEMOCRATIZES THE AUTOMOBILE

American inventors vied to be the first to create a workable automobile model before 1900. J. Frank and Charles E. Duryea are credited with manufacturing the United States' first working gasoline-powered automobile in 1893. The first commercial production of the Duryea car began in 1896. However, in the same year, the automobile revolutionary, Henry Ford, also successfully operated his first auto in Detroit. How would such inventions get to the consumer? By 1899 Percy Owen opened the first automobile salesroom in New York City. Auto shows soon followed. They helped to get information to the public about American manufacturers' interest in making the United States the world's first automobile nation.

The manufacture of automobiles quickly shifted from the efforts of independent inventors to become the world's largest industry. Manufacturers of many items experimented with mass production; however, automobiles became the first new product to be entirely defined by this new manufacturing process. Although Ford is often credited with first mass production of automobiles, Ransom E. Olds in 1901 became the first auto manufacturer to employ mass-production methods. In its first year, his company manufactured a shocking 400 vehicles, each selling for approximately $650. Unlike other manufacturing processes, mass-production

Model T: four-cylinder Model T Ford, 1908. Courtesy Library of Congress.

was a relatively vague term. It was impossible to patent. Therefore, other manufacturers, including Henry M. Leland and Ford, also experimented with applying mass-production processes to the manufacture of automobiles. However, other aspects of early automobiles proved to be extremely contentious.

The gas-powered engine, for instance, had been patented by George B. Selden, an American attorney, in 1879. The bulk of American manufacturers formed an association in 1903 that would recognize the Selden patent and pay him a royalty on each car that came off of their assembly lines. Ford, however, demonstrated his rebelliousness by refusing to go along with the other manufacturers. In fact, he filed suit to break Selden's hold on the manufacture of gas-powered engines. It was this independent sense of business that helped to make Ford a revolutionary figure in American industry. In 1911 Ford was vindicated when a court ruled that Selden's patent only applied to one engine design. Manufacturers were free to utilize other designs without paying Selden royalties (Kay, 154–58). In the interim, Ford had set the table for his great success.

Using mass production, Ford's assembly line produced the first of his famous Model T autos in 1908. During the next twenty years, Ford's plants manufactured more than 15 million Model Ts. Although it only came in one color and lacked pizzazz, the Model T, nicknamed the "flivver" and the "tin lizzie," revolutionized the automotive history. Although auto manufacturing came to a standstill during World War I, the nation emerged from the war more committed to the auto than ever before (Kay, 184–88).

No longer an extravagant novelty, the motorcar had become a necessity. By the early 1920s most of the basic mechanical problems of automotive engineering had been solved. Manufacturers set out to create a new variety of styles that would appeal to a variety of consumer needs. By the mid-1920s Henry Ford had decided to abandon the difficult to drive Model T and to replace it with the Model A, which was equipped with a more conventional gearshift. New consumers flocked to the new variation. Other manufacturers followed in the late 1920s, including Chrysler which began production of the Plymouth in 1928. Ford's uniform "tin lizzie," autos gave rise to a way for consumers to express who they were and who they wished to be.

Mass production made sure that by the 1920s the car was no longer a luxury but a necessity of American middle-class life. The landscape, however, had been designed around other modes of transport, including an urban scene dependent on foot travel. Cars promised an independence never before possible, if they could be supported by the necessary service structure. Massive architectural shifts were necessary to make way for the auto (Kay, 200–210).

REWORKING HUMAN CULTURE AT CONEY

It was only a matter of time until the increasing mechanization of industry began to creep into other parts of everyday life. Although the automobile became an indispensable tool in American life, other technologies also altered expectations of American life, including leisure. In 1893, the Columbian exposition had presented new ways that great machines would change American patterns of consumption. Some of these machines increased the scale and scope of industrial processes. The increased output altered patterns of American consumption. But technology also became linked to the lives that Americans lived outside of the workplace (Trachtenberg, 35). One of the greatest attractions at the Columbian Expo, for instance, was the first Ferris wheel. This innovation was completely intended for human leisure. The Ferris wheel began a century of technological leisure that began in the Ferris wheel's resting spot after the Columbian Exposition had closed: Coney Island, New York.

Coney Island proved that this new era of technology could link together diverse Americans. New, modern ways of doing things helped create portions of culture that were designed to appeal to the masses, which often helped people overcome differences of race, gender, ethnicity, and economic class. It was at places such as Coney Island that the nature of

Coney Island, 1910. Courtesy Library of Congress.

human contact with itself and the world around it changed dramatically. The new era of electricity helped to create this cultural commons, powering the attractions and bringing many visitors from throughout New York City when the subway system arrived in the early 1900s.

Coney began as an exclusive resort for the wealthy; however, new technological advances made Coney's beaches accessible for just pennies. The resort attracted 100,000 visitors on summer Sundays in 1900, but 500,000 daily during the 1910s and 1,000,000 per day by the 1920s. The ocean remained a primary attraction to visitors; however, the landscape of leisure that took shape included many additional elements as well, including Luna Park, Steeplechase Park, and a host of other attractions and food concessions (Kasson, 32).

NATURE AT WORK: CONEY DOGS AND THE MASSES EAT

Although the use of technology at Coney most often appeared as mechanically produced thrills, it also permeated other needs of the hordes of consumers who flocked to the parks. For instance, eating at Coney could be an event enjoyed by every visitor—at least in the form of a frankfurter. Coney Dogs, as they were called, could overcome the differences of ethnicities, race, and economic class. Feltman's, which was the most famous Coney food concession stand, charged 10 cents for a frankfurter. Coney's boom in the mid-1920s brought Feltman's hot dog business new success. At one point, he employed 1,200 men to serve 8,000 meals at a time in its frankfurter bars. During this era, Feltman boasted that their counters served 7,000,000 meals per year! (Kasson,38–40)

Initially, Nathan's challenged the 10-cent price for frankfurters by charging only a nickel for its "red hots." With these popular hot dogs, Nathan's also sold hundreds of gallons of root beer, Coca-Cola, and knishes (Jewish potato cakes flavored with onion and garlic and fried in oil). Breakthroughs such as the Coney dog made the visit to Coney Island more affordable and attractive to tourists from the working class.

The nickels coming from the masses of working-class visitors became a symbol of a new, "mass market" era. Millions of nickels would be spent for momentary diversion and enjoyment, whether a hot dog, a root beer, or a ride down the Steeple Chase. Often, the new technologies of the early 1900s made a moment at Coney a lifelong memory (Stanton).

THE TECHNOLOGY OF THRILL

The new machines of the early twentieth century altered the most basic aspects of the human's involvement in nature. Revolutions rippled through human limits including speed, gravity, and even ideas of fun. The basic definition of the thrill ride was that it must strain the laws of human existence. The Ferris wheel, of course, was about rising into the sky. More often, though, the thrills came from new speeds with which the human body could be flung through the air.

Historian Judith Adams writes that early Coney developers created rides and thrills that altered visitors. "Their muscles were loosened and their inhibitions shattered mostly by simple mechanical contrivances designed to strip visitors of all means of control" (Adams, 46). Rides including the Human Roulette wheel, which was a giant roulette wheel, spun humans into a moment of submission (carefully pressing males and females upon each other) and then spit them back into reality. Technology enabled the momentary escapes of Coney Island. In some rides, visitors traveled to the moon, witnessed disasters such as the Galveston and Johnstown floods, the eruption of Mt. Vesuvius, and the San Francisco earthquake, or saw exotic people from far-off lands.

In the nineteenth century, opportunities for escape relied on individual imagination, such as in literature, art, and storytelling. In the twentieth century, technology became a crucial new element for creating momentary escape and diversion. Technological diversions such as those at Coney Island helped to create American mass culture. Later innovations continued this development with film, television, and other media as well.

NATURE AT WORK: THE BOARDWALK AND CONNECTING WITH THE SEA

No matter which aspect of the modern world attracted visitors to Coney, the ocean remained a primary attraction. Planners created a new form to merge these worlds with the evolution of the boardwalk in the early 1900s. By 1923, the massive plank walkway had become a well-known promenade at a cost of more than $3,000,000. Technology, of course, made this leisure activity possible: groins were built into the ocean and sand was pumped in to create an extra 2,500,000 square feet of beach, free to the public (Stanton).

Boardwalks became popular throughout the Atlantic seaboard. Although they resembled wharves, they typically had no commercial use related to sea trades. Instead, they were a middle landscape for leisure and recreation that allowed visitors to enjoy the aesthetic of the ocean while still remaining dry and out of the sand. At Atlantic City, New Jersey, tourists had been arriving since the 1850s to enjoy the cool breezes of the ocean during hot summer days. Many visitors to the beach enjoyed bathing in the ocean; however, most beaches remained segregated by gender until Coney broke the barriers of gender and economic class in the early 1900s. Many beaches remained segregated by race until much later in the twentieth century (Stilgoe, *Alongshore*, 44–47).

OCEAN LINERS ALTER TIME, SPACE, AND TRADE

Just as technology impacted American patterns of leisure, it also changed America's place in the world. The many possible uses of petroleum combined with new marine technologies to lead America from the age of sail and into a more global society in which ocean liners redefined ideas of time and space and helped forge new connections throughout the world. Steamships had become more and more prominent for intercoastal trade after 1860, but the shift among ocean-going vessels was somewhat slower. Petroleum allowed ocean-going vessels to shift to steam more rapidly (Labaree, 390–91). The great trans-Atlantic liners were primarily made of iron and steel by British manufacturers. These liners became crucial devices for remaking the nature of human ideas of time, space, and connectivity by standardizing travel throughout the world.

Most important for the United States, steerage tickets made it possible for laboring-class immigrants to move more flexibly throughout the world. The "Golden Door," the United States's industrial growth, made it the most attractive destination for those in search of work. The early 1900s, therefore, became the period of greatest human migration in history, with massive numbers of Europeans arriving via New York City and other major ports. The sheer mass of immigrant arrivals led to the creation of American symbols such as the Statue of Liberty, designed to welcome the poor and hungry of other nations, and, of course, Ellis Island to organize and classify each new immigrant.

When new technologies carried Americans and their goods abroad with more ease, the United States also became more involved than ever before in new parts of the world. President Theodore Roosevelt's assertive approach to Latin America and the Caribbean was characterized as the "Big Stick" in the early years of the twentieth century. The primary tool for interacting with other nations, though, was a new American navy, which could reach even the most distant portions of the globe (Labaree, 441).

Primary to this assertive approach to global affairs was the document known as the Roosevelt Corollary to the Monroe Doctrine, which Theodore Roosevelt announced in 1904. In this document, Roosevelt announced to the world:

Our interests and those of our southern neighbors are in reality identical. They have great natural riches, and if within their borders the reign of law and justice obtains, prosperity is sure to come to them. While they thus obey the primary laws of civilized society they may rest assured that they will be treated by us in a spirit of cordial and helpful sympathy. We would interfere with them only in the last resort, and then only if it became evident that their inability or unwillingness to do justice at home and abroad had violated the rights of the United States or had invited foreign aggression to the detriment of the entire body of American nations. . . .

In asserting the Monroe Doctrine, in taking such steps as we have taken in regard to Cuba, Venezuela, and Panama, . . . we have acted in our own interest as well as in the interest of humanity at large. There are, however, cases in which, while our own interests are not greatly involved, strong appeal is made to our sympathies. . . . In extreme cases action may be justifiable and proper. What form the action shall take must depend upon the circumstances of the case; that is, upon the degree of the atrocity and upon our power to remedy it. (Roosevelt)

In order to reinforce the wishes of the United States, Roosevelt sent some of the navy's newest ships on a tour of the Pacific from 1907–1909. Known as the "Great White Fleet," the ships' tour emphasized Mexico, South America, and Asia. Burning petroleum and coal for steam power and with hulls of well-honed steel, the vessels were an awesome site at each of their ports of call. Symbolically, they bore witness to the world of the growing global presence of the United States (Labaree, 450).

THE PANAMA CANAL

One key to this changing role in the hemisphere concerned the management of topography in a profoundly new way. Roosevelt initiated plans for a canal through Panama that would greatly speed trade with Asia. The United States had been seriously interested in an isthmian canal since the Clayton-Bulwar treaty with Great Britain in 1850. Interest in constructing a canal in Panama actually dated back to 1524 when Charles V of Spain ordered the first survey of a proposed canal route through the isthmus of Panama. Even at this early date, people already realized the advantages and commercial value of a route that would avoid sailing the 10,000-mile journey around Cape Horn at the tip of South America. But more than three centuries passed before the first construction effort was attempted. In the interim, private interest groups tried to stimulate canal construction throughout Central America. Beginning in 1880, a private French Company (La Compagnie Universelle du Canal Interoceanique) pushed for construction of a canal at the isthmus of Panama. The second Walker Commission, the U.S. Isthmian Canal Commission of 1899–1902, ordered by President McKinley, favored a Nicaragua route, as did both popular and official U.S. support (McCullough, 15–20).

Instead, the United States helped Panama gain its independence and then signed the Bunau-Varilla Treaty, which granted the United States the right to build, operate, and defend a canal through Panama. The opening of the Panama Canal to world commerce on August 15, 1914, represented the realization of a dream of over 400 years. Construction by the United States of the 50-mile waterway bisecting the Republic of Panama was among the great technological innovations of the early twentieth century (McCullough, 30–5).

NATURE AT WORK: THE PANAMA CANAL AND MALARIA

Technological innovation did not only concern how to make a massive waterway function in the Panamanian jungle; first, an American work force needed to be able to survive heat and illnesses associated with the region. Specifically, the disease malaria, which was transmitted by mosquitoes in the jungle, proved to be the most difficult part of the project. Without chemical pesticides, Americans chose to first eradicate the habitat that bred the pests.

Scientists deduced that the disease was spread by the Anopheles mosquito. Assuming that the mosquito would be incapable of flying far without landing for at least a moment on some sort of vegetation, scientists ordered workers to clear a 200-yard-wide swath around areas in which people lived and worked. In addition, sanitation teams led other efforts to eradicate the areas in which the mosquitoes bred. This resulted in the drainage of more than 100 square miles of swamp. To better manage areas of standing water, the teams created nearly 1,000 miles of earthen ditching, some 300 miles of concrete ditch, 200 miles of rock-filled trench, and almost 200 miles of tile drain. Finally, scientists also ordered teams to spray standing water with thousands of gallons of oil, hatched and released thousands of minnows to eat the Anopheles larvae, and bred spiders, ants, and lizards to feed on adult insects (McNeil, 197).

When vegetation prevented the oil from spreading so that it could smother the larvae, barrels of poison (a mixture of carbolic acid, resin, and caustic soda) were applied monthly around the edges of many water pools and streams. These efforts reduced the mosquitoes' numbers sufficiently so that malaria incidents were significantly reduced in populated areas. Two hundred eleven employees died of malaria during fiscal year 1906–1907, declining significantly from a peak of 7.45 per 1,000 in 1906 to .30 per 1,000 in 1913. This achievement greatly increased American chances of canal-building success and also provided important new understandings about disease control.

WORLD WAR I: KILLING MACHINES

The rapid changes in technology were seen most persuasively when the great powers of the world squared off in the first large-scale war of the modern era. Just as the modernizing technologies impacted American life and leisure and redefined the human relationship with the natural world, so did they change the way war was fought. Events and agreements between nations brought Europe, the United States, and other nations to war in 1915. As each side used technology to attempt to win the war, World War I emerged as a transitional war in which new weapons were used in old forms of battle. The outcome was horrific trench warfare and unbelievable carnage. All totaled, approximately 10 million soldiers died worldwide as did an estimated 50 million civilians. Machines had been made to kill efficiently, just as they were also made to make car parts or stuff sausage casings.

The new era of killing technologies was defined by a gun that began with no use for hunting, the primary use of guns up to this point. Although versions of the machine gun had been used previously, World War I brought the machine gun into widespread application. The 1914 machine gun was quite difficult to use. Each gun had to be placed on a flat tripod and required a four to six man crew. Once in place, though, there had never been a weapon quite like it.

Models at the start of World War I fired 400 to 600 rounds per minute; by the end of the war, this capacity had doubled. High technology came at a price, however. Machine guns rapidly overheated. Without a cooling mechanism, the gun quickly became unusable. For this reason, the early guns were employed in short bursts and then allowed to cool. Strategically, armies worked around this limitation by grouping machine guns together and having them fire in shifts. Officials estimated that a properly positioned machine gun was worth approximately 60 to 100 rifles. They began the war as a defensive weapon, but, during the war, they were adapted for use on tanks, aircraft, and warships by 1915.

New technologies also expressed the desperation of what was referred to as "trench warfare." Faced with lengthy stalemates created by armies holding out in underground bunkers and trenches, World War I armies employed poison gas to force soldiers out from hiding (Russell, 146–50). Chlorine was used by the Germans on April 22, 1915 at the start of the second battle of Ypres. Within seconds of inhalation, the gas destroyed soldiers' respiratory organs. The Germans' use of chlorine gas was criticized worldwide. Just as they condemned the Germans, however, Britain also made plans to put gas to use on the battlefield. The Allies' retaliation began later in 1915. By 1917, each army had turned primarily to the use of mustard gas.

Although many new technologies emerged in World War I, the strategic fighting of war remained primitive in many ways. The most striking of these was the use of animals for transportation and other tasks. Although horses had been important to many wars in human history, World War I put more to work than any previous conflict. The British army acquired approximately 200,000 horses at the start of the war and reportedly added approximately 15,000 per month throughout the war. These animals were brought together from the United Kingdom, South Africa, New Zealand, India, Spain, and Portugal. Horses and mules carried ammunition, artillery, guns, and shells, as well as soldiers. In World War I alone, around 8 million horses, mules, and donkeys died.

Possibly the most famous animal participant in World War I was the messenger pigeon. Although radios began to be used during the war, soldiers sent most messages by messenger pigeon. Possibly, this transition in information transfer best represents the watershed change in technology by the end of the war.

New technologies wrought more damage and death than in any previous war. The toleration of humans to live in a world with technologies capable of killing masses set the stage for later developments, including nuclear weapons. As Thomas Edison and others lent their technical abilities to the war effort, though, a crucial connection was

During World War I, the federal government urged the consumption of fish among the American public. Courtesy Library of Congress.

permanently forged between technology, engineers and the military (Hughes, *Genesis*, 96–100). Technical innovation became indelibly linked to national security by the end of World War I.

MODERNISM AND EUROPEAN IDEAS

During the 1910s, Americans' relationship to nature was wholly reworked by the pervasiveness of new technologies. New machines and know-how seemed to put Americans firmly in control of creating their own world, which might function much more effectively than the one that naturally occurred around them. An extreme version of this view took root in Europe and eventually became known as modernism. In architectural circles, the product of modernism was called the International style.

After World War I, Europeans' International style infiltrated many other parts of the world. Although the arrival in the United States of European versions of modern art is normally dated to the New York City Armory Show of 1911, these ideas did not gel into the sleek steel and glass of the International style until the 1920s (Berman, 290–94).

Sometimes referred to as white architecture, this style is recognizable for its flat painted surfaces, box-like dimensions, and metal-framed windows that sit flush against the facade. International-style buildings are made with modern materials and contain no ornamentation or decorative flourishes. Architects often repeated shapes on the surface of a building to diminish the mass of the structure. The idea was to create the impression of space closed in by thin walls. These artificial environments often used a great deal of glass to allow for natural lighting and the impression of a wall-less space.

The works of these designers created a new generation of building that changed the American landscape during the twentieth century. Building technologies became simpler and more flexible by integrating the products of modern technology into new designs. Of course, this essentially meant that building could take place at an increased rate and scale.

NATURE AT WORK: STEEL SKELETONS AND THE SKYSCRAPER

By the end of the 1800s, urban areas spread over the landscape, leading to outlying areas now known as suburbs. Simultaneously, however, modern technology made it possible to expand urban centers by going upward. New technologies radically changed American building as the nineteenth century closed. For instance, in 1889, America's tallest building was New York's Trinity Church, near Wall Street. In 1890 the 26-story New York World Building seized the mantle of the nation's tallest building. As the skyscraper emerged on the American landscape, however, no building would hold this label for very long (Mumford, 322).

New technology helped architects to design in radically different ways. Brick, which had been used for most early urban construction, could not support a building of more than five or six stories. Steel frames, however, provided more support and allowed designers to consider reaching further into the sky. Other necessary technological advances included elevators and technology to move heat and water around the building.

The first building referred to as a skyscraper was built by William LeBaron Jenney, a Chicago architect, in 1884. The Home Life Insurance Building reached nine stories and was the first structure to be entirely supported by an iron frame. The first building to add elevators, pressurized plumbing and central heating, however, was New York City's Equitable Life Assurance Building, which was completed in 1898 (Roth, 161–62). As the price of steel fell in the late 1800s, it quickly became the architect's choice for framing tall buildings.

Additional technologies necessary to make the skyscraper emerged simultaneously. Elevator technology emerged in the 1870s. Early models were powered by steam engines that wound cables around a huge rotating drum. The limits of drum size meant that taller buildings needed a different technology. One of the first structures to use hydraulic-powered elevators was the Eiffel Tower, which was built in 1889. Electric elevators emerged as the most practical solution by the 1890s. For ventilation, early buildings used steam-powered fans to move air through ducts. Once again, electricity took over this process after 1890, and fans were driven by electricity. Plumbing to circulate water through the building relied on pressure created by electric pumps.

The evolution of skyscraper technology reached an early apogee when New York City's Empire State Building opened on May 1, 1931. A national symbol, the building's opening attracted President Herbert Hoover and New York Governor Franklin D. Roosevelt. The 102-story, 1,250-foot-high building had been constructed in only 13 months—a rate of more than one story per day. The completed building seemed to defy the nature of the human need to remain on Earth.

With the use of these new technologies, skyscrapers became a symbol for all modern technology and its ability to alter American life. These tall buildings

Empire State Building under construction showing steel frame built up to the 40th floor. Courtesy Library of Congress.

remade American cities by relieving urban congestion and allowing population and workplace concentration that had never been possible before. Technological innovation left very little unchanged in American life by the 1910s, and the skyscraper rose as one of the great symbols of the modern machine age (Smith, *Modern*, 242–43)

CONCLUSION: THE ENVIRONMENTAL ETHIC OF THE AMERICAN SUBURB

The skyscraper, of course, rose as the symbol of a technologically dominated era. However, this same era at times clearly used technological advances to elevate and enhance the role of the natural environment in everyday American life. The machine and the garden could achieve a reconciliation that resulted in what Marx called "the middle landscape,"—even during the era of modernity. This reconciliation is evident in the view of Frank Lloyd Wright's architectural creation, Fallingwater, which was discussed in the introduction. Wright's interest in nonmechanized details, organic materials, and the careful management of space were elements that helped to define changes in American living patterns after the 1900s. Interesting, this same ethic can be found in portions of the development of suburban living in the early 1900s.

When the idea of home-making and house-planning took shape in the United States around the turn of the twentieth century, designers sought a single style that embodied the evolving American ideals in a form that could be dispersed widely. Inspiration for such home design grew from modern sensibilities that were styled after a regressive tradition known as the Arts and Crafts movement. The enduring marriage of this blend was the well-known bungalow style house. Gustav Stickley's *Craftsman* magazine made plans for such homes widely available. The style was re-acquired by modernist designers. Frank Lloyd Wright used it to create a model design for homes that could be mimicked in any residential setting. His designs were grouped within the tradition known as the Prairie School. Accentuating horizontality and organization of internal spaces, the homes of the Prairie School sought to create models to inspire the homes of middle-class Americans.

The homes of such designs played directly into a growing interest in home management, referred to often as home economics. At the turn of the twentieth century, American women began to perceive of the home as a laboratory in which one could promote better health, families, and more satisfied individuals with better management and design. The leaders of the movement of domestic science endorsed simplifying the dwelling in both its structure and its amenities. Criticizing Victorian ornamentation, they sought something clean, new, and sensible. The bungalow fulfilled many of these needs perfectly.

The most familiar use of "bungalow," though, would arrive as city and village centers sprawled into the first suburbs for middle-class Americans.

These singular homes were often modeled after the original Stickley homes, or similar designs from *Ladies Home Journal.* The design would make it possible for the vast majority of Americans to own their own homes, thereby updating the Jeffersonian image of Americans as a landowning people. Housing the masses would evolve into the suburban revolution on the landscape; however, the change in the vision of the home can be traced to a specific type: the unassuming bungalow (Roth, 198).

Wright merged this style with a specific region when he began designing homes in the Prairie style from 1900 until 1915. The high point came in 1914 and was based in the American Midwest. During its formative years, the architects focused on suburban Chicago, but it would also reach into rural Illinois, Minnesota, Iowa, and Wisconsin. Emphasizing horizontality of design, the Prairie School was a regional manifestation of the more general, international revolt and reform occurring in the visual arts.

For Wright, the horizontal mimicking of the landscape allowed the form to become organic, concealed in the landscape, and satisfied his modernist desire for simplification. This link between structure and landscape was further stimulated by the management of inner and exterior space. The Prairie homes were designed to bring the inside of the home out and the surroundings inside. Patios, gardens, and windows were designed to facilitate this connectedness. Building materials were selected to include natural elements of the surroundings, such as wood, stone, stucco, brick, or the elemental sand, gravel, cement, and water that make up concrete. This was also true of the plants and landscape design of the elongated gardens and courtyards. The linking device between such spaces would often be stone fences that extended wall lines outward, but most often the most noticeable element was the elongated roof lines.

A product of cultural taste, the Prairie style's popularity petered out as preferences changed. *House Beautiful* illustrated its last prairie house in 1914. Stickley's journal ceased publication in 1916 as the Arts and Crafts movement itself also lost popularity. The Prairie style's great achievement is a mode of design universally applicable to every building type. Its influence can be seen in many other types of architecture of the twentieth century, particularly in gardens and courtyard designs. Many suburban homes, including the ubiquitous ranch house, strive for a similar link between the horizontal exterior space and the domestic living environment (Wright, 98). Unlike urban residences, suburban settings—at the very—prirortize space and contact with some form of nature.

2

THE DRIVE FOR PARKS

GETTING AWAY FROM IT ALL

As the mechanization of American life increased at the close of the 1800s,
it spurred a contrary reaction in American culture. For many Americans,

the growing intensity with which nature was put to use made them increasingly concerned with the wilderness that remained untouched. In addition, many Americans who appreciated roller coasters and other new leisure activities began also to better appreciate the antitechnological—the natural world. Although this movement occurred throughout the nation, its nexus grew from metropolitan New York and reached directly into one of the most accessible wild areas: the Adirondacks.

In the late 1800s, the Adirondacks became the center point in an intellectual reevaluation of nature's role in American life. Part of this was chance: with its proximity to New York City, the Adirondacks served as one of the most accessible vestiges of raw nature for urbanites. It was these upper-middle-class city dwellers who, by the 1890s, had created a reactionary cultural ripple to the massive use of technology discussed in Chapter 1. A major portion of this reaction was a rejection of mechanical progress and a new celebration of nature in its rawest forms.

The Adirondacks became the setting for many of these wealthy Americans to express their taste and civility by "roughing it"—at least briefly. Often, their ideas derived from romantic and transcendental leanings, such as the poem that began this chapter. However, as the

Hess Camp (i.e. Inn) cottages, Fulton Chain, Adirondack Mountains. Courtesy Library of Congress.

wealthy made retreating to nature trendy and tasteful, they also defined a grander vision than the tents and the hunting parties that occupied them in the 1870s and 1880s. By the late 1890s, the Adirondacks had reached its era of "Great Camps" (Terrie, 10–14).

Distinctive to New York State, the Adirondack camps illustrate a style of architecture that was meant to mimic nature. Most often, these camps were located on vast tracts of forested land in the Adirondack Mountains. The camps allowed the elite of New York City to use and enjoy the region's lakes, streams, and forests. The interest of upper-class Americans in the outdoors emerged at the end of the 1800s, which also marked the establishment of many of the Great Camps. Although their location was remote, the camps often made leisure and amenities available in a rustic setting.

Architectural historians use three characteristics to define the Adirondack camp: a distinctive compound plan consisting of separate buildings for separate functions; the close integration of camp buildings with existing natural features; and a rustic aesthetic of decoration, design, and building.

WILDERNESS IN THE 'DACKS

Although unclear in its original ethic or motives, the preservation effort in the Adirondacks eventually became more formal. By the mid-1890s, New York had created a model of legislative discussion that would have national implications. The movement to designate a park in the Adirondacks was spurred on by the writer Verplank Colvin, who wrote in 1885: "Had I my way, I would mark out a circle of a hundred miles in diameter, and throw around it the protecting aegis of the constitution. I would make it a forest forever. It would be a misdemeanor to chop down a tree and a felony to clear an acre within its boundaries" (Graham 70–78).

The effort to argue for a park in the Adirondacks did not make headway when it was based purely on romantic arguments about natural beauty. The key came when preservationists tied their argument to watershed preservation—especially that of New York City. Only then did the state government pay attention (Nash, 116–21). In short, preservation for its own sake was not attractive to nineteenth-century Americans. Ensuring good water supplies for the nation's most important urban area, however, was a tangible concern that interested preservationists (many of whom lived in the city). For this purpose, all the Adirondack land owned by the state (approximately 681,000 acres) was designated a Forest Preserve between 1883 an 1885. In order to make it simpler to acquire additional land, Governor David B. Hill urged the legislature to create an Adirondack park in 1890 (Terrie, 100–105).

The vote to establish a preserve came in 1892. The New York legislature voted to place a blue line on the map to denote the parts of the region that it hoped to acquire and include in the park. The total area covered more than 2.8 million acres. Many conservationists, however, immediately felt that the law was a mixed blessing. Although it created the park, it also weakened some earlier policies. The political winds continued to alter the park in 1893 when Governor Roswell P. Flower proposed a bill that authorized the park to sell trees from any part of the Forest Preserve. This idea, of course, undercut the whole concept for the forest preserve.

A major reaction came at a convention held in 1894. Nearly halfway through the meeting, David McClure proposed what became known as the "forever wild" amendment. After witnessing the threat of the 1893 Cutting Law, McClure and others wished to create a constitutional barrier that would block any similar efforts in the future. A committee convened to establish whether or not the Adirondacks merited amending the constitution. On the last day of the convention, the "forever wild" clause came to a vote. By a margin of 112 to 0, Article VII, Section 7 (which became Article XIV, Section 1 in 1938), was adopted into the New York State Constitution. Approved by New York state voters, the new Constitution went into effect in 1895 (Terrie, 95–100).

By 1900 the area of the Forest Preserve was over 1.2 million acres. Today, the Adirondack Preserve is composed of nearly 3 million acres. The nature of everyday life had changed for every American in the quiet Adirondacks (Terrie, 100–105).

DOCUMENT: THE ADIRONDACK "WILDERNESS CLAUSE"

The Adirondacks are responsible for the first legislation to mention the term "wild" or "wilderness." In 1894, voters added Article VII, Section 7 (which became Article XIV, Section 1 in 1938) to the state constitution, which reads:

> Section 1. The lands of the state, now owned or hereafter acquired, constituting the forest preserve as now fixed by law, shall be forever kept as wild forest lands. They shall not be leased, sold or exchanged, or be taken by any corporation, public or private, nor shall the timber thereon be sold, removed or destroyed.

DISAPPEARING SPECIES

Americans had clear indications by the end of the nineteenth century that the wasteful use of resources could result in their permanent loss. National forests were one example of this shift in American thought. Also, the trademark species of the continent, the American bison, became a symbol of the expansion westward and then of the gluttonous use of natural resources. The trade in buffalo had begun with the hide's use for robes in the early 1800s. Native Americans were involved in each part of the process, hunting and butchering, as well as tanning, which softened the robes. This process moved into factories after the Civil War.

Of course, this greatly increased the number of buffalo killed. Typically, a hunting team included a shooter who sat in wait with a large-caliber rifle. The shooter first killed the dominant cow. If this shot was successful, the hunter's ability to kill others in the herd was limited only by his reloading and ammunition. Two other men then worked as skinners. The carcasses were left behind. Manufacturers turned the hides into belts for machines that ran factories throughout the nation (White, *Misfortune*, 216–19).

The railroad altered the future of the bison herd forever. The tracks created a barrier to the bison and concentrated them in smaller areas. In 1884, the herd in eastern Montana numbered 75,000. An influx of approximately 5,000 hide hunters over the next year, however, reduced the herd to only a few hundred. Extinction seemed a likely outcome. Viewing the situation from an anthropocentric perspective, some onlookers knew that eradication of the bison held a positive outcome for American expansion: they felt that Native Americans could be more easily controlled without the bison.

The first impulse to conserve the bison population came from a trained scientist, zoologist William T. Hornaday, who needed additional bison specimens for the National Museum in Washington, DC. Fully aware of their growing scarcity, Hornaday was still shocked that during eight weeks in 1886 he could collect only 25 specimens in a region of Montana that just a few years earlier had supported tens of thousands of bison. He quickly became a leading opponent of the bison's imminent extinction. His efforts came not a moment too soon. By 1893, the population of bison that had numbered nearly 60 million was estimated to have plummeted to just 300 (Isenberg, 136–38).

Many upper-class Americans were ripe to hear Hornaday's conservation message. With consistent interest from urban areas in the northeastern United States, Hornaday worked with Theodore Roosevelt and others in 1905 to establish the American Bison Society. Their efforts helped to improve the bison's situation. During his presidency, Roosevelt persuaded Congress to establish a number of wildlife preserves. The Bison Society worked with a number of private ranch owners to raise bison that could be used to stock preserves and parks and to ultimately help the bison's numbers to rebound (Hays, *Gospel*, 141–44).

Bison were not alone in being threatened by the exploitation of American hunters. In the Midwest, for instance, game markets took shape to harvest a number of flocking birds. The most intense hunting focused on the passenger pigeon. The demise of the pigeon at the end of the nineteenth century directly stems from the growth of consumer markets. In the great flocks of pigeon, game hunters saw a steady and significant food resource for Eastern restaurants. In addition, though, nets could be employed to capture flocks of live pigeons and return them to hunting clubs for the upper-class hunters. From their nesting areas in the northern Midwest, live pigeons were sent to hunting clubs in cities in the region as well as Boston, New York, and Washington, D.C.

Although the waste of hunters of the era seems terrible by modern sensibilities, it was the excessive killing that spurred collective action. Alarm over the disappearance of these species and others fueled additional calls for conservation action among the American public (Price, 46–49).

THE POPULAR MOVEMENT FOR CONSERVATION

The movement for conservation was initiated by those who were using natural resources—hunters. Efforts to conserve wildlife began with fish. By 1870, hatcheries had been put in operation throughout the United States. Species ranging from shad, brook trout, and carp were reintroduced to depleted or polluted waters. In fact, seven years before George Perkins Marsh wrote *Man and Nature,* he was commissioned by sportsmen to study the feasibility of restoring fish populations lost from the Connecticut River (Reiger, 53).

In 1871, the issue of fish populations resulted in the establishment of the U.S. Fish Commission, the first federal conservation agency. Although this agency produced some of the earliest studies of fish population, most of the action was initiated by sportsmen's organizations. Typically, fish population was not stressed by these groups for the fishes' sake; instead, efforts were organized to preserve "fish culture." Although the population of fish is a critical component of such culture, their worth comes from humans being able to catch them. Historian John Reiger writes: "For sportsmen, [the fish culture idea] meant a restoration of angling opportunities; for farmers and ranchers, it meant a profitable sideline . . . , for commercial fishermen . . . it meant never-ending profits . . . ; and for the nation as a whole, it meant cheap food for the masses" (Reiger, 53).

Often, the efforts of early conservationists were inspired by a fairly self-serving rationale. Primarily, the goal was to ensure the supply of animals that could be hunted. Another branch of the sportsmen's efforts was the creation of hunting preserves, which began appearing in the 1870s (Hays, *Gospel,* 114–16). "Deer parks" date back to the colonial era; however, in the 1870s, sportsmen aware of the depleted stocks of certain choice game established their own preserves and stocked them. Two of the earliest examples were the Bisby Club and the Blooming Grove Park.

Located in Pike County, Pennsylvania, Blooming Grove spanned 12,000 acres. The founders of this preserve managed populations of game animals, fish, and forests to create the best environment for sportsmen. Reiger reports that it was in New York state where similar clubs in the Adirondacks began around 1890 (Reiger, 142).

NATURE GUIDE: GEORGE BIRD GRINNELL

When he was growing up, George Bird Grinnell had attended school in John James Audubon's mansion in Assigning, New York, where he developed a love for birds at an early age. George, as well as his brothers and sisters, knew the

Audubon family and were allowed to roam the grounds of their estate and play in the barn, which held large collections of bird specimens and skins.

Grinnell served as a naturalist on Custer's expedition to the Black Hills in 1874. Later, he became editor of a weekly magazine for sportsmen and naturalists called *Forest and Stream*. He used it to help him channel the dissatisfaction of outdoorsmen with disappearing habitats and dwindling game populations into a fight to conserve natural resources. He advocated for a game warden system that would finance effective enforcement of game laws by levying small fees on each hunter. His revolutionary regulation of hunting activity on the state level with financial support from the hunters themselves became a cornerstone for game management throughout the United States (Nash, 152–53).

On the national scene, however, Grinnell made one of the first battles for conservation one for the birds. Beginning in the late 1800s, Grinnell formed a society to fight the use of feathers, particularly in women's fashion. Hats decorated with feathers, bird parts, and even entire stuffed birds were a mainstay of the upper-class woman in France and England. Eight to 10 warblers were used on a single hat. Additionally, the long plumes of egrets or even the taxidermied heads of owls defined the well-dressed. Style reached broader audiences through advertisements in the magazines, including *Godey's Lady's Book* and *Harper's Bazaar*. Grinnell announced the formation of the Audubon Society in *Forest and Stream* on February 11, 1886:

> Very slowly the public are awakening to see that the fashion of wearing the feathers and skins of birds is abominable. There is, we think, no doubt that when the facts about this fashion are known, it will be frowned down and will cease to exist. Legislation of itself can do little against the barbarous practice, but if public sentiment can be aroused against it, it will die a speedy death. . . .
>
> The reform in America . . . must be inaugurated by women. . . . [But] Something more than this is needed. Men, women, and children all over our land should take the matter in hand, and urge its importance upon those with whom they are brought in contact. A general effort of this kind will not fail to awaken public interest, and information given to a right-thinking public will set the ball of reform in motion. . . .
>
> We propose the formation of an association for the protection of wild birds and their eggs, which shall be called the Audubon Society. (Rieger, 68–69)

The society was an instant success, attracting 50,000 members by 1888. Overwhelmed, Grinnell needed to choose between Audubon and *Forest and Stream*. In 1889, he disbanded the Audubon Society; however, others would form new chapters of the society within the decade. The new Audubons began in 1896 and had the social status and financial power of urban elite women behind them, starting in Boston and then extending to New York and other cities throughout the nation (Price, 75).

BOONE AND CROCKETT CLUB

Grinnell became close friends with Theodore Roosevelt during the 1880s, and together they began a group that marked an entirely new idea in Americans' relationship with nature. In *Forest and Stream* editorials, Grinnell wrote that he desired: "a [national] association of men bound together by their interest in game and fish, to take active charge of all matters pertaining to the enactment and carrying out of laws on the subject" (Rieger, 118). Roosevelt shared this opinion and invited many of his sportsmen friends to a meeting in Manhattan at which he suggested the formation of the group.

The Boone and Crockett Club had five organizing principles: to promote "manly" sport with the rifle; to promote travel to wild portions of the country; to work for preservation of large game; to stimulate interest in natural history and animal habits; and stimulate the exchange of ideas among members. As a forerunner of the Boy Scouts of America, the Boone and Crockett, obviously, placed a specific stress on hunting.

Extending from these elite New York high-society roots, Boone and Crockett spread its influence nationally, although almost always limited to upper-class portions of society. In the late 1890s, the organization began publishing books on conservation and hunting. The books, of course, also disseminated the sportsmen's code at the core of the organization. Most important, the code emphasized the need to use any animal that was killed (Nash, 152–53).

Boone and Crockett's ethical foundations were exhibited in the early 1890s when the group became involved with Yellowstone National Park.

"Now look pleasant teddy." Courtesy Library of Congress.

Critical of the mismanagement of game in the park, Boone and Crockett members considered taking over management themselves (Reiger, 125). The core of the issue was the effort to build a railroad through the park. Boone and Crockett members feared that this might increase the wholesale slaughter of game animals in the pristine area. This was just one example of the crossover between hunting and conservation. The efforts of hunters contributed to some of the earliest efforts at game management and land preservation.

NATURE GUIDE: THEODORE ROOSEVELT

The new American relationship with nature, of course, harkened back to more primitive times in American history. As life became more and more manufactured with the help of technology, wealthy Americans turned to hiking, hunting, and other outdoor activities as an outlet for leisure instead of as a necessity for survival. Personifying this new sensibility, President Theodore Roosevelt was possibly the nation's best-known outdoorsman. Although Roosevelt initiated new conservation policies regarding forests, national parks and monuments, and river management, he approached nature first as a leisure sportsmen. When he urged the nation to maintain a rigorous lifestyle, Roosevelt depicted himself with gun in hand searching for big game. He swung into the national political scene urging Americans to adopt an active lifestyle and not to "go soft."

At times, Roosevelt's actions contributed to his legend. He left government service, of course, to ride with a band of volunteer "rough riders" in Cuba during the War with Spain in 1898. In 1901, President William McKinley was shot in Buffalo and Vice President Roosevelt needed to be sworn in. But national headlines had to admit: "Mountains Searched for Roosevelt to no Avail" (Nash, 136). Roosevelt, who was hunting in the Adirondacks, could not be found initially. Eventually, he was sworn in after arriving in Buffalo (Morris, 12).

Possibly the most revealing tale connected with Roosevelt's outdoor exploits involved an injured bear. During one hunting expedition in the forests of the South, Roosevelt was told that his party had a bear cornered and they were waiting for him to make the kill. Biographer Edmund Morris writes that Roosevelt "was both disappointed and upset… to find a stunned, bloody, mud-caked runt tied to a tree." He refused to shoot it and another member of his party had to kill the bear. Although his hunt continued, cartoonists and journalists celebrated Roosevelt for his sporting ethic and his refusal to "kill just for killing's sake" (Morris, 175). Later that year, manufacturers of a new stuffed bear toy began to call it "Teddy" in honor of Roosevelt's act of compassion. Of course, the "Teddy Bear" became a popular toy for all American children. Figuratively and literally, Roosevelt brought nature into American lives in a profoundly new way.

PROGRESSIVISM AND ACTIVE CONSERVATION

The mandate for federal activity to regulate natural resource use took root early in the twentieth century. The progressive period energized many Americans to identify social ills and to use the government to correct them. The impulse to discontinue waste of resources and the pollution, physical and spiritual, of American communities rapidly became an expression of Americans' unique connection to the land.

The earliest interest in environmental policy grew out of wealthy urbanites of the Gilded Age who often combined an interest in hunting and fishing with efforts to maintain recreational sites. This also fueled efforts by women's groups to limit styles of fashion, which included the use of exotic birds and feathers as hat decorations. Efforts to manage the use of certain species and eliminate the practice altogether took root in the 1890s and extended into the early 1900s. Magazines on topics ranging from gardening to hunting fed Americans' interest. Magazines such as *The Horticulturalist, Field and Stream* (then known as *Forest and Stream), Godey's Lady's Book,* and *Better Homes and Gardens* helped to merge the women's

Gifford Pinchot and Theodore Roosevelt confer. Courtesy Library of Congress.

magazine with practical publications specifically concerned with home design. These popular interests, however, required a leader who could guide them toward concrete expression and policy initiatives.

The leadership of Roosevelt and his Chief of Forestry Gifford Pinchot galvanized the upper-class interest with national policies. The aesthetic appreciation of wealthy urbanites grew into progressive initiatives to create national forests and national parks with a unifying philosophy for each. These policies would develop in two directions, preservation and conservation. Roosevelt greatly admired the national parks as places where "bits of the old wilderness scenery and the old wilderness life are to be kept unspoiled for the benefit of our children's children." With his spiritual support, preservationists argued that a society that could exhibit the restraint to cordon off entire sections of itself had ascended to the level of great civilizations in world history (Fox, 19–25).

While Roosevelt possessed preservationist convictions, his main advisor on land management, Pinchot, argued otherwise for the good of the nation. Conservationists, such as Pinchot, sought to qualify the preservationist impulse with a dose of utilitarian reality. The mark of an ascendant society, they argued, was the awareness of limits and the use of the government to manage resources in danger of exhaustion. Forest resources would be primary to Pinchot's concern. The first practicing American forester, Pinchot urged Americans to manage forests differently than had Europe. Together, Roosevelt and Pinchot (as head of the National Forests) fueled the popular interest in nature. For instance, Pinchot had a national mailing list for the Forest Service of over 100,000 private citizens. He also made a specific effort to talk about forest issues in frequent public appearances, and he penned articles for popular magazines.

The conflict between preservation and conservation revolved around each side's emerging definitions of itself. Preservationists such as J. Horace McFarland urged that sites such as Niagara Falls required a hands-off policy that would maintain the natural aesthetic that they found so appealing. Roosevelt and others took a more practical approach that ultimately became known as conservation. Conservationists were buoyed by Roosevelt's vociferous and active ideas. In 1908 he stated some of these points in the nation's first Conference of Governors for Conservation:

The wise use of all of our natural resources, which are our national resources as well, is the great material question of today. I have asked you to come together now because the enormous consumption of these resources, and the threat of imminent exhaustion of some of them, due to reckless and wasteful use, . . . calls for common effort, common action.

The image of Roosevelt, the active conservationist, also contributed to the growing appreciation of "rustic" ways of life. His interest in a "vigorous life" and outdoor activity fed the development of organizations such as the Boy Scouts of America (Cutright, 191–95).

BOY SCOUTS AND EXPERIENCING THE OUTDOORS

The Gilded Age of the nineteenth century brought to wealthy Americans a genuine interest in rustic living and the outdoors. This was clearly demonstrated by the interest in Adirondack preservation. In addition, though, many wealthy urbanites began sending children to summer camps that could provide their children with a connection to the culture of outdoors that city living lacked. This sentiment was of specific interest to Roosevelt.

In addition to his policy initiatives, Roosevelt spurred a national interest in virility. He was concerned that young people growing up in a highly mechanized society would become soft. To keep this from happening, he worked with others to initiate various clubs and organizations, including the Boone and Crockett or Izaak Walton Clubs. Each group had an offspring for younger male members, with Sons of Daniel Boone proving the most popular. Neither, however, truly sought to reach young men of all economic classes. Ernest Thompson Seton, artist and wildlife expert, founded the Woodcraft Indians in 1902 (Nash, 147–48).

Seton chose to unveil the group through articles in *Ladies Home Journal.* Shortly afterward, Seton became the first chief scout of the Boy Scouts of America (BSA) when it was established by Robert Stephenson Smyth

Boy Scouts, 1919, cooking over an open fire at Camp Ranachqua. Courtesy Library of Congress.

Baden-Powell. The concern of BSA was the whole child. For instance, the first Boy Scout manual, *Scouting for Boys,* contained chapters titled Scoutcraft, Campaigning, Camp Life, Tracking, Woodcraft, Endurance for Scouts, Chivalry, Saving Lives, and Our Duties as Citizens. In 30 years the handbook sold an alleged seven million copies in the United States, second only to the Bible.

The Boy Scouts of America incorporated Feb. 8, 1910 and were granted a federal charter by Congress June 15, 1916. This organization is based on the principles established in England by scouting's founder, Lord Baden-Powell, in 1907 and modified to meet the needs of American youth. The purpose of the Boy Scouts of America is to provide for boys and young adults an effective educational program designed to build desirable qualities of character; to train them in the responsibility of participatory citizenship; and to develop in them physical and mental fitness.

Working in cooperation with the Young Men's Christian Association (YMCA), the BSA was popular from its outset. The BSA network spread throughout the nation and in 1912 included *Boys' Life,* which would grow into the nation's largest youth magazine. Most educators and parents welcomed scouting as a wholesome influence on youth. Scores of articles proclaimed such status in periodicals such as *Harper's Weekly, Outlook, Good Housekeeping,* and *Century.* Attitudes toward the outdoors were actively changing during the 1910s as Americans grew more and more aware of the benefits of contact with the natural environment.

Early scouting undoubtedly fostered male aggression; however, such feelings were to be channeled and applied to "wilderness" activities. Many scholars see such an impulse as a reaction to Frederick Jackson Turner's 1893 pronouncement that the frontier had "closed." Turner and many Americans wondered how the nation could continue to foster the aggressive, expansionist perspective that had contributed so much to its identity and success. The first BSA handbook explained that a century prior, all boys lived "close to nature." But since then the country had undergone an "unfortunate change" marked by industrialization and the "growth of immense cities." The resulting "degeneracy," instructed the handbook, could be altered by BSA leading boys back to nature (Fox, 347).

Roosevelt's personality guided many Americans to seek adventure in the outdoors and the military. BSA sought to acculturate young men into this culture with an unabashed connection to the military. Weapons and their careful use, as well as survival skills, constructed the basis for a great many of the activities and exercises conducted by Baden-Powell, a major-general in the British army. The original Boy Scout guidebook was partly based on the army manual that Baden-Powell had written for young recruits. World War I would only intensify youth involvement in scouting. The connection between "roughing it" in the wild and in the military demonstrated a new twist on the role of nature in everyday American life in the 1910s.

OLMSTED AND THE EFFORT TO DEFINE THE AMERICAN MOVEMENT FOR PARKS

Nature was clearly worth something to many Americans; however, most areas worth their attention were distant from where they lived and worked. How would this new interest in nature influence local environments?

Although the passion for nature in one's everyday life and the preservation interest in national parks each existed by 1900, they did not intersect and evolve into the modern parks movement until the 1910s. The growing interest in the natural environment did not immediately alter the places in which Americans chose to live. In fact, the American landscape urbanized at an increasingly rapid rate in the early 1900s. With the population concentration in more urban regions, the impulse to preserve accessible areas of nature became even more acute. These impulses drew a direct relation to those driving the design of Central Park, the nation's first planned park, and its designer, Frederick Law Olmsted, who was discussed in the Introduction for his design at the Columbian Exposition. Olmsted urged Americans to appreciate the psychological and restorative power of nature. His plans for additional urban parks and the early suburbs brought nature nearer to the lives of most Americans. Olmsted also worked to inspire a national set of parks that would celebrate the nation's symbolic appreciation of its natural resources (Roper, 122-40)

After making his name in New York City, Olmsted moved his practice to Brookline, Massachusetts in 1883. Olmsted had begun work on a park system for the city of Boston, and eventually he focused much of his time on the area known as the Emerald Necklace. In these plans as well as those for the 1893 World's Fair in Chicago, Olmsted sought to advance a shared sense of community. In Olmsted's mind, landscape architecture provided a critical opportunity for the natural environment to shape American life in healthy and productive ways. Particularly in congested urban areas, Olmsted believed parks offered an antidote to stress and artificiality and would help prevent mental decay. In "greenswards" and ornamental trees, Olmsted sought to spread calmness and democracy.

In addition to planning urban uses for natural elements, Olmsted took a pioneering role by defining the form of the emerging national park system. He had written the initial report to establish Yosemite National Park in 1865. Drawing on his Central Park experience, Olmsted viewed the valley's preservation as the creation of a work of art. Olmsted argues in terms of the psycho-sociological theory honed in the Central Park campaign:

It is a scientific fact that the occasional contemplation of natural scenes of an impressive character, particularly if this contemplation occurs in connection with relief from ordinary cares, change of air and change of habits, is favorable to the health and vigor of men and especially to the health and vigor of their intellect.

Without such recreation, in situations "where men and women are habitually pressed by their business and household cares," they are susceptible to "a class of disorders" that include such forms of "mental disability" as "softening of the brain, paralysis, palsy, monomania, or insanity" (Olmsted, *Civilizing*, 17).

THE EVOLUTION OF THE NATIONAL PARK SERVICE

The idea of parks as well as the growing number of natural areas set aside and placed under federal jurisdiction increased legislators' interest in formalizing the government's role in conservation. The effort to connect the growing interest in nature with the idea of national parks

Theodore Roosevelt and John Muir on Glacier Point, Yosemite Valley, California. Courtesy Library of Congress.

gained energy during the 1890s and early 1900s, Congress voted to create additional parks in Sequoia, Yosemite (to which California returned Yosemite Valley), Mount Rainier, Crater Lake, and Glacier (Fox, 111–17).

During these same years, western railroads helped spur tourism to the new parks by building large hotels and rail access. Simultaneously, Congress added other types of sites to the national collection. Prehistoric Indian ruins and artifacts were first preserved by Congress at Arizona's Casa Grande Ruin in 1889. In 1906 Congress added Mesa Verde National Park and passed the Antiquities Act that authorized presidents to set aside "historic and prehistoric structures, and other objects of historic or scientific interest" in federal custody as national monuments.

Behind many of these initiatives was President Roosevelt. He used the act to proclaim 18 national monuments, including El Morro, New Mexico, site of prehistoric petroglyphs and historic inscriptions, and natural features like Arizona's Petrified Forest and the Grand Canyon. Congress later converted many of these natural monuments to national parks. Although these new federal sites reflected the changing interest in preserving nature and history, there remained no unified ethic to tie together these sites (Runte, 88–95).

PINCHOT, MUIR, AND HETCH HETCHY

Due to the mixed motives and lack of organization in the creation of these early parks, it was inevitable that interested parties would soon clash over one site. The parks were vulnerable to competing interests, including industry and development. More surprising, however, early conservationists often squared off against preservationists on what the term "National Park" should mean. Utilitarian conservationists favoring regulated use rather than strict preservation of natural resources often advocated the construction of dams by public authorities for water supply, power, and irrigation purposes. The most memorable of these cases occurred when the city of San Francisco sought to dam Yosemite National Park's Hetch Hetchy Valley. John Muir and other park supporters openly fought the plan. However, in 1913, Congress permitted the dam (Fox, 147–49). Considered a disaster by many environmentalists, this episode forced preservationists to denote more specifically what it meant to call a place a "National Park."

The episode at Hetch Hetchy demonstrated the intellectual weakness of the American parks movement in relation to the idea of preservation. Grinnell, Pinchot, and Roosevelt had led the utilitarian perspective on conservation to a broad audience. Agencies including the U.S. Geological Survey and the Forest and Reclamation services gave the federal government a significant involvement in conservation. However, no comparable bureau in Washington spoke for preservation. A wealthy Chicago businessman named Stephen T. Mather recognized this shortcoming. When he brought it to the attention of Franklin K. Lane, the Secretary of the Interior,

Hetch Hetchy Valley, Sierra Nevada Mountains, California, 1911. Courtesy Library of Congress.

in 1915, Lane invited him to join him as his assistant and advisor. When Mather complained to Secretary of the Interior Franklin K. Lane about the parks' mismanagement, Lane invited him to come to work as his assistant in 1915.

NATURE GUIDE: A VOICE FOR WILDERNESS, JOHN MUIR

"Damming and submerging it 175 feet deep would enhance its beauty by forming a crystal-clear lake." Landscape gardens, places of recreation and worship, are never made beautiful by destroying and burying them. The beautiful sham lake, forsooth, should be only an eyesore, a dismal blot on the landscape, like many others to be seen in the Sierra. For, instead of keeping it at the same level all the year, allowing Nature centuries of time to make new shores, it would, of course, be full only a month or two in the spring, when the snow is melting fast; then it would be gradually drained, exposing the slimy sides of the basin and shallower parts of the bottom, with the gathered drift and waste, death and decay of the upper basins, caught here instead of being swept on to decent natural burial along the banks of the river or in the sea. Thus the Hetch Hetchy dam-lake would be only a rough imitation of a natural lake for a few of the spring months, an open sepulcher for the others.

"Hetch Hetchy water is the purest of all to be found in the Sierra, unpolluted, and forever unpollutable." On the contrary, excepting that of the Merced below Yosemite, it is less pure than that of most of the other Sierra streams, because of the sewerage of camp grounds draining into it, especially of the Big Tuolumne Meadows camp ground, occupied by hundreds of tourists and mountaineers, with their animals, for months every summer, soon to be followed by thousands from all the world.

These temple destroyers, devotees of ravaging commercialism, seem to have a perfect contempt for Nature, and, instead of lifting their eyes to the God of the mountains, lift them to the Almighty Dollar.

Dam Hetch Hetchy! As well dam for water-tanks the people's cathedrals and churches, for no holier temple has ever been consecrated by the heart of man. (Muir, *Yosemite*, 255–57; 260–62)

MAKING IT OFFICIAL: NATIONAL PARK ACT, 1916

As is often the case, the battle over Hetch Hetchy marked a loss for preservationists while also clarifying the route for future policy initiatives. The shortcomings of the environmental movement that were shown by the Hetch Hetchy episode focused future efforts of environmentalists to clarify and sharpen the definition and meaning of "the term national park."

Crusading for an independent federal bureau to oversee the U.S. national parks, Mather and Horace Albright effectively blurred the distinction between utilitarian conservation and preservation by emphasizing the economic value of parks as tourist attractions that might spur economic development. Mather initiated a vigorous public relations campaign that led to widespread media coverage in popular magazines. Mather also used funds from western railroads to produce *The National Parks Portfolio,* a lavishly illustrated publication that he sent to congressmen and other influential citizens (Sellars, 48–50).

Even though the Interior Department was responsible for 14 national parks and 21 national monuments by 1916, it had no organization to manage them. Typically, parks were staffed by the army—not for security purposes but because they were the only available federal employees. In Yellowstone and in the California parks, military staff developed park roads and buildings, and enforced regulations against hunting, grazing, timber cutting, and vandalism. They had little or no ability to educate or advise visitors; therefore, national parks included little of what today is referred to as "interpretation."

Congress quickly responded to Mather's publicity campaign. President Woodrow Wilson signed legislation on August 25, 1916 that created the National Park Service and placed it within the Interior Department. The act made the bureau responsible for Interior's national parks and monuments, as well as Hot Springs Reservation in Arkansas (made a national park in 1921), and other national parks and reservations of like character" that would subsequently be created by Congress. The act also stipulated how the Park Service was to carry out site management. The agency's efforts, read the act, "[will include] . . . to conserve the scenery and the natural and historic objects and the wild life therein and to provide for the enjoyment of the same in such manner and by such means as will leave them unimpaired for the enjoyment of future generations."

Mather was chosen to be the first director of the Park Service. His assistant, Horace Albright, became the assistant director (and would eventually become director). Early initiatives clearly laid out a dual mission for the bureau: conserving park resources and providing for their enjoyment. While the bureau's existence emphasized the idea of preservation, the rationale for setting sites aside was for their future use and enjoyment by the general American public. For instance, automobiles, which were not permitted in Yellowstone, would now be allowed throughout the system. Roads would be built to assist tourists in accessing sites by vehicle (Sellars, 55–61).

DOCUMENT: THE NATIONAL PARK SERVICE ORGANIC ACT (1917)

The National Park Service Organic Act stipulated that the Park Service should:
> promote and regulate the use of the Federal areas known as national parks, monuments, and reservations hereinafter specified by such means and measures as conform to the fundamental purposes of the said parks, monuments, and reservations, which purpose is to conserve the scenery and the natural and historic objects and the wildlife therein and to provide for the enjoyment of the same in such manner and by such means as will leave them unimpaired for the enjoyment of future generations.

The secretary was specifically given the right to:
> sell or dispose of timber in those cases where in his judgment the cutting of such timber is required in order to control the attacks of insects or diseases or otherwise conserve the scenery or the natural or historic objects in any such park, monument, or reservation. He may also provide in his discretion for the destruction of such animals and of such plant life as may be detrimental to the use of any of said parks, monuments, or reservations. He may also grant privileges, leases, and permits for the use of land for the accommodation of visitors in the various parks, monuments, or other reservations herein provided for, but for periods not exceeding thirty years; and no natural curiosities, wonders, or objects of interest shall be leased, rented, or granted to anyone on such terms as to interfere with free access to them by the public.

A NEW ETHIC FOR AMERICAN PARKS?

With this unified mission, the national parks changed significantly during ensuing decades. One primary change, though, was in the accessibility of new parks. For a variety of reasons, before 1916 the national parks were primarily in the western United States. Although the existence of such parks demonstrated an ethical change in the American relationship with nature, it did not necessarily change the everyday lives of the majority of Americans. During the 1920s, however, the national park system added Shenandoah, Great Smoky Mountains, and Mammoth Cave National Parks in the Appalachian region but required that their lands be donated. Private donors, including John D. Rockefeller Jr. and other philanthropists, joined with the involved states to slowly acquire and turn over to the federal government the bulk of the lands that would combine to make new parks during the next decade (Sellars, 108).

The Park Service also took on another eastern-U.S.-based mandate by accepting oversight of many historic sites during the 1930s. Starting in 1890, Congress had directed the War Department to manage historic battlefields, forts, and memorials as national military parks and monuments. These included sites such as Gettysburg, Chickamauga, and Chattanooga. After succeeding Mather as director in 1929, Albright succeeded in carrying out his predecessor's desire to have Congress move military parks to the jurisdiction of the National Park Service. The popular, largely-Eastern sites increased the Park Service's annual visitation. Over time, however, they also complicated what the service intended by carrying out "preservation." The efforts to maintain certain aspects of the natural surroundings in Yellowstone, for instance, were a very different mission from facilitating visitors' interpretation of Pickett's Charge at the Gettysburg battlefield.

AUTOMOBILITY AND AMERICANS' PARK USE

The intellectual formation of ideas of wilderness at the Adirondacks in the late 1800s was one of the first expressions of the public's growing interest in nature preservation. This same sentiment, however, would soon attract interested Americans westward to existing national parks. Railroads seized this potential and began to develop lines that could specifically take advantage of the American passion for wilderness at the end of the 1800s. Often, the railroad constructed lodges in the parks that were modeled after the Adirondacks' rustic camps.

By the 1910s, park areas had begun to be accessed on an individual basis thanks to a new technology made possible by the petroleum discovery at Spindletop—the automobile. Ironically, the access to wild areas grew from a technology that would ultimately prove injurious to the environment.

The interest in the outdoors, writes historian Paul Sutter, stemmed from a variety of cultural forces, including: "fears of Anglo-Saxon racial degenerations"; feminization caused by urban living; and a culture of authenticity to combat the mass productions of modern technology (Sutter, 22). Individuals became specifically interested in spending leisure time outdoors and, potentially, in wild areas between 1880 and 1920. This era coincides with the popularization of the automobile in the United States.

By the 1920s, the *New York Times* estimated that at least five million autos per year were being used for auto-camping (particularly surprising given that there were a total of approximately 10 million cars on the road) (Sutter, 30). Before roads had been improved, driving long distances was a certain version of a survival experience in its own right. Referred to as auto-camping or "gypsying," drivers often stopped to sleep in open fields or along the side of the road. By the 1930s, pull-along campers (including

Mammoth public auto camp. Courtesy Library of Congress.

the well-known Airstream) had gone into production and helped to make traveling by car even simpler. The development of this impulse included national conferences organized by President Calvin Coolidge in 1924 and 1926, which were each dubbed the National Conference on Outdoor Recreation (Sutter, 39–41).

Some travelers sought the outdoors only to escape the "civilized" world. Others sought out activities such as hunting and fishing. Each of these constituents played an important role in defining the role of nature in everyday American life.

CONCLUSION: MAKING THE RUSTIC AN ALTERNATIVE TO THE MODERN

Many of these impulses congealed into complicated forms that were related to the "rustic" and "wilderness" characteristics that were part of the cultural interest in locales such as the Adirondacks. The use of natural forms in design and home layout was a well-established portion of traditions such as English gardens and urban parks, which were advocated by A. J. Downing and others during the mid-1800s. The blending

One of many New Deal posters to celebrate America's tradition
of National Parks. Courtesy Library of Congress.

of this current with modern sensibilities, however, produced a uniquely
American rustic aesthetic that had never before been applied with such
intensity to buildings.

For instance, as tourists became increasingly interested in visiting national parks, the architectural example used by the NPS often
derived almost directly from the Adirondack camps. The kind of pole-
work closely associated with Adirondack camps was copied elsewhere
in rustic resorts and recreational architecture, appearing in signs, gate-
ways, bridges, and cabins from the White Mountains to Camp Curry in
Yellowstone by the turn of the century. A number of the early hotels in
national parks, such as those of Glacier National Park and Yellowstone
National Park's Old Faithful Inn, were influenced by the architecture

as well as the decorative arts characteristic of the Adirondack camps (Carr, 189–90).

What began the century as a token interest of the wealthy had grown into a federal mandate for the conservation of America's natural resources by 1920. It was not a perfect ethic: priorities still included park tourists over ecology or any natural inhabitants. But the stage was set for American society to begin to consider the human role in nature in a more complicated fashion than it had ever been capable of previously.

3

POLLUTION AND CITY LIFE

EVERYDAY SETTING: PITTSBURGH, PA

Excerpts from the Pittsburgh Survey, 1914

The factory inspector has seemed to most Pennsylvania employers and to all working children a remote and inaccessible dignitary. In Pittsburgh, center of thousands of industrial establishments, there was during the year of the Survey no office of the state government charged with the supervision of these industries, and the number of inspectors was sadly insufficient. It was difficult to find inspectors. Had the Pennsylvania statutes been as effectual as the best laws of any state and had the chief inspector been inspired by modern ideas and labor legislation, it would still be true that his staff of five officers assigned to the Pittsburgh District could not by reason of insufficient numbers cover the ground [which included Braddock, Homestead, and McKeesport]. . . . There was in the city no local collection of records, of certificates of inspection, suits pending, work done by individual deputies, or other current material of interest to citizens whose work closely interlocks with that of the department of factory inspection, such as local boards of health and education, and co-operating voluntary agencies which have to do with working people. (Vol. 3, 189)

Among dust-producing occupations examined in Pittsburgh are stogy making, garment and mattress making, mirror polishing, broom, cork, and soap making. Most of these occupations are productive of vegetable dust. The high percentage of tuberculosis among tobacco workers, second only to that among stone cutters, has led to the supposition that there is something inherently dangerous in the trade itself. The amount of dust varies greatly, however, according as the tobacco is dried by air or by heat. . . . With reference to present conditions, Dr. Kober states that "Workers in tobacco suffer more or less from nasal, conjunctival and bronchial catarrh, and digestive and nervous derangements, and although the mucous membranes gradually become accustomed to the irritation of the dust and fumens, the occupation appears to be dangerous." (Vol. 1, 359)

Industrial work and environment must induce health and not disease if the future shall justify us in employing women in factories. Processes can be made harmless if we work at the problem long enough; workrooms can be made wholesome, speed cut short before the point of depletion. In such an industrial city as Pittsburgh, the medical profession or the department of factory inspectors might take the initial steps toward overcoming the tendency to trade disease by giving employers and legislators more facts about industrial hygiene, exact knowledge of what and how a trade contributes to ill health. (Vol. 1, 366)

I began my study of the industry with no preconceived ideas as to health. . . . I discovered that there is always a fine dust in the air of the steel mill. It was not very noticeable at first, but after being in a mill or around the furnaces for a time, I always found my coat covered with minute, shining grains. A visitor experiences no ill effect after a few hours in a mill, but the steel workers notice it and then declare that it gives rise to throat trouble. . . . Many a workman justifies his daily glass of whiskey on the ground that it "takes the dust out of my throat."

I began to notice after a time that the men with whom I talked were often a little hard of hearing. It was some time before I connected this fact with the noise of the mill. The rolling mills are all noisy, the blooming mills and the plate mills especially so, while the cold saw bites in the steel with a screech that is fairly maddening. When I finally began to make inquiries I found that among the men I met, partial or slight deafness was quite common, and that they all attributed it to the noise.

On a street car the men who are employed where the heat strikes their faces can often be singled out because of their peculiar complexion. Sometimes their faces are red, sometimes covered with pimples and the skin is nearly always rough. (Vol. 4, 58–62)

ENVIRONMENTAL REFORM AT THE GROUND LEVEL

New understandings about nature in American life combined slowly with modern efforts to use technology to solve problems. The first application of such a reformist ethic was seen in American cities, which had borne the brunt of rapid industrial development. In the late 1800s, cities were more often viewed as entities for producing economic development than as places to live. Reformers called for change beginning in the early 1900s.

Today, environmental policies regulate many different aspects of the world around us. This is particularly true of industries and factories that produce air, water, and other types of pollution. Today, we even know that there are different types of pollution: point, which effects the area immediately adjacent to the pollution's creation; and non-point, which effects a wider region—possibly even distant portions of the Earth such as Antarctica. Scientists have given us a much clearer idea about how such pollution damages the surrounding environment as well as the human body.

These ideas, of course, are radically different from those of the nineteenth century, when few questions were asked of economic development. Personal injuries or health problems were considered by many to be the price of having a job. This expectation began to change during the progressive era of the early twentieth century. Muckraking journalists alerted the public and politicians to examples in which industry exploited resources, including the natural environment and the human worker. Unions called for more attention to be paid to workers' rights. In each case, the focus of concern became the massive factories that could be found concentrated in many American cities. Few cities possessed more polluting industries than Pittsburgh, Pennsylvania.

RUSSELL SAGE FOUNDATION STUDIES THE STEEL CITY

New technology had long been accepted blindly as a national good by most Americans. Shifting from this stance was more about new expectations than about new technologies. Experts from a variety of fields began to ask new questions about industrialization. Many of the answers to these questions demanded reform.

When sociologists working for the Russell Sage Foundation looked for a city in which to study the human effects of industrialization and pollution, they immediately found Pittsburgh to be the best case study. Here is how Paul U. Kellogg described the process:

The Pittsburgh Survey has been a rapid, close range investigation of living conditions in the Pennsylvania steel district. . . . It has been made practicable by co-operation from two quarters,—from a remarkable group of leaders and organizations in social and sanitary movements in different parts of the United States, who entered upon the field work as a piece of national good citizenship; and from men, women and organizations in Pittsburgh who were large-minded enough to regard their local situation as not private and peculiar, but a part of the American problem of city building.

The main work was set under way in September, 1907, when a company of men and women of established reputation as students of social and industrial problems, spent the month in Pittsburgh. On the basis of their diagnosis, a series of specialized investigations was projected along a few of the lines which promised significant results. The staff has included not only trained investigators but also representatives of the different races who make up so large a share of the working population dealt with. Limitations of time and money set definite bounds to the work, which will become clear as the findings are presented. The experimental nature of the undertaking, and the unfavorable trade conditions which during the past year have reacted upon economic life in all its phases, have set other limits. Our inquiries have dealt with the wage-earners of Pittsburgh (a) in their relation to the community as a whole, and (b) in their relation to industry. Under the former we have studied the genesis and racial make-up of the population; its physical setting and its social institutions; under the latter we have studied the general labor situation; hours, wages, and labor control in the steel industry; child labor, industrial education, women in industry, the cost of living, and industrial accidents. (Kellogg)

The findings of the Pittsburgh Survey remain one of the best represen-tations of the ills of unregulated industrialization. This study was an important step in the efforts of reformers to help make everyday life in American cities safer from industrial hazards.

Clearly from the excerpts above, the Pittsburgh Survey demanded that industry be scrutinized for its sociological and health costs, and, whenever possible, that companies must make amends to those afflicted because of its pollution or other types of impacts (Tarr, *Devastation*, 64-6).

Steelworker and family in Pittsburgh, Pennsylvania, 1935. Courtesy Library of Congress

NATURE GUIDE: JACOB RIIS URBAN REFORM IN THE PROGRESSIVE ERA

As early as 1890, individual Americans voiced concerns such as those that the Russell Sage Foundation set out to study. In New York City, Jacob Riis, a writer and artist, observed that "three-fourths of [the city's residents] live in the tenements, and the nineteenth-century drift of the population to the cities is sending ever-increasing multitudes to crowd them. . . . We know now that there is no way out; that the 'system' that was the evil offspring of public neglect and private greed has come to stay, a storm-centre forever of our civilization" (Riis).

As an early social reformer, Riis's concern with problems in cities would eventually inspire attention from groups such as the Russell Sage Foundation. Through his sketches and writing, Riis sought to create attention for the causes that he had identified. He showed his intention by titling his book on urban life *How the Other Half Lives*—obviously, he wished to inform the nonurban, nonpoor half of society. By alerting wealthy or middle-class Americans (particularly women) to the living conditions among many workers living in New York City, Riis initiated a social reform movement that would sweep through every American city by the 1920s. This movement, however, relied at least partly on the Gilded Age's ingrained elitism and class division. Many of the reformers and activists of the era held very conservative views of society, including the inability of specific ethnic groups to succeed in American society.

CLASS AND SOCIAL DARWINISM

In this complicated fashion, the nature of urban reform in the early 1900s is intertwined with the bias and racism inherent in American culture of the era. Reformers had to make the assumption that the poverty-stricken were somehow morally, and by extension civically deficient. During the Gilded Age, this concept had combined with the popularity of Charles Darwin's theories of survival of the fittest and Edward Spenser's translation of these ideas into the social realm. Historian Paul Boyer writes: "Common to almost all the reformers . . . was the conviction—explicit or implicit—that the city, although obviously different from the village . . . should nevertheless replicate the moral order of the village. City dwellers, they believed, must somehow be brought to perceive themselves as members of cohesive communities knit together by shared moral and social values" (City Beautiful, vii).

These beliefs were given quasi-scientific status (particularly among upper-class Americans) under the term "Social Darwinism." Although they applied the concepts to early 1900s American life, social Darwinists legitimized social inequality by reaching back to the writings of Herbert Spencer. In *Progress: Its Law and Cause* (1857) Spencer wrote:

this law of organic progress is the law of all progress. Whether it be in the development of the Earth, in the development of Life upon its surface, the development

New York, New York. A tenement house in Harlem in early 1910s. Courtesy Library of Congress.

of Society, of Government, . . . this same evolution of the simple into the complex, through a process of continuous differentiation, holds throughout.

While such notions of unidirectional progress are not identical to those described in Darwin's *Origin of Species*, many Americans made a connection. Particularly among the wealthy whites who had benefited from the economic disparity of the Gilded Age, social Darwinism helped to assuage any guilt that they might feel about their opulence. In the social form of Darwinism, different types of humans (cultures and ethnicities) were more fit to succeed than others. The less desirable types of humans, went the dangerous logic, including Native peoples and Africans, were less capable of succeeding in society and should be given menial labor tasks to perform. Such loose, social rankings were also applied to white-skinned, European immigrants based on their country of origin. This allowed informal—and, at times, formal—ranking systems for those hiring factory workers.

In an era when technological change occurred so rapidly, many social ideas lagged behind modern sensibilities. During the early 1900s, these misconceptions influenced the majority of Americans' ideas about social class and race.

DOCUMENT: LIFE IN THE SHOP, BY CLARA LEMLICH

This piece was first published in the *New York Evening Journal,* November 28, 1909. The grueling life of a young, newly-emigrated female factory worker is seen in the account of Clara Lemlich.

First let me tell you something about the way we work and what we are paid. There are two kinds of work—regular, that is salary work, and piecework. The regular work pays about $6 a week and the girls have to be at their machines at 7 o'clock in the morning and they stay at them until 8 o'clock at night, with just one-half hour for lunch in that time.

The shops. Well, there is just one row of machines that the daylight ever gets to—that is the front row, nearest the window. The girls at all the other rows of machines back in the shops have to work by gaslight, by day as well as by night. Oh, yes, the shops keep the work going at night, too.

The bosses in the shops are hardly what you would call educated men, and the girls to them are part of the machines they are running. They yell at the girls and they "call them down" even worse than I imagine the Negro slaves were in the South.

There are no dressing rooms for the girls in the shops. They have to hang up their hats and coats—such as they are—on hooks along the walls. Sometimes a girl has a new hat. It never is much to look at because it never costs more than 50 cents, that means that we have gone for weeks on two-cent lunches—dry cake and nothing else.

The shops are unsanitary—that's the word that is generally used, but there ought to be a worse one used. Whenever we tear or damage any of the goods we sew on, or whenever it is found damaged after we are through with it, whether we have done it or not, we are charged for the piece and sometimes for a whole yard of the material.

At the beginning of every slow season, $2 is deducted from our salaries. We have never been able to find out what this is for. (Lemlich)

NATURE GUIDE: FREDERICK WINSLOW TAYLOR AND THE AMERICAN NATURE OF WORK

With so much emphasis on factories and industrial labor, it is logical that the early 1900s ushered in new ideas to make workers and workplaces function more effectively. Some industrialists such as Ford and Carnegie sought efficiency at least partly to increase their own profits. However, the field of management emerged from the work of America's first bone fide management consultant, Frederick Winslow Taylor. Taylor called his ideas "scientific management" (though they were commonly referred to as "Taylorism"), and he made his services available to business leaders throughout the nation.

Taylor was not the originator of many of his ideas; however, he was able to synthesize the work of others and to promote their ideas to business owners in search of solutions. In the late-nineteenth-century workplace, managers had little interaction with the actual activities of the factory. Taylor urged managers to actively observe the processes of their workplaces in order to establish more effective methods. Ultimately, he formed his observations into a few scientific principles. These basic ideas included clear delineation of authority, responsibility, separation of planning from operations, incentive schemes for workers, management by exception, and task specialization. (Hughes, *Genesis*, 187–201).

Time studies were one of the basic elements of Taylor's analysis of work. He timed workers at tasks in order to establish reasons for better or worse times. In such analysis, of course, little allowance is made for a host of variables. Critics came to believe that Taylor's analysis was often cruel in that it clearly viewed humans as a portion of the industrial process and often expected rigid consistency from their performance just as one might from a machine. For some business owners, however, this was just the type of information they wished to obtain.

FACTORY LIFE

Playing into ideas such as social Darwinism, Taylor remade the human worker into less of a human and more of a machine. Many business owners of the early twentieth century were particularly concerned with the bottom line, and Taylor's ideas gave them good reason to treat workers harshly and to cycle through employees in order to hire cheaper, immigrant labor.

Overall, the years following the American Civil War were a time of industrial and technological expansion in the United States unlike any the world had seen previously. Job creation and industrial development were unequivocally considered to be social goods, in a fashion distinct from any previous era. The heroes of the age were industrial titans with names such as Carnegie, Rockefeller, and Morgan, who would later be called "robber barons" because of their uncompromising commitment to their own fortune. By and large, the political leaders of the era gave way to the whims of these entrepreneurs. In such an environment, unions were shunned by business owners and workers were given few rights. With no regulative agency, consumers bought at their own risk. If a consumer noticed a problem with a certain item, she had no available information technology to alert others. Clearly, the nineteenth century was a frontier-like—"no safety nets"—era of consumption (Trachtenberg, 30).

Faced with little recourse and few rights, many workers struck back in a variety of ways. Lemlich, who was quoted above, sparked the 1909 walkout of shirtwaist makers with her call for a strike. The cloakmakers' strike of 1910 helped workers to establish a grievance system within the garment industry. Only with this system in place were workers in these shops granted the ability to formally complain to their supervisors without losing their jobs. Although many shops remained under the control of owners who disregarded basic workers' rights and imposed unsafe working conditions on their employees, the cloakmakers' strike marked an important step in the workers' rights movement.

THE TRIANGLE SHIRTWAIST FACTORY FIRE

On March 25, 1911, a fire, which broke out on the top floors of the 10-story Asch Building in lower Manhattan, New York, created the type of lesson that made every American reconsider the ethics with which factories were governed. The Triangle Shirtwaist Company was a fairly typical "sweat-shop" factory in the heart of Manhattan, at 23–29 Washington Place, at the northern corner of Washington Square East.

Workers suffered with low wages, excessively long hours, and unsanitary and dangerous working conditions. If they registered a complaint, they were typically fired and replaced with cheaper workers. In this case, when the fire broke out, the exits had been blocked in order to keep workers from going outside on breaks. Unable to flee, many of the workers died in the flames. The fire killed 146 of the 500 employees of the Triangle Shirtwaist Company in one of the worst industrial disasters in the nation's history.

These factory workers, mostly young female immigrants from Europe working long hours for low wages, died because of inadequate safety precautions and lack of fire escapes. As a result of the Triangle fire, the

In the early 1910s, the unions helped to provide striking workers with materials to fulfill their basic needs. This photo shows the commissary during the Chicago garment workers strike. Courtesy Library of Congress.

International Ladies' Garment Workers Union stepped up its organizing efforts and fought to improve working conditions for garment workers. Also a public outcry prompted the New York State Legislature to appoint a commission to investigate the causes of the fire. The commission's investigation, and union organizing, eventually led to the introduction of fire-prevention legislation, factory inspections, liability insurance, and better working conditions for all workers.

MUCKRAKERS AND PROGRESSIVE REFORM

In response to Social Darwinism and the bias of the Gilded Age workplace, a new breed of journalism became both a tool and an expression of social change. Writing fiction, documentaries, and serialized articles, these socially concerned writers began to critically consider the corruption and exploitation involving large companies. The term "muckrakers" was coined by Theodore Roosevelt in 1906 in reference to their ability to uncover "dirt." Roosevelt borrowed the word from John Bunyan's Puritan story *Pilgrim's Progress,* which spoke of a man with a "Muck-rake in his hand" who raked filth rather than look up to nobler things. Roosevelt recognized the muckrakers' key role in publicizing the need for progressive reform but demanded that they also know when to stop in order to avoid stirring up radical unrest.

Many fine writers made their names during the muckraking era of the 1890s and early 1900s. A crucial device in this movement was *McClure's* magazine, which began running installments of muckraking investigations before they were released as books. Ida Tarbell had been at work for years on her history of the Standard Oil Company, and it began to run in *McClure's* in November 1902.

McClure's remained at the heart of this new journalistic form. In the 1880s, S.S. McClure had dropped the price of his general-interest magazine to only 15 cents. He hoped to create a magazine that would appeal to the growing reading masses in the United States. *McClure's* circulation climbed, and it became one of many magazines constructing a new, mass culture that was not restricted to elite Americans. Muckraking articles played directly into this change in readership. From 1902 to 1912, over 1,000 such articles were published in magazines specializing in the genre, including *McClure's, Everybody's,* and *Collier's.* Their efforts caused substantive change to the American view of business and social responsibility.

TARBELL AND SINCLAIR SET THE TONE

Muckrakers demanded action. In at least two cases, the writers received swift and dramatic action. Ida Tarbell was born in the oil regions of northwestern Pennsylvania. She watched as her father's oil tank business failed due to the unfair practices of one company in particular, the Standard Oil

Trust. To Tarbell, the efforts of John D. Rockefeller to place his company in control of the nation's energy, in the early 1870s, formed a turning point for the nation. In the episode known as "the Oil War," Rockefeller sought to dominate petroleum markets worldwide.

Initially, small producers banded together and defeated his efforts. But Rockefeller built his Standard Oil Trust from the ashes of this initial setback. By the end of the 1870s, Standard controlled roughly 80 percent of the world's oil supply. By dominating transportation and refining, Rockefeller dominated the market.

An alarming picture of "Big Oil" took shape as Standard used ruthless business practices, including rollbacks and insider pricing, to squeeze out its competitors. Tarbell, who had become a successful journalist and editor, went to work in order to show Americans what Rockefeller was really doing. Across the nation, readers awaited each installment of the story serialized in 19 installments by *McClure's* between 1902 and 1904. Although Tarbell teemed with bitterness for what Rockefeller had done to the private businessmen of Pennsylvania's oil industry, she appreciated the value of allowing the details of the story to express her point of view. The articles were compiled into the *History of the Standard Oil Company* (1904) and President Theodore Roosevelt, who succeeded McKinley in 1901, used the public furor to pursue a federal investigation. Tarbell's investigation inspired new efforts to enforce antitrust laws. In 1911, the Supreme Court ordered the dissolution of Standard Oil.

Upton Sinclair also achieved significant changes through his writing. Although Sinclair's most famous book, *The Jungle,* was published after Tarbell's, the book's topic gained almost immediate action. *The Jungle* described the meatpacking industry of Chicago, Illinois. Sinclair made the industry the setting for the tale of a Lithuanian immigrant, Jurgis Rudkus. Although Sinclair made the difficult experience of new immigrants the primary theme of the narrative, readers were drawn to the squalid setting in which their meat and other food was prepared. In the end, *The Jungle* exposed to a wide audience the horrors of the Chicago meatpacking plants and the immigrants who were worked to death in them.

The meatpackers protested Sinclair's characterization. "We regret that if you feel confident the report of your commissioners is true, you did not make the investigation more thorough, so that the American public and the world at large might know that there are packers and packers and that if some are unworthy of public confidence, there are others whose methods are above board and whose goods are of such high quality as to be a credit to the American nation"(Cronon, 251–55). However, the public reacted so strongly that the government launched an investigation of the meatpacking plants of Chicago.

Although there was little scientific about Sinclair's account, the public reacted so strongly that the government launched an investigation of the meatpacking plants of Chicago. Working with Dr. Harvey W. Wiley,

In the sheep department, Armour's great packing house, Union Stock Yards, Chicago. Courtesy Library of Congress.

Roosevelt helped press a debated bill into becoming law. The 1906 law forbade interstate and foreign commerce in adulterated and misbranded food and drugs. Offending products could be seized and condemned; offending persons could be fined and jailed. Drugs had either to abide by standards of purity and quality set forth in guidebooks prepared by committees of physicians and pharmacists, or meet individual standards chosen by their manufacturers and stated on their labels.

The exact implications of the law remained unclear for some time. However, clearly, the law empowered Wiley's Bureau of Chemistry to police for violations. When violators were found, the bureau needed to prepare cases for the courts. It was one of the first moments in which progressivism placed the responsibility for protecting citizens' everyday lives on the federal government. Throughout the twentieth century, this expectation consistently increased. As president, Roosevelt held the ideal that the government should be the great arbiter of the conflicting economic forces in the nation, especially between capital and labor, guaranteeing justice to each and dispensing favors to none.

AN ACTIVIST ROLE FOR GOVERNMENT

Spurred by the muckrakers, Roosevelt created a responsive federal government that appeared to be concerned about the welfare of "common" people. However, he remained dubious of the journalists' tendency toward sensationalism. Similar to investigative journalists today, muckrakers could sell more papers or copies by shocking readers. Despite such tendencies, the writing of muckrakers forever altered the role of American journalism and spurred the continued growth of a social consciousness in the United States.

In general, the writings of this era resulted in a political movement known as progressivism. Leaders such as Roosevelt and Gifford Pinchot argued vociferously that the government had a responsibility to its citizens. Some of this social change derived from moralism, which some critics viewed as sanctimonious. Supporters of muckraking and the progressive movement, however, argued that writers such as Sinclair were reformers who were upholding American values and the American way of life.

Roosevelt boldly steered government into its first open confrontation with big business. Roosevelt's reputation as a progressive grew in 1902 when Pennsylvania coal miners went on strike for higher wages and better working conditions. Roosevelt threatened to send in the army to operate mines unless the owners agreed to arbitration. Some people said that this governmental interference went against the U.S. Constitution. They argued that the government had no right to take command of public property. Roosevelt replied, "The Constitution was made for the people, not the people for the Constitution."

Next, Roosevelt attacked a few giant business trusts. These trusts were becoming too powerful, he said, and were preventing economic competition. While some business leaders were angered, many Americans cheered Roosevelt and nicknamed him the "trust-buster." Roosevelt said that he wanted to give a "square deal" to the seller, consumer, employer, and employee. He did this by utilizing the Sherman Anti-Trust Act, which had been enacted in 1890 but largely left unused.

Roosevelt had tapped into a spirit of the times. He perceived the impact of reformers and journalists and appropriated it as part of his progressive initiatives. Progressives argued for an activist government that foresaw problems and acted aggressively to prevent calamities before they occurred rather than reacting to damage already done. Thus they demanded safety legislation, closer regulation of public health issues, and better management of things like public utilities.

By 1906 the combined sales of the 10 magazines that concentrated on investigative journalism reached a total circulation of three million. Writers and publishers associated with this investigative journalism movement between 1890 and 1914 included Henry Demarest Lloyd, Nellie Bly, Riis, Frank Norris, Tarbell, Lincoln Steffens, David Graham Phillips, C. P. Connolly, Benjamin Hampton, Sinclair, Thomas Lawson, Alfred Henry Lewis, and Ray Stannard Baker. Many of these investigative journalists objected when Roosevelt described them as "muckrakers." Some of the journalists felt that the president had betrayed them after they had helped improve his political standing. Lincoln Steffens told him: "Well, you have put an end to all these journalistic investigations that have made you."

In addition to taking on big oil and meatpackers, these muckrakers can be credited with initiating a movement that created significant change between 1900 and 1915. The convict and peonage systems were destroyed in some states, prison reforms were carried out, a federal pure food act was passed in 1906, child labor laws were adopted by many states, a federal employers' liability act was passed in 1906, forest reserves were set aside, the Newlands Act of 1902 made reclamation of millions of acres of land possible, a policy of the conservation of natural resources was followed, eight-hour labor laws for women were passed in some states, race-track gambling was prohibited, 20 states passed mothers' pension acts between 1908 and 1913, 25 states had workmen's compensation laws in 1915, and an income tax amendment was added to the Constitution.

NATURE GUIDE: ALICE HAMILTON AND PUBLIC HEALTH

Although Roosevelt and his progressive allies worked to change laws to help Americans in general, other progressive reformers worked at the grassroots level to help urban Americans. One of the best known was Alice Hamilton, the founder of occupational medicine, the first woman professor at Harvard Medical School, and the first woman to receive the Lasker Award in public health (Opie, 286).

After taking her first academic appointment in 1897, Hamilton was appointed professor of pathology at the Women's Medical School of Northwestern University in Evanston, Illinois, and in 1902 she accepted a position as a bacteriologist at the Memorial Institute for Infectious Diseases in Chicago, Illinois. Dr. Hamilton became familiar with Jane Addams's Hull House, where she began to apply her medical knowledge to the needs of the urban poor. During her stay at the Hull House, she established medical education classes and a well-baby clinic.

During the typhoid fever epidemic in Chicago in 1902, it was Hamilton who connected improper sewage disposal and the role of flies in transmitting the disease. Based on her findings, the Chicago Health Department was entirely reorganized. She then noted that the health problems of many of the immigrant poor were due to unsafe conditions and noxious chemicals, especially lead dust, to which they were being exposed in the course of their employment. In 1910, the state of Illinois created the world's first Commission on Occupational Disease with Hamilton as its director. The commission led to new laws and regulations for Illinois and contributed to the workers' rights movement in the United States. They introduced a new notion that workers were entitled to compensation for health impairment and injuries sustained on the job.

Because of her work in Illinois, Hamilton was asked by the U.S. commissioner of labor to replicate her research on a national level. She noted hazards from exposure to lead, arsenic, mercury, and organic solvents, as well as to radium, which was used in manufacture of watch dials. Although many reformers argued that the industrial environment had become unsafe, Hamilton was one of the first scientists to prove it.

NATURE IN EVERYDAY LIFE: "LEAD MAKES YOUR ENGINE SING"

Voices such as Hamilton's rose up against the preferences and priorities of many other Americans. Many Americans—very likely the vast majority—were just getting used to the conveniences of the modern era. The idea of questioning their worth or safety was lessened by the immediate gratification of the possible. One example of this is the use of lead in gasoline.

Charles "Boss" Kettering had made a name for himself by inventing the self-starting ignition system that eliminated the hand crank used to start early autos. While reformers such as Hamilton focused on elements of human health, Kettering set about to solve a technological ill that plagued the new automobile culture: engine knock, which he referred to as "the noisy bugbear." As vice president of research at General Motors, Kettering guided the scientific team that in December 1921 unveiled a gasoline additive that diminished the knocking sound that came from poorly running engines. GM teamed with DuPont and Standard Oil to market Ethyl, their brand name for the first leaded gasoline on the market.

As tests were run on Ethyl at a Standard Oil facility in 1924, several workers died from a form of sudden lead poisoning in which they became delirious and violent. Reports surfaced that DuPont workers had suffered similar deaths. These incidents gave credence to complaints already being voiced by public health reformers. Public outcry followed when it was learned that Standard Oil had already put Ethyl on the market based only on the results of its own tests with the substance. In some communities, boards of health blocked any sale of Ethyl until it had been further tested.

Unfortunately, there was no federal entity that could investigate the new fuel without bias. Examining the of the impacts of Ethyl's use fell to the U.S. Surgeon General's office. At this time, the Surgeon General was overseen by the Treasury Department. In May 1925 Surgeon General Hugh Cumming formed a panel of experts to consider the new fuel compound, Ethyl.

Also indicative of the era, the hearings were dominated by the corporate entities who had been responsible for developing and testing the new gasoline. The hearing heard experts report that the workers who had died from manufacturing Ethyl breathed much greater amounts of lead than would the general public from the burning of such fuel. Although reformers pointed out the clearly-proven dangers of lead poisoning—citing significant health risks from just small amounts of lead— the corporate effort to prove Ethyl's safety was overwhelming. One Standard Oil

British Petroleum Ethyl anti-knock controls horsepower. Courtesy Library of Congress.

spokesman likened Ethyl to a "gift of God." Leaded gasoline, they explained, would significantly increase the utility of American automobiles. Ultimately, the panel agreed to lift the ban on the sale of leaded gasoline (Gorman, 139–40).

Although the effort to control lead failed, the attempt to place expectations relating to health on large American industries proved a harbinger of things to come. Unfortunately, in the 1920s, the federal government often could not muster the influence to fully control powerful corporations, such as the petroleum and automobile manufacturers. There were, however, some important areas in which the regulative authority of the federal government could have great sway.

FEDERALIZING HEALTH AND DIET

The connection between science and the health of the American public evolved late in the nineteenth century. The first federal efforts at monitoring health focused on one of the most important sectors of the nation's population in the late 1700s: seamen. From 1798–1902, when national security and global trade relied on the stability of this segment of the population, the Marine Hospital Service (MHS)—and from 1902–1912 the Public Health and Marine Hospital Service—made sure sailors had the best health care the nation could muster. Members of the maritime industries, of course, are not government employees; however, their well-being had a direct impact on the nation's economy. Seamen traveled widely and often became sick at sea or in foreign nations. Therefore, their health care became a national problem.

In 1798, Congress established a network of marine hospitals in port cities around the world. Here, doctors cared for these sick and disabled seamen in facilities financed by taxing American seamen 20 cents per month. This payment was one of the nation's first direct taxes, as well as its first medical insurance program.

The progressive era of the late 1800s and early 1900s brought new calls from the public for the federal government to help improve the American standard of living. Of primary concern were well-known epidemics of contagious diseases, such as small pox, yellow fever, and cholera that had caused many deaths worldwide. Congress's interest in enacting laws to stop the importation and spread of such diseases resulted in a significant expansion of the responsibilities of the MHS.

The increase in passenger travel by steamship, for instance, meant that the MHS was responsible for supervising national quarantine, including ship inspection and disinfection, the medical inspection of immigrants, the prevention of interstate spread of disease, and general investigations in the field of public health, including yellow fever epidemics.

The effort to diagnose and treat infectious disease required the application of new science. To help inspect and diagnose passengers of incoming ships, the MHS established a small bacteriology laboratory in 1887. The Hygienic Laboratory was first located at the marine hospital on Staten Island, New York, and then later moved to Washington, D.C., where it ultimately became the National Institutes of Health.

In 1902, Congress passed an act to expand the scientific research work at the Hygienic Laboratory and to provide it with reliable funding. In an effort to spread the impact of good health practices, the bill also required the Surgeon General to organize annual conferences of local and national health officials. To reflect these new responsibilities, the name of the MHS became the Public Health and Marine Hospital Services. Finally, the Public Health Service was established in 1912, just in time to confront one of the nation's most serious health issues (Health).

INFLUENZA PANDEMIC

Increasing interactions because of global trade increased the occurrence and awareness of disease. Although World War I was a global tragedy, it also contributed to one of the most significant pandemics in world history. The influenza (flu) pandemic of 1918–1919 killed between 20 and 40 million people. It has been cited as the most devastating epidemic in recorded world history. More people died of influenza in a single year than in four years of the black death bubonic plague from 1347 to 1351. Known as "Spanish Flu" or "La Grippe," the influenza of 1918–1919 was a global health disaster (Crosby, 23–9).

Ultimately, influenza in the fall of 1918 infected approximately one-fifth of the world's population. The flu usually most affects the elderly and the young, but this strand hit hardest on people aged 20 to 40. It infected 28 percent of all Americans, killing an estimated 675,000. The flu's connection to World War I was clear: of the U.S. soldiers who died in Europe, half of them fell to the influenza virus—an estimated 43,000 servicemen. *The Journal of the American Medical Association* wrote in 1918: "The effect of the influenza epidemic was so severe that the average life span in the US was depressed by 10 years. The death rate for 15 to 34-year-olds of influenza and pneumonia were 20 times higher in 1918 than in previous years" (Influenza).

As the influenza pandemic circled the globe, there were very few regions that did not feel its effects. Primarily, the spread of the flu followed the path of its human carriers along trade routes and shipping lines. Outbreaks swept through North America, Europe, Asia, Africa, Brazil, and the South Pacific in 1919. In India the mortality rate was extremely high at around 50 deaths from influenza per 1,000 people.

Ports such as Boston, where materials were shipped out to the battlefront, were the most heavily affected American cities. The flu first arrived in Boston in September of 1918. Then, however, the disease became more diffuse when soldiers brought the virus with them to those they contacted. In October 1918 alone, the virus killed almost 200,000. As

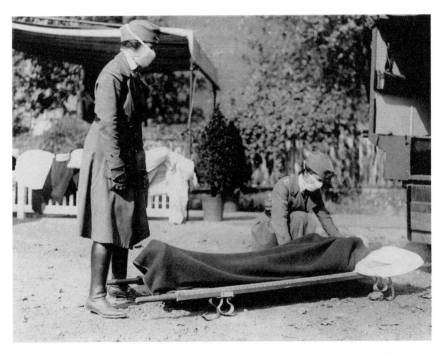

Demonstration at the Red Cross Emergency Ambulance Station in Washington, D.C., during the influenza pandemic of 1918. Courtesy Library of Congress.

people celebrated the end of the war on Armistice Day with parades and large parties, many U.S. cities suffered from public health emergencies. Throughout the winter, millions became infected and thousands died.

In one effort to stall the spread of the disease, public health departments distributed gauze masks to be worn in public. Basic parts of everyday life changed: places of business closed, funerals were limited to 15 minutes in order to fit in more services, and some towns and railroads required a signed certificate to enter. Bodies pilled up throughout the nation. Besides the lack of health care workers and medical supplies, there was a shortage of coffins, morticians, and gravediggers. The public emergency very closely resembled the black death of the Middle Ages (Crosby,15–25).

Philadelphia, the hardest hit of all U.S. cities, was struck in October 1918. By the end of the first week 700 residents were dead; 2,600 died by October 12, and the death toll continued to rise. Although no single group or neighborhood was entirely spared, immigrant neighborhoods—where basic sanitation and overall health were poorest—were the hardest hit. By November 2, the death toll in Philadelphia from the flu reached a staggering 12,162 people.

Through this public health disaster, Americans learned a valuable lesson: the federal government needed to be used proactively to assist in preventing such outbreaks and helping to ensure and educate Americans on better health practices.

IMPACTS OF AUTO MANUFACTURING

Industry and new technology continued to lead the American economy forward while the federal government attempted to establish a balance that would allow it some control for the sake of issues such as human health. The greatest example of this rapid industrial growth could be seen around Detroit, Michigan, the hub of the nation's emerging automobile industry.

The scale of auto manufacturing was unlike any manufacturing undertaking that the nation had ever seen before. Ford's plants around Detroit, Michigan created the model of the single-factory site that could combine the assorted materials and tasks necessary to turn out mass-produced automobiles. The most famous of these manufacturing sites was the River Rouge Plant. To create the ideal environment for his ideas of mass production, Ford created the Rouge Plant in the late 1920s and early 1930s. It was the world's largest industrial complex, containing cutting edge technology of many types. By concentrating the entire manufacturing process at one site, Ford continued his effort to rationalize and simplify industrial processes. Efficiency was his goal (Brinkley, 200).

One aspect of Ford's pursuit of efficiency was independence. He wanted his manufacturing of autos to be as free as possible from the constraints of other businesses and regions. Therefore, the Rouge Plant was

Ford Plant, 1936: aerial view of Dearborn, Michigan, showing Rouge River Plant of Ford Motor Co., Ford rotunda in lower center, and surrounding area. Courtesy Library of Congress.

built as a nearly self-sufficient and self-contained industrial city. After a decade of construction, the Rouge Plant released the new Model A Ford in September 1927. At that time, the facility contained 93 structures, 90 miles of railroad tracks, 27 miles of conveyors, and 53,000 machine tools. The Rouge Plant alone employed 75,000 employees. By the early 1940s, the Rouge Plant had produced more than 15 million cars.

In order to realize Ford's dreams of efficiency, the Rouge plant incorporated all phases of auto production, including steel forging and stamping operations, manufacturing of parts, and assembling automobiles. In addition, the Rouge Plant included its own power plant, glass plant, cement plant, and a byproducts plant, which produced petroleum products such as paints, fertilizers, and charcoal. To feed the factory's fires, Ford used his own iron ore mines in northern Michigan and Minnesota and coal mines in Kentucky and West Virginia. To transport these raw materials, Ford used his own railroad lines or ships. Over the years, Ford even established a lumber operation in northern Michigan and a rubber plantation in Brazil for tire production.

Remarkably, the Rouge Plant grew even larger during the next decade. In the 1940s, when it employed more than 100,000 workers, the factory

Retrofitted to create jeeps for the war effort during World War II, the Ford River Rouge plant increased production. Courtesy Library of Congress.

grew to include 30 miles of internal roads and 120 miles of conveyors. During the war years, each day the Rouge Plant consumed 5,500 tons of coal and 538 million gallons of water. With this input, the plant could smelt more than 6,000 tons of iron and roll 13.4 miles of glass each day. At its most efficient, Ford estimated that the Rouge Plant produced a new car every 49 seconds. (Brinkley, 154).

Concentrating the production also concentrated the byproducts of manufacturing. Heavy manufacturing created toxic byproducts, soot, and smoke wherever it took place. In the case of the Rouge Plant, the concentration of production ability corresponded with concentrated levels of pollution in the area. When other manufacturers concentrated their production facilities in Detroit, Michigan as well, this region was destined for decades of environmental problems (Hurley, 2–14)

MASS PRODUCTION AND MAIL ORDER

The sweatshops of the early 1900s and the mass-production factories of the 1920s were each profitable ways of organizing industrial enterprises. In the workplace, Americans were becoming part of mechanical processes at a rapid pace. The same change was occurring to many Americans outside of the workplace. Systems emerged to organize many portions of American life. In hindsight, some of these—such as mass production—made humans part of mechanical processes in a way that seemed to dehumanize them. Other examples of domestic systems, though, seemed to have a democratizing effect on American life.

As technology allowed Americans to shrink time and distance, many Americans living in rural areas still enjoyed few of the amenities that were changing life so quickly in urban areas. For rural America, however, change was coming. The first symbol of these new ways of living arrived thanks to Montgomery Ward, the first mail-order house. Starting as a one-page circular in 1872, Montgomery Ward used the parcel post system to develop a mail-order catalog that would become one of the most important articles in the homesteader's world. Often referred to as "The Homesteader's Bible" or "The Wish Book," the catalogue used the mail service to connect outlying areas to American mass culture. By 1893, Montgomery Ward had been joined by Sears, Roebuck and Company.

To increase the usefulness of these catalogues, the U.S. mail service created a new system of delivery that would bring mail to rural residences instead of making them come to centralized post offices. Rural free delivery (RFD) is credited to Pennsylvanian John Wanamaker who was

Ordering from Sears Roebuck catalogue, Pie Town, New Mexico, because of the distance to the nearest store. Courtesy Library of Congress.

the first postmaster general to argue for its need. Experiments with RFD service in West Virginia began in 1896. The West Virginia experiment then expanded, and by 1897 Sears boasted that thanks to RFD it was selling four suits and a watch every minute, a revolver every two minutes, and a buggy every ten minutes (Cronon, 334–40).

A byproduct of RFD was the stimulation it provided to the development of the great American system of roads and highways. A prerequisite for rural delivery was good infrastructure by which the mail could travel. In the early years, the Post Office turned down many petitions for rural delivery because of unserviceable and inaccessible roads. With the desire for mail, however, many local governments designated extensive funds for such improvement. Between 1897 and 1908, these local governments spent an estimated $72 million on bridges, culverts, and other improvements. Such improvements helped to link the nation together as never before (Cronon, 340).

SCOPES TRIAL AND THE THEORY OF EVOLUTION

The inconsistent reach of scientific knowledge and modern ways of thinking about the human's place in the world was never more obvious than in the Tennessee trial of 1925 that became known as the "Scope's Monkey Trial." The school board brought suit against a Tennessee biology teacher who insisted on teaching evolution. In the early 1920s, the older Victorians worried that the traditions that they valued were ending while younger modernists sought to apply the new intellectual revelations that took shape. Intellectual experimentation flourished. Americans danced to the sound of the Jazz Age, showed their contempt for the prohibition of alcohol, and debated abstract art and Freudian theories. In a response to the new social patterns set in motion by modernism, a wave of revivalism developed, becoming especially strong in the American South. The nature of the human species became one of the primary battlegrounds for these groups of Americans.

In the Dayton, Tennessee courtroom during the summer of 1925, John Scopes defended the teaching of a nature-based theory of evolution against the teachings of the Judeo-Christian Bible. His opponent was represented by William Jennings Bryan, three-time Democratic candidate for president and a well-known populist. With his oratorical skills, Bryan led a Fundamentalist crusade to banish Darwin's theory of evolution from American classrooms. In the courtroom, Bryan squared off against the well-known attorney Clarence Darrow, who defended Scopes.

The Scopes trial revealed deep divisions in the nation's interest in and abilities to conceive of scientific findings that might challenge the religious convictions of many citizens. Viewed in this light, Social Darwinism and even segregation become part of a complicated cultural reaction to modern ideas.

Clarence Darrow at the Scopes evolution trial, Dayton, Tennessee, July 1925. Courtesy Library of Congress.

TUSKEGEE INSTITUTE AND THEORIES OF AFRICAN AMERICAN ADVANCEMENT

In a post-Reconstruction era marked by growing segregation and disfranchisement of blacks, the spirit of Booker T. Washington's ideas grew from stark realism. "The opportunity to earn a dollar in a factory just now," he observed, "is worth infinitely more than the opportunity to spend a dollar in an opera house" (Washington, Atlanta Addresss).

Washington began his work at the ground-level in 1881 at a school in Mississippi. Little more than a run-down church, the school housed thirty students. Using the model of the Hampton Institute in Georgia, Washington established basic objectives for the school that became known as the Tuskegee Institute. His goals were: to educate teachers who could return to the agricultural areas of the South; to have students learn by doing while constructing the additional facilities for the Institute; and to provide former slaves with basic concepts of hygiene, manners, and appearance.

Washington's approach won him support in both the North and South. This helped him to raise additional funds for Tuskegee. Ultimately, many benefactors donated buildings and funds to the Institute. Donors

A weaving class, Tuskegee Institute, Tuskegee, Alabama. Courtesy Library of Congress.

whose names were found on buildings included Andrew Carnegie, Collis P. Huntington, and John D. Rockefeller. Such donors agreed with Washington's approach and believed it offered freed slaves the best hope for a prosperous future.

However, not everyone agreed with Washington. For instance, sociologist W.E.B. Du Bois argued that African Americans, like any other population of humans, possess a "talented tenth" who would excel in the arts and other creative enterprises. These skilled thinkers, argued Du Bois, were short-changed by Washington's approach to equality. Other critics called for similar efforts to help develop African-American skills in the arts. Ultimately, these critics helped to stimulate an oasis of artistic and cultural opportunity for black Americans in New York City. By the 1920s, this concentrated activity became known as the Harlem Renaissance.

George Washington Carver, of Tuskegee Institute, studies soils to assess their agricultural capability. Courtesy Library of Congress.

THE GREAT MIGRATION AND ENVIRONMENTAL RACISM

Opportunities such as the Harlem Renaissance worked in tandem with economics to fuel a movement of black Americans out of rural areas of the South and into cities from 1890–1930. The lack of opportunity in the agricultural regions in which most blacks had lived previously contributed to the demographic shift that became known as the Great Migration. In 1890, almost 95 percent of all African Americans lived in the South and some 90 percent of them lived in rural areas. By the 1960s, 90 percent of all African Americans lived outside the South and 95 percent lived in urban areas. African Americans came north to fill the jobs in growing industries throughout the Midwest. Pressures inside the South such as Jim Crow laws and the weakness of southern agriculture also led African

Americans to move north. In a society where lynchings and the legal system prohibited both advancement and protest, abandoning the South provided an opportunity to do both.

Of course, the concentration of blacks in urban areas meant that they suffered a disproportionate contact with the environmental and health hazards of city life. In the early 1900s, the racial composition of the nation's cities underwent a decisive change—particularly during and after World War I. Scholars estimate that in 1910 approximately 3 out of every 4 black Americans lived on farms, and 9 out of 10 lived in the South. Hoping to escape tenant farming, sharecropping, and peonage after World War I, 1.5 million southern blacks moved to cities in the late 1910s and the 1920s. During this period, for instance, Chicago's black population grew 148 percent, Cleveland's by 307 percent, and Detroit's by 611 percent (Lemann, 4–16).

When racial equality was resisted by most Americans and even the federal government, many blacks rebelled. Riots and other problems related to segregation were also concentrated in urban areas, beginning with the 1908 riot in Springfield, Illinois, which spurred the formation of the National Association for the Advancement of Colored People (NAACP). Under the influence of Du Bois and others, the NAACP established its headquarters in Harlem and helped to lay the foundation for the Harlem Renaissance. The Urban League was formed in 1910 to protect the interests of these migrants in northern cities. Confined to all-black neighborhoods, African Americans created cities-within-cities during the 1920s. Harlem, in upper Manhattan, was the largest, with an estimated population of 200,000 African Americans. This concentration created social and political power not available before.

AFRICAN AMERICAN URBAN PROTESTS

How could the nature of Americans' ideas of race and the human species be changed? The groundwork for this social shift grew out of the urban enclaves, which provided African Americans with some of the first opportunities to develop a unique culture in the United States. Most often, the culture was distant from the agrarian life in which most blacks had spent their first years in the United States. Now they were an urban people, and the city would present the first opportunities for equality.

When African Americans returned from fighting in World War I, they faced the "Red Summer" of 1919, in which hundreds of blacks were lynched by whites hoping to reject their interest in equality and spur fear among blacks. Instead, urban blacks took part in a series of large-scale riots and public protests. The reaction took many forms and it brought significant changes, almost all of which emanated from the urban interior.

While urban groups rioted, the NAACP fought to change the nation's laws that enforced the color line, and other urban blacks looked to abandon the United States altogether. A flamboyant and charismatic figure from Jamaica, Marcus Garvey, rejected integration and preached racial pride and black self help. By 1917, Garvey's movement had been formally organized as the Universal Negro Improvement Association (UNIA). Based in Harlem, Garvey's organization eventually had 700 branches in 38 states and the West Indies. The UNIA operated grocery stores, laundries, restaurants, printing plants, and clothing factories. Garvey even had the UNIA purchase a steamship line in order to facilitate a return to Africa for any blacks who were interested.

Around the UNIA in Harlem, an enclave took shape that allowed blacks—and particularly the "talented tenth" about whom DuBois had written—their first real chance to develop their talents. The enclave of Harlem was a "safe" place where black artists could develop their talents. Soon, reform-minded young whites—referred to as Negrotarians—began frequenting the clubs of Harlem. The movement for black pride found its cultural expression in the Harlem Renaissance—the first self-conscious literary and artistic movement in African American history.

Very often, the nature of African American life after 1930 became entirely urban, with the memory of slavery helping blacks to almost entirely reject the land and the natural environment. This did, however, contribute to the development of an early wing of the environmental movement that grew from health concerns. With the concentration of industry and pollutants in the urban centers where blacks also were concentrated, clear patterns of pollution-related health problems could be observed. Eventually, protest and litigation resulted in improved corporate, government, and industrial oversight. By the 1970s, the term given to such cases was "environmental racism."

NATURE GUIDE: THE DONORA SMOG, 1948

The perception of environmental hazards in the 1920s and 1930s was very crude. Primarily, Hamilton and other early critics of urban pollution concentrated on the observable and easily traceable impacts that industry had on urban populations. An important event in this progression occurred on October 30–31, 1948. Up to this point, air pollution was suspected to cause significant health problems around many factories; however, it had proven to be difficult to specifically trace. On these days in 1948, atmospheric conditions in the vicinity of Donora, Pennsylvania, helped to concentrate toxic emissions and contributed to the deaths of 19 people within a 24-hour period. Of the fatalities, two had active pulmonary tuberculosis. The other 17 were known to have had chronic heart disease or asthma. All were between 52 and 85 years of age. In addition, approximately 500 residents of the area became ill, reporting symptoms of respiratory problems. No doubt, countless others suffered in silence (Opie, 454).

Around 1900, Donora had become a prototype of many other industrial cities of the modern era. Incorporated in 1901, its name combined that of Nora Mellon, wife of R. B. Mellon, and W. H. Donner, the purchasers of the land along the river

Strange fog (the Donora smog) brings death to 20 in Donora, Pennsylvania. Courtesy Library of Congress.

on which their Union Steel Company constructed a rod mill that later became the American Steel and Wire Works. In 1902, the Carnegie Steel Company completed a facility that consisted of two blast furnaces, 12 open hearth furnaces, and a 40-foot blooming mill furnace. At the same time, the Matthew Woven Wire Fence Company erected a facility. A third rod mill was constructed in 1916. A year earlier the Donora Zinc Works began production. Such industrial expansion required more effective transportation facilities than the river barges and short-line railroads could provide. The Pennsylvania Railroad bought what had been the Monongahela Valley Company and expanded rail service. By 1908, the Donora station had the largest volume of freight in the "Mon Valley." Of course, these industries needed workers, and job-seekers flocked to the area, especially recently arrived immigrants. In 1948, 14,000 people resided in Donora, and additional thousands lived in towns in the immediate vicinity.

For years prior to 1948, residents complained about the industrial pollutants. An investigation by the state government's Bureau of Industrial Hygiene revealed an extraordinarily high level of sulfur dioxide, soluble sulphants, and fluorides in the air. According to the agency's report and complaints by residents, such contamination of the atmosphere was caused by different portions of the steel-making process, including the zinc smelting plant, steel mills' open hearth furnaces, a sulfuric acid plant, slag dumps, coal-burning steam locomotives, and river boats. Typically, the surrounding hills kept such pollutants from dissipating very quickly. But in addition in October, 1948, an unusually dense fog combined with these other factors and kept the pollutants close to the earth's surface where the residents inhaled them, killing 19.

The Donora Smog Disaster attracted attention to the potential problems related to air pollution from industrial plants. Donora's experience was an odd confluence of factors; however, similar environmental contaminants could be found around many American communities. As a result of the Donora events, Pennsylvania established the Division of Air Pollution Control to study the matter in 1949.

The mechanisms for creating laws and agencies to make significant changes on the federal level, though, were decades away. Eventually, members of Pennsylvania's General Assembly felt the pressure to cleanse Pennsylvania's atmosphere of harmful substances. Consequently, the legislature passed the clean streams law in 1965 and began to enact statewide clean air regulations in 1966.

CONCLUSION: PARKS AND THE CITY BEAUTIFUL

Clearly, in the early 1900s, Americans developed new expectations for their own health and safety. For many decades, though, these expectations remained limited by economic class: wealthier Americans demanded and received reform, while many working-class communities remained unsafe through much of the twentieth century.

Cities, which had long been centers of economic concentration and production, began to be understood more as residential environments by the early 1900s. Although this same era saw a rise in suburbanization, noticeable improvements occurred within American cities as well. From 1860 to 1910 the number of Americans living in cities increased by 46 percent. (Hines, 81). With population centering in urban areas, Americans began to consider issues of crime, health, and poverty with added urgency.

The connection between nature and health was most obvious in the effort to plan natural areas into many cities. The American Park and Outdoor Art Association, begun in 1897, championed outdoor art and the cultivation of beautiful landscapes in great city parks. It consisted of about 230 landscape architects, park superintendents, commissioners, and laypeople who were inspired by Frederick Law Olmsted's park designs. They met annually and encouraged "proper" principles of park development, landscaping of factory grounds, school yards, railroad-station sites, and city streets. They railed against billboards and pleaded for state parks and forest preservation. They emphasized piecemeal, practical projects.

Between 1900 and 1904, a social reform movement took shape that became known as the City Beautiful movement. Planners and reformers designed ideal landscapes—much like that of the Columbian Exposition—within cities in an effort to incorporate municipal art, civic improvement, and outdoor art associations into every city. These efforts joined in the American Civic Association to promote elaborate "model cities," including the design of the 1904 St. Louis World's Fair. Soon, though, the priorities of the City Beautiful effort could be seen in every American city as well as in the development of new suburbs and roadways to connect them. The common theme was planning and design for human living with an aesthetic priority on natural forms.

4

RESOURCE MANAGEMENT AND CONSERVATION

EVERYDAY SETTING: FLEEING THE SOUTHERN PLAINS

From John Steinbeck, *The Grapes of Wrath*

The cars of the migrant people crawled out of the side roads onto the great cross-country highway, and they took the migrant way to the West. In the daylight they scuttled like bugs to the westward, and as the dark caught them, they clustered like bugs near to shelter and to water. And because they were lonely and perplexed [confused], because they had all come from a place of sadness and worry and defeat, and because they huddled together; they talked together; they shared their lives, their food, and the things they hoped for in the new country. . . .

Thus it might be that one family camped near a spring, and another camped for the spring and for company, and a third because two families had pioneered the place and found it good. And when the sun went down, perhaps twenty families and twenty cars were there. . . .

A certain physical pattern is needed for the building of this world [the camp]— water, a river bank, a stream, a spring, or even a faucet unguarded. And there is needed enough flat land to pitch the tents, a little brush or wood to build fires. If there is a garbage dump not too far off, all the better; for there can be found equipment—stove tops, a curved fender to shelter the fire, and cans to cook in and to eat from. . . .

In the evening a strange thing happened: the twenty families became one family, the children were the children of all. The loss of home became one loss, and the golden time in the West was one dream. . . . In the evening, sitting about the fires, the twenty were one. A guitar unwrapped from a blanket and tuned—and the songs, which were all of the people, were sung in the night. . . .

In the morning the tents came down, the canvas was folded, . . . the beds put in place on top of the cars . . . and the cars moved westward. . . .

Thus they changed their . . . life. [T]hey were not farm men any more, but migrant men. And the thought, the planning, the long staring silence that had gone out to the fields, went now to the roads. . . . Eyes watched the tires, ears listened to the clattering motors, and minds struggled with oil, with gasoline. . . . Then a broken gear was a tragedy. . . . The fears that had once apprehended [surrounded] drought or flood now lingered with anything that might stop the westward crawling.

WESTERN EXPANSION AND AGRICULTURE

The climatic event that stripped much of the midwestern United States of topsoil is called the Dust Bowl. This ecological disaster awakened Americans to the need for a change in the ethic with which it used and managed its supply of natural resources. The dust storms were partly weather phenomena; however, as historian Donald Worster writes, they were also a product of a culture working perfectly. He writes, "It cannot be blamed on illiteracy or overpopulation or social disorder. It came about because the culture was operating in precisely the way it was supposed to" (Worster, *Dust Bowl*, 4). This expansionist ethic had largely governed settlement and agriculture on the Great Plains in the early 1900s. The expansionist zeal behind the 1893 Columbian Exposition led a nation to tear away the grasses that naturally preserved the rich soils of the Midwest in order to clear the way for agriculture.

By World War I, the nation's agriculture had settled into basic patterns based primarily on region and climate but also containing important elements of cultural traditions. In areas such as the upper Midwest, this meant dairy farming (since ancestors had begun the tradition). In the Great Plains from Texas to the Canadian border, however, agricultural traditions grew at least partly from national cultural patterns. Here, in the country's breadbasket, settlers had been assured that vast fields of wheat were the best way of making a profit from the vast expanse of flat lands. Their crop relied on railroads to carry grain to distribution centers such as Chicago, Illinois. Most often, the crop required more moisture than what fell from the sky (Worster, *Dust Bowl*, 34).

Although American agriculture was extremely productive relative to that of other nations, most farmers were not prosperous. In 1900 income per worker in agriculture was only $260 annually compared to $622 for nonagricultural workers. Tenancy increased from 25 to 35 percent between 1880 and 1900. World War I brought a great boon to wheat farmers as the federal government urged that "Wheat will win the War!" The demand for farm commodities increased and land values rose. In addition, the federal government offered farmers subsidies to help pay for tractors and other new agricultural technology that could increase production.

Dust storms on the Great Plains. Courtesy Library of Congress.

The period of 1900 to 1920 went down as a golden age for Great Plains agriculture (Opie, 357–59).

What followed, however, was worse than anyone could have imagined. Postwar price drops hit Great Plains farmers particularly hard. Although federal assistance was considered, it did not arrive until the 1933 Agricultural Adjustment Act that inaugurated a wide range of federal assistance programs, including the stabilization of the prices of basic agricultural commodities, encouragement of soil conservation, and subsidizing of exports. But it became clear in the early 1930s that the golden 1920s had taken a toll on Plains farming.

The introduction of the gasoline tractor brought a close to the era of farming with horses and other animals. In addition, the development of bigger and better machines, like the grain combine harvester and the mechanical cotton picker, continued to reduce the amount of labor needed in agriculture. In each case, technology overcame limitations that the regions climate placed on farmers—they could now grow more and spread their crop over larger areas. These changes set the stage for a fairly typical climatic event of the region: drought. During the 1930s, the Great Plains experienced a lack of rainfall that created perfect conditions for an agricultural calamity. Federal efforts to help began during the 1930s and continued throughout the twentieth century. Government payments to farmers in 1934 totaled $134 million; by 1961 they had increased to $1.5 billion, and by 1987 to $22 billion (Schlebecker, 295–300).

During the 1930s, author John Steinbeck wrote about the dreams and the difficulties of the thousands of American farmers who, no longer able to earn livings in their former homes, began a mass exodus to California where they hoped to find work as migrant field hands. In March 1938 Steinbeck toured migrant worker camps in California with a photographer. His assignment was to write a photo essay for *Life* magazine, but he decided the story was too important; and he wrote a novel instead. *The Grapes of Wrath*, an excerpt from which opened this chapter, became an American classic.

INCREASING TECHNOLOGY ON THE FARM

Although many American romanticize the pioneer spirit that allowed settlers to establish agriculture in inhospitable regions, a more realistic perspective had become evident on the ground level by the early 1900s. For instance, W.A. Peffer published his *The Farmer's Side* in 1891 to suggest the real power structure in agricultural regions of the West.

The railroad builder, the banker, the money changer, and the manufacturer undermined the farmer. . . . The manufacturer came with his woolen mill, his carding mill, his broom factory, his rope factory, his wooden-ware factory, his cotton factory, his pork-packing establishment, his canning factory and fruit-preserving houses; the little shop on the farm has given place to the large shop in town; the wagon-maker's shop in the neighborhood has given way to the large establishment in the city where men by the thousand work and where a hundred or two hundred wagons are made in a week; the shoemaker's shop has given way to large establishments in the cities where most of the work is done by machines; the old smoke house has given way to the packing house, and the fruit cellars have been displaced by preserving factories. The farmer now is compelled to go to town for nearly everything that he wants. . . . And what is worse than all, if he needs a little more money than he has about him, he is compelled to go to town to borrow it. But he does not find the money there; in place of it he finds an agent who will "negotiate" a loan for him. The money is in the East . . . five thousand miles away. He pays the agent his commission, pays all the expenses of looking through the records and furnishing abstracts, pays for every postage stamp used in the transaction, and finally receives a draft for the amount of money required, minus these expenses. In this way the farmers of the country today are maintaining an army of middlemen, loan agents, bankers, and others, who are absolutely worthless for all good purposes in the community. . . .

From this array of testimony the reader need have no difficulty in determining for himself "how we got here." The hand of the money changer is upon us. Money dictates our financial policy; money controls the business of the country; money is despoiling the people. . . . These men of Wall Street . . . hold the bonds of nearly every state, county, city and township in the Union; every railroad owes them more than it is worth. Corners in grain and other products of toil are the legitimate fruits of Wall Street methods. (Peffer, 42, 56, 58–63, 121–23)

CONSERVING FORESTS BECOMES A FEDERAL JOB

The concept of conservation in the United States began far from the Great Plains and in an ecosystem altogether dissimilar from the prairie. The term was used most in reference to forest reserves, which trace their origin to an 1876 act of Congress that created the Forest Service. Based on the lessons of European nations, this act authorized the Department of Agriculture to hire a forestry agent who would investigate the present and future supply of timber. In addition, he studied the methods employed by other nations attempting to manage or conserve timber supplies. Although federal forest lands were not set aside until 15 years later, a Division of Forestry was set up in 1881. The first head of the agency was a Prussian-educated forester named Bernhard E. Hough. Compiling many reports about American forest use past and present, Hough was very critical of American patterns of use. He urged the nation to adopt regulations to "secure an economical use" (Hays, *Gospel*, 28–30).

Although the division began as primarily a disseminator of information, by the 1890s it provided forestry assistance to states and to private forest land owners. In 1891, Congress granted the president the authority to establish forest reserves from the existing public domain lands under the jurisdiction of the Interior Department. The Organic Administration Act of 1897 stipulated that forest reserves were intended: "to improve and protect the forest within the reservation, or for the purpose of securing favorable water flows, and to furnish a continuous supply of timber for the use and necessities of the citizens of the United States." By the early 1900s, this office administered approximately 56 million acres. However, the agency was about to take a leading role in the broader American conservation movement (Hays, 30–33).

NATURE GUIDE: GIFFORD PINCHOT, AMERICA'S FIRST FORESTER

Forest conservation was the business of Gifford Pinchot, America's first native professionally trained forester. He had returned from forestry school in Germany to establish one of the United States's first model forests, which lay on the Biltmore estate of Cornelius Vanderbilt in North Carolina. He took over administration of the National Forests in 1898 and became first chief of the renamed Forest Service in 1905, when the agency took over the forest reserves from the Department of the Interior's General Land Office. The agency was renamed the U.S. Forest Service and, ultimately, forest reserves were renamed national forests. Pinchot voiced a refrain of the conservation movement when he instructed Secretary of Agriculture James Wilson that the goal of forest administration needed to be based on "the greatest good for the greatest number in the long run" (Opie, 389–90).

Pinchot's real fame came when his close friend Theodore Roosevelt became president in 1901. Together, they oriented the Forest Service toward the wise use of timber resources. This guideline was the forerunner of the multiple-use and sustained-yield principles that have guided forest management in recent years. These principles stress the need to balance the uses that are made of the major resources and benefits of the forests—timber, water supplies, recreation, livestock forage, wildlife and fish, and minerals—in the best public interest.

With Roosevelt's support, the 1905 act transferred the Forestry Division from the Department of the Interior to the Department of Agriculture and combined it with the larger Bureau of Forestry. Roosevelt and Pinchot more than doubled the forest reserve acreage in the two years following the merger, to a total of 151 million acres by 1907. This total included 16 million acres that were squeezed through after Congress placed limits on the president's authority to proclaim additional forest reserves. Without congressional approval, Roosevelt designated these areas in defiance of Congress. When he left office in 1909, there were 195 million acres of National Forest (Nash, 152–59).

EDUCATING FORESTERS

By the model set by the new Forest Service, Americans learned to view forests very differently than they once had. Pinchot made sure that applicants to work for the Forest Service needed to demonstrate a mix of formal education and practical aptitude. These new types of foresters, he hoped, would approach old problems differently. Primarily, science would now be included in efforts to solve some of the service's most pressing problems, including fires, overgrazing by cattle and sheep, soil disturbance and stream pollution caused by mining, and insect and disease impacts.

In 1908, the Forest Service established its first experimental station near Flagstaff, Arizona. Other stations were later added throughout the West and eventually in other regions. The Forest Service also established its laboratory to experiment with new products that could be manufactured from forests, while also establishing the framework that would allow states to use the proceeds from any products made from their national forests to be used locally for new schools and other services. With science at its core, the Forest Service initiated some of the nation's first efforts to set aside wilderness and primitive areas. The most famous of these efforts was the Gila Wilderness in New Mexico, which was the first primitive area in the service set in 1930 (Hays, *Gospel*, 44–48).

Forest research got a big boost in 1928 through the McSweeney-McNary Act, which authorized a broad permanent program of research and the first comprehensive nationwide survey of forest resources on all public and private lands. Tree planting in national forests was expanded under the Knutson-Vandenberg Act of 1930. The Forest Service also operated more than 1,300 Civilian Conservation Corps (CCC) camps in national forests during the 1930s New Deal. More than 2 million unemployed young men in the CCC program performed a vast amount of forest protection, watershed restoration, erosion control, and other improvement work, including the planting of 2.25 billion tree seedlings. Although the administration of forests would shift with the political wind, a core ethic had crept into the Forest Service that emphasized conservation of lumber supplies and, at times, administration of national forests as complex ecological sites (Hays, *Gospel,* 264–68).

WHO OWNS A FEDERAL RESOURCE?

Although the government had begun to exert control over the nation's industrial and economic powers by the 1920s, agriculture and other endeavors remained deeply beholden to established financial interests. Clearly, a large segment of the nation continued to view natural resources as raw material for development. Federally owned resources were most susceptible. With the large-scale growth in petroleum use nationwide, many petroleum companies scoured federal lands for any supply of black gold.

By and large, oil exploration continued to be based in western areas. By the 1870s, oil fever had swept specifically into the public domain of California. In the early 1890s, oil was discovered near Coalinga, California, and in 1892 E. L. Doheny drilled the first successful well in Los Angeles. The Placer Act of 1870 included "all forms of deposit" except veins of quartz. The Department of the Interior debated whether this act applied to petroleum and, then, in order to clarify the situation, in 1897 Congress passed another version of the Placer Act that specified its application to oil lands. With this legal framework established, in 1909, President Taft temporarily withdrew three million acres of potential oil lands from the public domain (Oliens, 127–29).

Similar to Roosevelt's coal withdrawals, Taft's act garnered a great amount of debate—particularly in the West. Congress then passed the Pickett Act in 1910 to allow presidents to withdraw public lands for examination and reclassification for various "public purposes." During the 1910s, this act enabled the president to withdraw nearly all of the known oil lands. In order to conserve an adequate supply of oil for the navy, two naval reserves were established by Executive Order in 1912, in Elk Hills and Buena Vista Hills, California. Similar to a forest reserve, the oil supply, administrators believed, was best preserved if left in the ground. These withdrawals were then followed in 1915 by reserves at Teapot Dome, Wyoming and in 1916 by the naval oil shale reserves in Colorado and Utah. In 1923, a similar reserve was created in Alaska (Oliens, 129–31).

While most of the public debate centered on the right of the executive branch to make such withdrawals, other issues emerged as well, including whether the land should be sold or leased to oil companies, whether or not land previously patented to railroad companies could be withdrawn by the federal government as well, and whether or not oil companies had any standing if the federal government wished to withdraw land that they had already leased. These issues, of course, took on greater importance as the United States observed and then participated in World War I at the end of the decade. Petroleum had many military uses, including powering most of the ships of the new navy.

Historian John Ise was one of the loudest critics of such government policy. His argument, however, differed from most of the critics. He wrote in 1926: "During this time there was always overproduction of oil from privately owned lands and there was never any need or justification for opening any public lands" (Ise, 327). While this argument shifted to the fore by the end of the twentieth century, there was little public support for the idea of conservation. Western lawmakers focused on insuring federal supplies of petroleum on public lands when Congress passed the Mineral Leasing Act of 1920, otherwise known as the Smoot Bill. Congress intended this act to bring relief to some of these issues and to offer more equal treatment to interests of the Western United States. In the naval reserves, leases were given only on producing wells, unless the president chose to lease the remainder (Ise, 320–21).

NATURE GUIDE: ALBERT FALL AND TEAPOT DOME

Within six months after the passage of the Mineral Leasing Act, the secretary of the navy was granted extensive jurisdiction over the naval reserves. In 1921, Albert B. Fall, a senator from New Mexico, was appointed secretary of the interior by Warren G. Harding. In short order, Fall convinced Secretary of the Navy Edwin Denby to relinquish control of the reserves and had Harding sign a secret presidential order to this effect. Within a few months, word leaked to the public that Fall had leased reserves in California and Wyoming to his friends in the oil business.

This episode, which transpired in full view of the public, became the primary test of jurisdiction and law regarding energy development and the West. In the scandal known as Teapot Dome, a congressional committee found that Fall had acted secretly and without competitive bidding to lease the Teapot Dome to Harry Sinclair and the California tract to E. L. Doheny. Allowing a private company to develop naval oil reserves, Fall went outside the boundaries of existing law. As a result, he was one of the first members of a presidential cabinet to serve a jail term, convicted of bribery and ordered to serve a year in prison as well as to pay a $100,000 fine.

Fall represented the western interests who felt betrayed by the overly zealous control of the federal government over the development of public lands. Before Warren Harding appointed him as secretary of the interior, Fall had gained experience in farming and ranching. In New Mexico, he owned a ranch that spanned more than 55 miles in length and 35 miles in width. He had been a judge and a sheriff. Throughout his public life in New Mexico, Fall referred to the territory as "corporation country." He hated government interference in business, and he did not have to struggle with torn loyalties when he became a federal employee.

"I have long believed," Fall said in 1918, "that the laws should protect . . . capital and should be so enforced as to offer an inducement for its investment" (Stratton, 40–46). In giving business the advantage of governmental favors, Fall had, however, acted as a man of a certain faith. The core of his faith was simple: since nature's resources were unending, there was no need for humanity to restrain its ambitions and desires. "All natural resources should be made as easy of access as possible to the present generation," Fall declared. "Man cannot exhaust the resources of nature and never will." This, of course, included those resources falling within the public domain (Stratton, 61–64).

When Americans began to hear about Teapot Dome in news reports in the 1920s, much of the public shared a growing appreciation of nature. Fall's feelings were well known to many observers. Upon his appointment in 1921, one newspaper wrote: "To us Fall smells of petroleum and we know what that means among . . . politicians." Another paper, also prior to the Teapot Dome scandal, described the new administrator of federal lands as a man who found "wise conservation of natural resources . . . hateful to his every instinct."

While Fall would be held accountable for his abuse of power on the federal lands, his basic idea of unfettered development and unending abundance remains a reality today. This has been a major portion of the debate over petroleum development on federal throughout the lands.

CORPS OF ENGINEERS

The other emphasis of early conservation ideas was rivers. These efforts, however, clearly stretched modern environmental interpretations of the term *conservation* even more than did forest management. Most typically, river management emphasized development of human communities and how best to control and limit their impact on rivers. Possibly no organization influenced nature in flood-prone areas more than the Army Corps of Engineers. Though the organization was most active in the mid-1900s, it has a long history that began in 1879 when Congress created the Mississippi River Commission. This group of engineers mixed advice from both the military and civilian communities in order to improve the Mississippi River for navigation and flood control (Opie, 308–10).

Cooperating with local levee districts, the Mississippi River Commission oversaw the construction of many levees along the river. Later, dredging would become an additional duty in order to prolong the effectiveness of the levees. In order to slow or stop erosion along this portion of the river, the commission used mattresses made from willow branches. Experiments with concrete mattresses eventually helped the corps to develop the articulated concrete revetment that has been used for several decades to protect the banks of the lower Mississippi River (Hays, *Gospel*, 96, 212).

THE FLOODING MISSISSIPPI OF 1927

Repeated flooding along the Mississippi forced the corps to try a variety of new measures; however, the floods of 1912 and 1913 paled in comparison to what the region endured in 1927. The 1927 flood displaced at least 700,000 and ended any hope of truly controlling the river. This event left a lasting imprint on American politics, society, and on management strategies for the Mississippi and other U.S. rivers (Barry, 13–17). Some planners and historians have argued that the federal effort to recover from the 1927 flood will provide a template for any effort to help the region recover after Hurricane Katrina in 2005. Ironically, however, a significant number of the decisions made as a response to the 1927 flood resulted in the flooding of New Orleans in 2005.

Until 1927, the U.S. Army Corps of Engineers had bypassed secondary channels and outlets and attempted a heavy-handed effort to steer the river where they wanted it to go. The primary mechanism was the levee. In August 1926, the Mississippi began rising, and by January 1, 1927, the river had passed flood stage at Cairo, Illinois. It is estimated that the river remained in its flood stage for 153 consecutive days. The flood shattered most of the levee system from Illinois to the Gulf of Mexico. The flood inundated approximately 27,000 square miles of land in the midwestern United States. The corps managed to keep New Orleans from flooding by dynamiting levees and creating intentional floods at other points. Until that time, the U.S. federal government had left relief from natural disasters in local and private hands. The flood of 1927 was so severe, however, that the government was forced to step in, ushering in the subsequent era of increasing federal involvement in disaster relief and recovery.

The flood of 1927 was most disastrous in the lower Mississippi valley. An area of about 26,000 square miles was inundated. Levees were breached, and cities, towns, and farms were laid waste. Crops were destroyed, and industries and transportation were left at a standstill. The relief effort was massive but uneven, with inequities largely falling along racial lines. Property damage amounted to about $1.5 billion at today's prices. Out of it grew the Flood Control Act of 1928, which committed the federal government to a definite program of flood control. This legislation authorized the Mississippi River and Tributaries (MR&T) Project, the nation's first comprehensive flood control and navigation act. With these new policies came a change in the strategy for federal flood control.

With the old "levees only" policy definitely swept away, there gradually emerged the multifaceted structural approach that remains in place today (Barry, 403–8).

NATURE AT WORK: REMAKING THE MISSISSIPPI

With the Army Corps of Engineers functioning as the nation's beavers, engineers set out to "solve" the problematic Mississippi River. The four major elements of the Mississippi River and Tributaries Project are: levees for containing flood flows; floodways for the passage of excess flows past critical reaches of the Mississippi; channel improvement and stabilization for stabilizing the channel in order to provide an efficient navigation alignment, increase the flood-carrying capacity of the river, and for protection of the levees system; and tributary basin improvements for major drainage and for flood control, such as dams and reservoirs, pumping plants, auxiliary channels, etc. (Colten, 84–86).

The Mississippi River levees are designed to protect the alluvial valley against projected floods by confining flow to the leveed channel, except where it enters the natural blackwater areas or is diverted purposely into the floodway areas. The main stem levee system spans 2,203 miles and is comprised of levees, floodwalls, and various control structures. This system reaches 1,607 miles along the Mississippi River and then along 596 miles of the Arkansas and Red Rivers. During the twentieth century, construction of the levees was financed by the federal government. Once constructed, though, the levees were maintained by local interests with government assistance during major floods. The U.S. Army Corps of Engineers is responsible for inspecting the system in cooperation with local authorities.

Communities from Cairo, Illinois, to New Madrid, Missouri, have grown around the massive banks and levees that are employed to protect them from seasonal floodwaters. Throughout much of this area, the corps created an additional setback levee about five miles west of the riverfront levee. In many communities, such as New Orleans, residents have grown to take these barriers for granted. Hurricane Katrina in 2005 demonstrated how important a tool such levees have become (Colten, 100–101).

FEDERALIZING WESTERN WATER DEVELOPMENT

The Corps of Engineers typically used river conservation plans to assist or maintain existing human communities. When progressive politicians began to see the capabilities of dams, it did not take long for their gaze to turn to the arid regions of the American West. With the Newlands or Reclamation Act of 1902, river engineering was connected to a federal effort to overcome the rainfall deficiencies of the American West and allow it to be "reclaimed" for human development. Although these intrusive projects significantly manipulated western environments, they are typically included under the term "conservation" because they necessitated the careful management and maintenance of natural resources.

The Newlands' Reclamation Act of 1902 was predominantly relevant to irrigation developments in the American West, but it also set the precedent for the Bureau of Reclamation and U.S. Corps of Engineers to use federal funds for hydraulic development of the West, including dams to generate electricity (Riesner, 110–15).In addition, President Roosevelt also appointed an Inland Waterways Commission in 1907, which subsequently issued a report advocating a national policy of planned development of water resources, including both navigable streams and nonnavigable streams on public lands. Multiple uses of the nation's waterways were proposed and were to be financed through the sale of electric power. A conference on natural resources held at the White House in 1908 stressed the necessity of exploiting more fully the nation's hydroelectric power capacity of more than 30 million horsepower in order to conserve nonrenewable fossil fuels.

Originally, the Bureau of Reclamation came to the field of hydropower simply to create revenue while achieving its larger goal of managing the water resource in the arid West. Government planners realized that Reclamation dams could provide inexpensive electricity, which might also stimulate regional growth. Reclamation's first hydroelectric power plant was built to aid construction of the Theodore Roosevelt Dam. Even prior to fully constructing the dam, the bureau installed small hydroelectric generators to manufacture energy for building the dam and running equipment. Surplus power was sold to the community, and this helped citizens to quickly fall in line to support expansion of the dam's hydroelectric capacity.

In 1909, the Theodore Roosevelt Powerplant became one of the first large power facilities constructed by the federal government. Initially, the plant provided the Phoenix area with 4,500 kilowatts before being expanded to over 36,000 kilowatts. Power, first developed for building the dam and for pumping irrigation water, also helped pay for construction, enhanced the lives of farmers and city dwellers, and attracted new industry to the Phoenix area (Reisner, 84–89).

By the early 1900s, hydroelectric power accounted for more than 40 percent of the United States's supply of electricity. In the 1940s hydropower provided about 75 percent of all the electricity consumed in the West and Pacific Northwest, and about one third of the total United States's electrical energy. With the increase in development of other forms of electric power generation, hydropower's percentage has slowly declined and today provides about one-tenth of the United States's electricity.

NATURE AT WORK: HOOVER DAM

The new era of hydro-development in the West received its greatest symbol in 1935, when the Hoover Dam was completed. The large dam and the completeness

Boulder Dam, later known as Hoover Dam, nears completion.
Courtesy Library of Congress.

with which it turned the unruly river to human good sent shockwaves around
the world. In fact, Hoover Dam served as a symbol of the efficiency of modern
technology in general—not just hydroelectric development. The dam, which has
long since repaid the $165 million cost for construction, is a National Historic
Landmark and has been rated by the American Society of Civil Engineers as one
of America's Seven Modern Civil Engineering Wonders. The structure contains
over 4 million cubic yards of concrete, which if placed in a monument 100 feet
square would reach 2.5 miles high—higher than the Empire State Building.

As proposed in the 1910s, the mammoth Boulder Dam (as it was first referred
to) served as the linchpin of a western land-use policy designed to "reclaim" dry,
barren regions by applying human ingenuity. This ingenuity would be applied
to the region's few existing waterways, including the Colorado River. In 1922,
five western states agreed on the Colorado Compact, which parceled up the great
river's flow among the signers—including at least two states that never made

contact with the river. Most of the flow, including the electricity made at Hoover Dam, would be managed by the Six Companies contractors to power development over 300 miles away in Southern California. Today, the majority of Hoover Dam's power is passed over wires to Los Angeles.

The symbolic significance of this immense structure became obvious immediately, which led developers to name it after President Herbert Hoover (an engineer who had been a great supporter of the project). Upon its completion in 1935, Hoover Dam became a symbol of America's technological prowess, firmly placing the United States with the great civilizations in world history. More importantly, however, conservationists had adopted a policy format that included scientific management based in ecological understanding. This perspective viewed technology, such as dams, as a tool of conservation.

EMERGENCE OF ECOLOGY: THINKING IN ECOSYSTEMS

While conservation was taking active form during the early 1900s, an intellectual revolution was changing the scientific ideas of humans' relationship to the natural world. Ultimately, these ideas would converge; however, during this era, conservation remained largely focused on managed development and the science of ecology remained limited to the biology community. This would begin to change in the 1930s (Worster, *Nature's Economy*, 221–24). The intellectual shift, however, had roots in the late 1800s.

Centered around the midwestern United States, a group of scientists participated in and eventually led to the development of the field of ecology. Henry Chandler Cowles, a plant ecologist, helped to lead this group of scientists. When he began graduate studies in 1895, his faculty at the University of Chicago introduced him to the ideas of a Danish scientist named Eugenius Warming. Cowles supplemented his study of botany with the science of physiography. This combination helped him to better appreciate the importance of landforms as a factor in the shaping patterns of plant life. He incorporated these combined approaches to form a theory of dynamic "vegetational succession" that he first expressed in his 1898 Ph.D. thesis, "The Ecological Relations of the Vegetation on the Sand Dunes of Lake Michigan" (Worster, *Nature's Economy*, 206–9).

In his thesis, Cowles used the southern shore of Lake Michigan, which is an area of beaches, sand dunes, bogs, and woods, to demonstrate that the natural succession of plant forms over time could be traced in physical space as one moved inland from the open lake beach across ancient shorelines through the shifting dunes to the interior forest. Along this route, scrubby beach grass would give way to flowers and more substantial woody plants, cottonwoods and pines would be seen yielding to oaks and hickories, and one would finally encounter the climax forest of beeches and maples. If left alone, Cowles argued, nature had a systematic structure of growth and development all of its own (Cowles). Of course, this made it clear that humans were a disturbing agent in the natural world. Cowles's thesis had an immediate and far-reaching impact. Published serially in 1899 in the *Botanical Gazette*, "Ecological Relations" became one of the most influential works in American plant science and quickly established Cowles's reputation as a pioneering American ecologist.

Cowles went on to apply the theory of ecology that he had developed in the Indiana Dunes to the entire range of plant communities found throughout the Midwest. He demonstrated that the natural processes of succession and climax were not confined to the isolated dunes. This demonstrated that plant life in any setting had a great deal in common. Therefore, the patterns of change in plant communities could be more effectively tied to climatic or regional variables.

Cowles and his theories attracted students from all over the world. As these former students became active scientists, the influence of Cowles' ideas grew larger. One study of scientific influences by Douglas Sprugel in 1980 concluded that of the 77 recognized American scientists dominant in the field of ecology from 1900 to the early 1950s, no fewer than 46 were students of Cowles or were directly influenced by professional mentors who had been students of Cowles (Cowles).

These new concepts possessed an intrinsically new way of viewing nature outside of human existence. Although it would not immediately impact American life, the intellectual principles clearly constructed a worldview that relegated humans to simply being one part in a larger natural story.

NATURE GUIDE: CLEMENTS'S IDEA OF PLANT SUCCESSION

Cowles was not alone in recognizing the significance of dynamic succession for the study of plant communities. Independently, Frederic E. Clements (1874–1945) of the University of Nebraska and the University of Minnesota developed the principles of ecology and based them on his studies of the grasslands and sand hills of Nebraska. Simultaneously, Cowles's former student Victor E. Shelford extended ecological theory into the realm of animal communities.

Clements began his ecological work shortly after Cowles published his influential work. In his own work, Clements argued that vegetation must be understood as a complex organism. Beginning in 1913, Clements and his wife established a lab on Pikes Peak in Colorado where they began conducting systematic studies of plant succession (or self replacement) in the surrounding mountains. Clements documented the environmental influences (temperature, sunlight, evaporation, etc.) on specific plants so that any shift could be explained. Their work demonstrated the complex interrelationship that mountain plants have with surrounding insects and animals. Ultimately, his work established verifiable natural patterns for succession within plant species.

In Shelford's work, he applied Cowles' theories of ecology to the animal world. Specifically, Shelford analyzed the impact of ecological variables on the life histories and habits of tiger beetles. His later studies applied these ideas to species including fishes, moths, antelope, lemmings, owls, and termites. Ultimately, Clements and Shelford combined their ideas of plant and animal ecology in, *Bio-Ecology* (1939).

Their essential argument was that neither plants nor animals exist in a vacuum; instead, they must be understood within a complex set of factors and variables. This was a crucial step toward creating the ecosystem concept that would organize ecological thought. Ultimately, these ecological ideas would form the foundation of all of environmental thought (Worster, *Nature's Economy*, 209–18).

THE INTERNATIONAL PHYTOGEOGRAPHIC EXCURSION OF 1913

The United States acted as an incubator for some of these new scientific understandings that eventually moved abroad. One catalyst for the spread of these ideas occurred from July 1913 to September 1913, when American ecologists led by Cowles hosted the International Phytogeographic Excursion in America. The excursion was a scientific tour of significant natural environments in the United States by a visiting party of the leading European botanical experts of the time (Worster, *Nature's Economy*, 209).

Members of the party traveled between cities by rail and made tours of local environments and plant communities. The route of the excursion was east to west, beginning in New York City on July 27 (Tansley). English botanist and ecologist Arthur Tansley reported on the International Phytogeographic Excursion and wrote: "Certainly no member of the international party will ever forget the overwhelming impressions we received of American landscapes and vegetation, designed truly on the grand scale." In particular, he praised the work of American ecologists when he wrote:

In the vast field of ecology America has secured a commanding position and from the energy and spirit with which the subject is being pursued by very numerous workers and in its most varied aspects, there can be little doubt that her present pre-eminence in this branch of biology—one of the most promising of all modern developments—will be maintained. (Tansley)

Ultimately, ecology spread the concept of ecosystems throughout the biological sciences. The term *ecosystem* is credited to Tansley, who in the 1940s argued that nature occurred in self-sufficient (except for solar energy), ecological systems. He would go on to add that such systems could overlap and interrelate. The existence of such systems, of course, began to suggest that the human agent existed as the interloper in any system. Although the spread of ecological understanding among scientists was a significant change in humans' relationship with nature, the new ideas of ecology now needed to find their way to the general public.

NATURE GUIDE: ALDO LEOPOLD AND THE LAND ETHIC

The ideal of wilderness received scientific definition through the growing science of ecology and the related development of the concept of ecosystems. One important figure who carried forward the ideas of Clements, Cowles, and others was Aldo Leopold. Eventually, Leopold would be one of the earliest voices to bring these new scientific principles to the public.

After completing a degree in forestry at Yale in 1909 (from the school of forestry begun by Pinchot), Leopold worked for the U.S. Forest Service for 19 years. Primarily, Leopold worked in the Southwest (New Mexico and Arizona) until he was transferred in 1924 to the Forest Products Lab in Madison, Wisconsin. It was while working in the Gila National Forest that Leopold came to a new understanding about the role of the U.S. Forest Service in managing nature. Leopold writes:

> We were eating lunch on a high rimrock, at the foot of which a turbulent river elbowed its way. We saw what we thought was a doe fording the torrent, her breast awash in white water. When she climbed the bank toward us and shook out her tail, we realized our error: it was a wolf. A half-dozen others, evidently grown pups, sprang from the willows and all joined in a welcoming melee of wagging tails and playful maulings. What was literally a pile of wolves writhed and tumbled in the center of an open flat at the foot of our rimrock.
>
> In those days we had never heard of passing up a chance to kill a wolf. In a second we were pumping lead into the pack, but with more excitement than accuracy; how to aim a steep downhill shot is always confusing. When our rifles were empty, the old wolf was down, and a pup was dragging a leg into impassable side-rocks.
>
> We reached the old wolf in time to watch a fierce green fire dying in her eyes. I realized then, and have known ever since, that there was something new to me in those eyes—something known only to her and to the mountain. I was young then, and full of trigger-itch; I thought that because fewer wolves meant more deer, that no wolves would mean hunters' paradise. But after seeing the green fire die, I sensed that neither the wolf nor the mountain agreed with such a view.
>
> Since then I have lived to see state after state extirpate its wolves. I have watched the face of many a newly wolfless mountain, and seen the south-facing slopes wrinkle with a maze of new deer trails. I have seen every edible bush and seedling browsed, first to anaemic desuetude, and then to death. I have seen every edible tree defoliated to the height of a saddlehorn. Such a mountain looks as if someone had given God a new pruning shears, and forbidden Him all other exercise. In the end the starved bones of the hoped-for deer herd, dead of its own too-much, bleach with the bones of the dead sage, or molder under the high-lined junipers. (Leopold, 129–32)

In 1928, Leopold quit the Forest Service and in 1933 he was appointed professor of game management in the agricultural economics department at the University of Wisconsin, Madison. Leopold taught at the University of Wisconsin until his death in 1948. While in Wisconsin, he purchased a worn-out farm and began to experiment with ways of reinvigorating the soils and of managing the site as a cohesive ecosystem. His efforts may have been the first such ecological preservation effort in the U.S. (Worster, *Nature's Economy*, 271–74).

While working in Wisconsin, Aldo Leopold wrote his best known work, *A Sand County Almanac*, which was published in 1949. A volume of nature sketches and philosophical essays, the Almanac is now recognized as one of the enduring expressions of an ecological attitude toward people and the land. Within its pages, Leopold penned a concept known as the "land ethic," which was rooted in his perception of the human's need to itself as one component in a larger environment. Ultimately, the land ethic simply enlarges the boundaries of the human community to include soils, waters, plants, and animals, or collectively: the land.

Contemporary environmentalists use this ethic as a way of measuring the impact and implications of human activity on the environment. They ask: can we say that we are giving equal standing to soils, bugs, and the air and water? Can we give standing to an element of nature—such as a species of snail or a fish—when it slows or limits human opportunity and development? The land ethic strives to give more equal standing to these other elements of nature. Contemporary environmentalists who are able to fully commit to this ethic often refer to themselves as "deep ecologists." Throughout the late 20th century, though, some variation of Leopold's land ethic could be found in much of the environmental policies that became a normal part of American life.

While Leopold' s writing would construct a new environmental ethic for generations to come, federal programs had begun applying some of the lessons of the new ecology by the 1930s. However, these early efforts rarely reached far enough to meet with approval from Leopold and other idealists.

FORMALIZING A VOICE FOR WILDERNESS

As Leopold and other visionaries applied a new understanding on human's relationships with the natural world, many grew increasingly frustrated with the limits of what was known in the 1930s as "conservation." Although the New Deal initiated many new ways of applying ideas of conservation to the landscape, the alternative ethic of preservation also found new energy. Leopold and others combined the new ideas of ecology with Muir's conception of preservation to organize their efforts around the idea of wilderness.

Robert Marshall, a young wealthy outdoorsman, led the formation of the Wilderness Society. He joined efforts with two other visionaries who were frustrated with their work for in New Deal conservation: Robert Sterling Yard and Benton MacKaye. In early 1935, these three environmentalists joined with Leopold to form an organization committed to the preservation of a wondrous idea: wilderness. Utopian in its conception, the Wilderness Society embodied the ideas expressed by Marshall when he said: "There is just one hope of repulsing the tyrannical ambition of civilization to conquer every niche on the whole earth. That hope is the organization of spirited people who will fight for the freedom of the wilderness." The concept of wilderness prioritized a lack of human impact; however, there was otherwise little definition to the concept or the organization's efforts. This would change during the next three decades.

FRANKLIN D. ROOSEVELT CREATES CONSERVATION POLICY

Ecology only emerged as a bona fide field in the 1930s; however, it quickly became the basis of portions of the massive works projects of the New Deal. When Franklin D. Roosevelt (FDR) took office in 1933, he sought the advice of modern-thinking experts in many fields. Looking into colleges and universities, FDR inserted intellectuals immediately into the emergency of the Great Depression. Both he and the American people expected results. With a long-term interest in the science of forestry and resource management, FDR was particularly struck by the waste of American natural resources at a time of great need. In his inaugural address, FDR stated: "Nature still offers her bounty and human efforts have multiplied it. Plenty is at our doorstep, but a generous use of it languishes in the very sight of the supply." His initiatives sought to intelligently utilize these resources while creating jobs for out-of-work Americans (Henderson, 35).

These policies incorporated ecology with federal policies to manage watersheds, maintain forests, teach agriculture, and hold fast the flying soils of the southern plains. The main impetus for federal action derived from a national surge in joblessness. The economic collapse of 1929 left millions of Americans incapable of making a living. Nowhere was this more evident than on the American southern plains (Worster, *Dust Bowl*, 182–85).

Terrible drought combined with economic difficulty to make many farmers in the rural midwestern United States incapable of farming. Residents of Oklahoma (nicknamed Okies) fled westward to California, creating resettlement problems as well. In the southern plains, the loose topsoil was lifted by heavy winds creating dust storms of epic proportions. Press coverage of the Dust Bowl of the 1930s presented a natural disaster caused by drought and bad luck. Through government-made documentary films such as *The Plow That Broke the Plains,* the New Deal, however, infused a bit of ecological background to explain desertification and agricultural practices that can be used to combat it. In the process of a natural disaster, the American public learned a great deal about its role within the natural environment. Proper land use could be taught, and the federal government installed extension agents to do so.

This was also apparent in New Deal river projects, particularly the Tennessee Valley Authority. Finally, Franklin Roosevelt's pet project, the Civilian Conservation Corps (CCC), merged the earlier Roosevelt's trust in the importance of work in the outdoors for the development of young Americans with scientific understandings of agriculture and watershed management. CCC projects often grew from lessons of ecology—for instance, the need to construct "shelter belts" of trees to help block the wind on the plains and to keep topsoil in place—but their most important priority was creating employment opportunities for young men.

Overall, the emergence of ecology had brought a new utility for science in the everyday life of Americans. Scientific knowledge, however, was still largely controlled by experts—often working for the federal government. During World War II, science would be placed more in the public eye than ever before (Worster, *Nature's Economy*, 339–41).

TENNESSEE VALLEY AUTHORITY CREATES A MODEL OF PLANNING

Moving beyond City Beautiful, aesthetic design merged with science and sociology during the 1930s into a bona fide scholarly field known as "planning." Although many CCC efforts fell under the rubric of planning, the greatest example of New Deal planning was the Tennessee Valley

TVA multi-use dams each resembled the best-known TVA dam, Norris Dam, seen with its powerhouse in this night view. Courtesy Library of Congress.

Authority (TVA). The entire watershed of the Tennessee River contributed to flooding problems on its banks and along the Mississippi River before 1933. In this year, Franklin Delano Roosevelt created the TVA to manage the entire watershed through a system of dams and other structures. The land management system, based in ecology, would restore lost topsoil, prevent floods, stabilize transportation possibilities, and create the opportunity for recreation (Henderson, 182–24).

TVA was an idea based in idealism, and the New Deal offered the forum through which utopian schemes might be put into practice. The TVA Act of 1933 called for the U.S. government to finance, plan, and carry out the revitalization of a depleted region by constructing a series of dams along the Tennessee River to harness the river's potential for generating power while also tempering its flow to prevent flooding. The first TVA project, Norris Dam, cost $34 million to erect. During the 1930s, the United States invested $300 million in TVA projects, creating eight dams along the Tennessee. By 1945, TVA would double the number of dams and in the process put thousands of people to work. These projects, of course, also created controversy by pushing hundreds of residents from their homes.

From the TVA perspective, untrained humans could no longer be entrusted with the vulnerable ecological legacy. Such planning was based on the conservation ethic of efficiency and functionality but especially on limiting waste. In his inaugural address, Franklin Delano Roosevelt revealed the forces that would drive many of his New Deal policies, when he said: "Nature still offers her bounty and human efforts have multiplied it. Plenty is at our doorstep, but a generous use of it languishes in the very sight of the supply." The wealth was available, he suggested, if the management of such resources were conducted with more care.

TVA began with similar aspirations in the minds of Senator George Norris of Nebraska and Arthur Morgan, the founding director of TVA. The regional planning movement grew out of the modern field of human engineering that Norris and others believed could resurrect a downtrodden portion of society. Morgan arrived as a visionary engineer with extensive experience in river management. For his chief planner, Morgan, the utopian dam builder, resisted pressure by Lewis Mumford, the modernist thinker and designer, and others to hire a regional planning enthusiast; instead, Morgan chose Earle Draper, a landscape architect.

Unlike many previous products of landscape architecture, however, the TVA landscape was intended as a multi-use area based in conservation. Morgan and Draper's TVA represented a national trend. As journals for planning were founded and 42 state planning boards were established under the guidance of one national planning board in the 1920s, planners and landscape architects found themselves in great demand. The magical hand of federal authority gave designers carte-blanche to make this valley an ideal, no matter if the plan necessitated moving families, towns, or forests to more convenient locations.

Taming the river led to many ancillary duties, including relocation, town planning, power distribution, and recreational administration. The Electric Home and Farm Authority, for instance, facilitated the purchase of low-cost appliances that could be powered by TVA electricity. Before TVA, 97 percent of those living in the area had no electricity. TVA's control of the river had other accomplishments beyond flood control, including the reduction of cases of malaria, which was thought to be endemic to the region. With these additional duties in mind, TVA conceived of its purpose in a much more far-sighted fashion than simply constructing dams. Once the river was controlled and soil runoff eased, TVA planners set out to make sure that the land would not be depleted again. This was to be accomplished through education.

TVA EDUCATES THE NATION ON CONSERVATION

For 1930s Americans, the practices and products of TVA acted as concrete symbols or archetypes to help the public understand conservation as a concept. The public's education represented the clearest way to solidify support of TVA and conservation. The visual aesthetic of well-managed land, specifically landscape architecture, knitted TVA's system of conservation into a cohesive form and impressed Americans with its pleasing appearance. Landscape architects carried out this vision as they shaped the scenery and functionality of the 41,000 square miles of the Tennessee Valley.

Undoubtedly, TVA designers construed their dams much differently than had the Corps of Engineers or Bureau of Reclamation. The act of stopping a river becomes so momentous that observers equate all such structures with this awesome intention. However, there is a great deal of structural diversity within dam design, and many of these variations suggest different intentions motivating construction. Dams of TVA were neither planned as landmarks nor intended to dominate the natural environment; instead, they were a portion of an integrated system of managed nature that would conserve the resources of the entire river valley. They were a cog in the machine of conservation.

In addition to controlling the floods and erosion of the Tennessee, TVA dams helped to solidify the effectiveness of scientifically based planning and land use in the popular consciousness. One 1940 observer commented that TVA had perfected "the architecture of public relations." For the first time, conservation was able to be envisioned clearly as a distinct scientific act of planning followed by action that led to improved natural resources.

THE LEGACY OF TVA

These systems of recovery, development, and conservation proved revolutionary in American land use. However, the idea for a national system of regional planning authorities dissolved in the shadow of TVA experience. The legal fights that befell TVA in the late 1930s crystallized the American discomfort with the blurring of the line between government and private economic development (these cases essentially involved the right of the federal agency to seize private property in order to build facilities such as dams and power plants). Indeed, such wrangling seems a precursor of current angst focused against the Environmental Protection Agency and general environmental regulation.

Following legal decisions favoring TVA, it may have been possible for regional planning to regain the support seen in the early 1930s; however, World War II forever changed TVA and also, by association, took with it the dreams of utopian planning. In essence, the war burst the original aspirations of planning and quickly changed the job and image of TVA to that of a war-time agency. The outbreak of World War II brought more power needs to TVA, including that needed by the Oak Ridge facility to produce atomic weapons from uranium 235. TVA's power capacity more than doubled to 2.5 million kilowatts in 1946. TVA also diversified its modes of energy production to include coal mining, particularly large-scale strip-mining. The emphasis on energy production made TVA's original mandate fade, permanently divorcing the agency from its utopian roots in regional planning.

"The usefulness of the entire Tennessee River," President Franklin D. Roosevelt had instructed in 1933, "transcends mere power development; it enters the wide fields of flood control, soil erosion, reforestation, elimination from agricultural use of marginal lands, and distribution and diversification of industry" (Henderson, 150). By 1945, TVA by most assessments had accomplished these goals and more. These early accomplishments place TVA as a watershed in American land-use planning, even suggesting an important role for TVA in the development of modern environmentalism. But as TVA's mandate shifted to emphasize power generation after World II, it rightfully earned the ire of many environmentalists, causing most observers to forget its crucial early role in redefining the federal government's role in planning the use of the natural environment.

TVA's role in the complicated twentieth-century movement toward federal environmental regulation suggests the limits of engineering and planning in social or ethical change in American society. The ethical role of the TVA utopia only functioned while it was supported by New Deal rhetoric and propaganda. These ideas linger in American society but find new applications and vehicles. TVA's planned landscape, instead of symbolizing effective conservation, has become an accepted, functioning portion of the natural landscape. TVA's basic legacy has become a defining role for the federal government in regulating and orchestrating the American relationship with the natural environment (Henderson, 148).

CONCLUSION: THE DEPRESSION AND MODERN LAND PLANNING

TVA marked a linkage between ecological regions and community development. However, planning was also being applied to residential communities that would ultimately become an important step in the growth of the American suburb after World War II. In the 1910s, philanthropists and investors launched the first two experiments in Letchworth and Welwyn, England, and then in the 1920s came Radburn, New Jersey. These projects marked the beginning of a new genre of community planning. The emergency of the Great Depression and the Dust Bowl brought the need for extreme measures in planning and development. Under the auspices of Roosevelt's New Deal, Rexford Tugwell initiated the Farm Resettlement Administration, which planned the construction of four greenbelt towns, which prioritized new ideas for community design. The first of these would be named Greenbelt, Maryland, which proved to be the largest New Deal project in the Washington, D.C. area.

The economic difficulties of the 1930s resulted in a significant displacement of rural Americans. The primary goal of the Resettlement Administration was to establish, maintain, and operate communities for the resettlement of destitute or low-income families. For Greenbelt, the Resettlement Administration acquired 19 square miles near Berwyn, Maryland. In 1937 and 1938, approximately 9,000 workers constructed the new community at a price of approximately $13 million.

As the New Deal's chief model of community development and most ambitious experiment in public housing, Greenbelt faced opposition from other political parties. The centralized authority that was necessary for any large-scale ecological or community planning immediately stimulated calls of communism and socialism. Anti-New Dealists dubbed Greenbelt "the first communist town in America" (Callicott, 73). Enemies of the project protested the excessive power the government would gain over the development of the community. In 1952, Congress forced the government to sell the experiment. Before this, however, a community had been formed and informed by the innovative planning and design elements incorporated into the fabric of Greenbelt.

After World War II, American housing became dominated by prefabricated suburbs; however, in the late twentieth century architects and designers searched for a better model. The greenbelt towns provided an important example that resembled the ecosystem concept. Green planners sought to create a human living environment that possessed the least possible impact on the surrounding environment. Eventually, these planned communities inspired architects to design more sustainable communities, a project described as "New Urbanism."

In housing and other areas, the inter-war years had brought ideas of conservation to action. Combined with strands of the ecological ideas reforming the biological sciences during these years, human planning and resource management took on a scientific quality not seen previously. Most often, the conservation impulse required the involvement of the federal government as an authoritative or regulative influence. Although this model met with some success in the 1920s and 1930s, it also linked environmental planning to politics in a way that would remain volatile. Throughout the twentieth century, the government's ability to integrate and administer new scientific understanding would vary with factors ranging from social moods to foreign affairs.

5

EXPANSIVE POSSIBILITIES: LIFE WITH THE BOMB

EVERYDAY SETTING: THE ATOMIC WEST

From Terry Tempest-Williams, *Refuge*

"The Clan of One-Breasted Women: Epilogue"

I belong to a Clan of One-Breasted Women. My mother, my grandmothers, and six aunts have all had mastectomies. Seven are dead. The two who survive have just completed rounds of chemotherapy and radiation.

I've had my own problems: two biopsies for breast cancer and a small tumor removed between my ribs diagnosed as "a borderline malignancy."

This is my family history.

Most statistics tell us breast cancer is genetic, hereditary, with rising percentages attached to fatty diets, childlessness, or becoming pregnant after 30. What they don't say is living in Utah may be the greatest hazard of all.

Over dessert, I shared a recurring dream of mine. I told my father that for years, as long as I could remember, I saw this flash of light in the night in the desert. That this image had so permeated my being, I could not venture south without seeing it again, on the horizon, illuminating buttes and mesas.

"You did see it," he said.

"Saw what?" I asked, a bit tentative.

"The bomb. The cloud. We were driving home from Riverside, California. You were sitting on your mother's lap. She was pregnant. In fact, I remember the date, September 7, 1957. We had just gotten out of the Service. We were driving north,

past Las Vegas. It was an hour or so before dawn, when this explosion went off. We not only heard it, but felt it. I thought the oil tanker in front of us had blown up. We pulled over and suddenly, rising from the desert floor, we saw it clearly, this golden-stemmed cloud, the mushroom. The sky seemed to vibrate with an eerie pink glow. Within a few minutes, a light ash was raining on the car."

I stared at my father. This was new information to me.

"I thought you knew that," my father said. "It was a common occurrence in the fifties."

It was at that moment I realized the deceit I had been living under. Children growing up in the American Southwest, drinking contaminated milk from con-taminated cows, even from the contaminated breasts of their mothers, my mother— members, years later, of the Clan of one-Breasted Women.

It is a well-known story in the Desert West, "The Day We Bombed Utah," or perhaps, "The Years We Bombed Utah." Aboveground atomic testing in Nevada took place from January 27, 1951, through July 11, 1962. The winds were blowing north, covering "low use segments of the population" in Utah with fallout and leaving sheep dead in their tracks, and the climate was right. The United States of the 1950s was red, white, and blue. The Korean War was raging. McCarthyism was rampant. Ike was it and the Cold War was hot. If you were against nuclear testing, you were for a Communist regime. (Tempest-Williams)

ATOMIC TECHNOLOGY AND THE "AMERICAN CENTURY"

When the first atomic weapons exploded over Japan in 1945, observers from all over the world knew that human life had changed in an instant. In the years since, proponents of nuclear technology have struggled to over-come its dangerous potential and to have it be identified as a public good. While technology rapidly became a tool for environmental action, it also presented a downside that inadvertently helped to propel environmental concern. Nothing else embodies this development like atomic technology, including the bombs developed to end World War II. However, this era of nuclear successes created an exuberance for many other technologies as well. Together, the technological developments of the post-World War II era brought the United States a standard of living unrivaled in the world. Atomic technology serves as a symbol of the emergence of the United States as a world power based on its ingenuity and technological develop-ment. Although these strengths translated into economic progress, they also fueled military dominance.

The technology of nuclear weapons and energy began under the control of the military; however, its implications influenced every American— and they continue to do so today. The dangerous implications of nuclear reactions have made it an important part of domestic politics since the 1960s. All of this together illustrates that twentieth-century life has been significantly influenced by "the bomb," even though it has been used sparingly—nearly not at all. A broader legacy of atomic technology can be seen on the landscape, from Chernobyl to the Bikini Atoll or from

Aerial view of atomic bomb test on Bikini Atoll, 1946. Courtesy Library of Congress.

Hiroshima to Hanford, Washington. With this broader legacy in mind, nuclear technology may have impacted everyday nature more than any other innovation. In fact, between its explosive ability and its toxic products, atomic technology changed the order of the natural world, clearly placing with humans the ability to destroy everything.

During the Cold War era, Americans focused on stabilizing everyday life and improving the quality of living for the growing middle class. Nuclear weapons were an important part of this stability. Atomic bombs, which were being tested in the American West, were not known to be a threat to the environment. Information about radiation was not released to the American public. In the opening excerpt from *Refuge*, Terry Tempest Williams describes the plight of many westerners who became "downwinders." Although it is difficult or impossible to prove that their illness and cancer derives from radioactive fallout from nuclear testing, many residents of the region share Williams's perspective that they were unwittingly part of the cost of the technological effort to win the Cold War.

VICTORY GARDENS AND THE HOME FRONT

World War II presented a time of global panic possibly unlike any seen before or since. As powerful, imperialist nations sought to dominate the world, much of the free world—including the United States—lived in fear of attack. Once the attack on Pearl Harbor pulled the United States into the fighting, civilian Americans rallied to support the war effort like never before. Severe rationing was imposed in order to conserve materials needed for the war effort. Many Americans living in urban and suburban areas took a page from the nation's agrarian past and grew many of their own produce in gardens. These came to be called "Victory Gardens."

In 1941 the Agriculture Department startled most Americans by suggesting that if they wanted fresh vegetables on their dinner tables they should plant a Victory Garden. Many urban Americans had little experience with growing a garden. Many novice gardeners experimented with hoe and shovel in order to do their part in the war effort. Armed with seeds and shovels, millions of small town backyard and city rooftop gardens suddenly sprouted across the country. The government reported that by 1943 these "Sunday Farmers" had planted over 20 million Victory Gardens. Their gardens were estimated to produce 8 million tons of food. During the war, this production accounted for over 50 percent of all the fresh vegetables consumed in the United States.

Other efforts on the home front included increased manufacturing and the emergence of women as a force in factory labor. Many of these factories, particularly in the Pacific Northwest and in California, created new models of mass production, especially those manufacturing aircraft. In other areas, though, America's strength in industrial manufacturing combined with cutting-edge theoretical thought to make a weapon not just capable of fighting the Axis powers, but also of defeating them.

WORLD WAR II AND THE EINSTEIN LETTER

World War II was a war with many fronts, including scientific laboratories on each side of the conflict. Physicists in Nazi Germany worked furiously to harness the explosive possibilities of fissioning uranium. Leo Szilard, a Hungarian physicist, in particular was afraid the Germans would produce a bomb first and, with fellow Hungarian physicist Edward Teller, he approached the world-famous Albert Einstein . They asked this great scientist to discuss this danger with U.S. President Franklin D. Roosevelt. In a letter to the president in August of 1939 Einstein told him that "this new phenomenon [a nuclear chain reaction] would also lead to the construction of bombs, and it is conceivable—though much less certain—that extremely powerful bombs of a new type may thus be constructed." Roosevelt initiated one of the greatest efforts in world history to combine military and scientific know-how (Hughes, *Genesis,* 381–85). Ironically, the final decision to develop the bomb did not occur until December 6, 1941, the day before the Japanese bombed Pearl Harbor.

The pursuit of this scientific discovery required one of the most complex industrial research arrangements in history. Officially, the world entered the atomic age on December 2, 1942, at 3:25 P.M. when a team of scientists led by Enrico Fermi were the first in history to initiate a self-sustaining nuclear chain reaction and maintain it under control. Fermi's atomic pile was built underneath the West Stands of Stagg Field, the athletic stadium of the University of Chicago. It had been assembled by football players from the university, who were hired by the scientists for their strength. This technology now needed to be applied to a bomb delivery system.

Eventually, science and the military would be linked in a way never before seen. However, first scientists needed to demonstrate the viability of such a reaction. Under the leadership of General Leslie Groves in February 1943, the U.S. military acquired 500,000 acres of land near Hanford, Washington. This served as one of three primary locations in "Project Trinity," each of which was assigned a portion of the duty to produce useful atomic technology. The coordinated activity of these three sites under the auspices of the U.S. military became a path-breaking illustration of the planning and strategy that would define many modern corporations. Hanford used water power to separate plutonium and produce the grade necessary for weapons use. Oak Ridge in Tennessee coordinated the production of uranium. These production facilities then fueled the heart of the undertaking, contained in Los Alamos, New Mexico, under the direction of Robert Oppenheimer, a California professor of theoretical physics.

The scientists at Los Alamos produced two bomb designs, one using uranium 235 and another using plutonium. Little Boy, the uranium bomb, was a simple gun-type weapon, which the scientists were confident would work and which did not require testing. Gadget, the plutonium-cored implosion bomb, was more complex. The design worked by compressing the plutonium into a critical mass, which could sustain a chain reaction. The compression of the plutonium ball was to be accomplished by surrounding it with lens-shaped charges of conventional high explosives, which had been precision-cast for the purpose. They were designed to all explode at the same instant. The force was directed inward, thus crushing the plutonium core and increasing the density of the sphere. This would have to be tested—experimental verification of the projected results was important since a number of new design principles were involved.

Success came with the first test at 5:29:45 A.M., on July 16, 1945. Code-named Trinity, the explosion took place 210 miles south of the Manhattan Project laboratory at Los Alamos. The results were telegraphed to

President Truman on the evening of the second day of the Potsdam Conference. In a prearranged code, the message read: "Operated on this morning. Diagnosis not yet complete, but results seem satisfactory and already exceed expectations. Local press release necessary as interest extends great distance. Dr. Groves pleased. He returns tomorrow. I will keep you posted" (Hughes, *Genesis,* 390).

To most observers the brilliance of the light from the explosion—watched through dark glasses—overshadowed the shock wave and sound that arrived later. This was a revolution, a giant leap in destructive power. Its yield was the equivalent of 21 kilotons of TNT. The tower that had held the bomb had been evaporated and replaced by a crater 2.9 meters deep and 335 meters across. Residents of Santa Fe and El Paso could see the flash. The shock broke windows 120 miles away and was felt by many at least 160 miles away. Brigadier General Thomas F. Farrell recalled:

In that brief instant in the remote New Mexico desert the tremendous effort of the brains and brawn of all these people came suddenly and startlingly to the fullest fruition. Dr. Oppenheimer, on whom has rested a very heavy burden, grew tenser as the last seconds ticked off. He scarcely breathed. He held on to a post to steady himself. For the last few seconds, he stared directly ahead and then when the announcer shouted "Now!" and there came a tremendous burst of light followed shortly thereafter by the deep growling roar of the explosion, his face relaxed into an expression of tremendous relief. Several of the observers standing back of the shelter to watch the lighting effects were knocked flat by the blast . . . All seemed to feel that they had been present at the birth of a new age—The Age of Atomic Energy—and felt their profound responsibility to help in guiding into the right channels the tremendous forces which had been unlocked for the first time in history. (Groves)

BEGINNING AS A BOMB

By 1944, World War II had wrought a terrible price on the world. The European theater would soon close with Germany's surrender. While Germany's pursuit of atomic weapons technology had fueled the efforts of American scientists, the surrender did not end the project. The Pacific front remained active, and Japan did not accept offers to surrender. "Project Trinity" moved forward, and it would involve Japanese cities, Hiroshima and Nagasaki, as the test laboratories of initial atomic bomb explosions. *Enola Gay* released a uranium bomb on the city of Hiroshima on August 6 and *Bock's Car* released a plutonium bomb on Nagasaki on August 9. Death tolls vary between 300,000 and 500,000, and most were Japanese civilians. The atomic age, and life with the bomb, had begun.

The war ended with the emperor's announcement to the Japanese people on August 15, 1945; however, bomb production did not cease with the cease-fire. The nuclear age had begun and this technology would help to define the rest of the twentieth century. Although nuclear weapons and technology would play a defining role in making the twentieth century the "American century," the symbol of American success would become the standard of living with which we lived: a middle class with technologies not even available to the wealthiest members of many other societies.

AUTOMOBILITY AND SUBURBANIZATION

Living with the bomb altered American life in many ways, but there were other technologies that more directly influenced Americans' interaction with the natural environment. Growing out of the same interest in creating a modern world that integrated new technologies into everyday life, automobility—the reliance on automobiles—presented one of the most ubiquitous technologies in American history. With each passing year in the twentieth century, the American landscape seemed to transform itself in various ways that would better accommodate the automobile and the living patterns that were connected with it.

With the national future clearly tied to cars, planners began perfecting ways of further integrating the car into American domestic life. Initially, these tactics were quite literal. In the early twentieth century, many homes of wealthy Americans soon required the ability to store vehicles. Most often these homes had carriage houses or stables that could be converted. Soon, of course, architects devised an appendage to the home and gave it the French name, garage. From this early point, housing in the United States closely followed the integration of the auto and roads into American life.

Upper- and middle-class Americans had begun moving to suburban areas in the late 1800s. The first suburban developments, such as Llewellyn Park, New Jersey (1856), followed train lines or the corridors of other early mass transit. The automobile allowed access to vast areas between and beyond these corridors. Suddenly, the suburban hinterland around every city compounded. As early as 1940, about 13 million people lived in communities beyond the reach of public transportation. Because of these changes, suburbs could be planned for less wealthy Americans. Modeled after the original Gustav Stickley homes, or similar designs from *Ladies Home Journal* and other popular magazines, middle-class suburbs appealed to working and middle-class Americans. The bungalow became one of the most popular designs in the nation. When new construction halted during the Great Depression, the stage was set for new ideas. As new construction subsequently began, more recent ideas and designs (such as the ranch house) re-made the American suburb.

Planners used home styles such as these to develop one site after another, with the automobile linking each one to the outside world. The ticky-tacky world of Levittown (the first of which was constructed in 1947) involved a complete dependence on automobile travel. This shift to suburban living became the hallmark of the late twentieth century, with over half of the nation residing in suburbs by the 1990s. The planning system that supported this residential world, however, involved much more than roads. The services necessary to support outlying, suburban communities also needed to be integrated by planners.

Instead of the Main Street prototype for obtaining consumer goods, the auto suburbs demanded a new form. Initially, planners such as Jesse Clyde Nichols devised shopping areas such as Kansas City's Country Club Plaza that appeared a hybrid of previous forms. Soon, however, the "strip" had evolved as the commercial corridor of the future. These sites quickly became part of suburban development, in order to provide basic services close to home. A shopper rarely arrived without an automobile; therefore, the car needed to be part of the design program. The most obvious architectural development for speed was signage: integrated into the overall site plan would be towering neon signs that identified services. Also, parking lots and drive-through windows suggest the integral role of transportation in this new style of commerce (Jackson, 159).

In the United States roads initiated related social trends that added to Americans' dependence on petroleum. Most important, between 1945 and 1954, nine million people moved to suburbs. The majority of the

Aerial view of Levittown, New York. Courtesy Library of Congress.

suburbs were connected to urban access by only the automobile. Between 1950 and 1976, central city population grew by 10 million while suburban growth was 85 million. Housing developments and the shopping/ strip-mall culture that accompanied decentralization of the population made the automobile a virtual necessity. Shopping malls, suburbs, and fast-food restaurants became the American norm through the end of the twentieth century, making American reliance on petroleum complete (Kay, 220–25).

HITTING THE ROAD

The earliest suburbs did not necessitate infrastructure such as road construction. However, the rapid expansion of American interest in living outside of urban areas combined with the growing American passion for the automobile by the 1920s to require the development of American roads. Although the motorcar was the quintessential private instrument, its owners had to operate it over public spaces. Who would pay for these public thoroughfares? After a period of acclimation, Americans viewed highway building as a form of social and economic development that was necessary for almost any community to succeed. They justified public financing for such projects on the theory that roadway improvements would pay for themselves by increasing property-tax revenues along the route. At this time, asphalt, macadam, and concrete were each used on different roadways.

By the 1920s, the congested streets of urban areas pressed road building into other areas. Most urban regions soon proposed express streets without stop lights or intersections. These aesthetically conceived roadways, normally following the natural topography of the land, soon took the name parkways. Long Island and Westchester County, New York, used parkways with bridges and tunnels to separate them from local cross-traffic. The Bronx River Parkway (1906), for instance, follows a river park and forest; it also is the first roadway to be declared a national historic site. In addition to pleasure driving, such roads stimulated automobile commuting (Jackson, *Crabgrass*, 166).

The Federal Road Act of 1916 offered funds to states that organized highway departments, designating 200,000 miles of road as primary and thus eligible for federal funds. More importantly, ensuing legislation also created a Bureau of Public Roads to plan a highway network to connect all cities of 50,000 or more inhabitants. Some states adopted gasoline taxes to help finance the new roads. By 1925 the value of highway construction projects exceeded $1 billion. Expansion continued through the Great Depression, with road building becoming integral to city and town development.

Robert Moses of New York defined a new role as road builder and social planner. Through his work in the greater New York City area from

Toll roads, such as the Pennsylvania Turnpike, presented a vision of the automobile future when they began to appear in the 1940s. Courtesy Library of Congress.

1928–1960, Moses created a model for a metropolis that included and even emphasized the automobile as opposed to mass transportation. This was a dramatic change in the motivation of urban design. Historian Clay McShane writes: "in their headlong search for modernity through mobility, American urbanites made a decision to destroy the living environments of nineteenth-century neighborhoods by converting their gathering places into traffic jams, their playgrounds into motorways, and their shopping places into elongated parking lots" (McShane, 38).

NATURE AT WORK: THE INTERSTATE HIGHWAY SYSTEM

The Federal Road Act of 1916 began a century of road building that some historians have called the "largest construction feat of human history," and the American road system unfolded throughout the early twentieth century. Highway building was intensified in the 1950s when President Dwight D. Eisenhower included a national system of roads in his preparedness plans for nuclear attack. Road development for this purpose became a vital portion of Cold War economic growth in the interrelated economy that Ike dubbed the "military-industrial complex." This connection cleared the way for the federal funds to create the world's greatest highway system: the Interstate Highway Act spanned the nation with large-scale roads that could aid with mass evacuations in the event of a nuclear war. In the meantime, though, the roads became the corridor for trade and industry that allowed trucking to supplement and eventually replace railroading (Lewis, 6–12).

Why did such inspiration come to Ike? In 1920, Eisenhower had led troops across the American road system in a military call for new roads. Then he had witnessed the spectacle of Hitler's Autobahn first-hand. When he became president, he worked with automobile manufacturers and others to devise a 1956 plan to connect America's future to the automobile. The Interstate highway system was the most expensive public works project in human history. The public rationale for this hefty project revolved around fear of nuclear war: such roadways would assist in exiting urban centers in the event of such a calamity. The emphasis, however, was clearly economic expansion. At the cost of many older urban neighborhoods—often occupied by minority groups—the huge wave of concrete was unrolled that linked all the major cities of the nation.

THE AUTO ENVIRONMENT

During the twentieth century, planners and designers gave Americans what they wanted: a life and landscape married to the automobile. Most details of the new, planned landscape reflected this social dynamic. For instance, while drivers through the 1930s often slept in roadside yards, developers soon took advantage of this opportunity by devising the roadside camp or motel. Independently owned tourist camps graduated from tents to cabins, which were often called Motor Courts. After World War II, the form became a motel in which all the rooms were tied together in one structure. Still independently owned, by 1956 there were 70,000 motels nationwide. Best Western and Holiday Inn soon used ideas of prefabrication to create chains of motels throughout the nation. Holiday Inn defined this new part of the auto landscape by emphasizing uniformity so that travelers felt as if they were in a familiar environment no matter where they traveled (Belasco, 44–56).

The auto landscape, of course, needed to effectively incorporate its essential raw material—petroleum. The gas station, which originally existed as little more than a roadside shack, mirrors the evolution of the automobile-related architecture in general. By the 1920s filling stations had integrated garages and service facilities. These facilities were privately owned and uniquely constructed. By the mid-1930s, oil giants such as Shell and Texaco developed a range of prototype gas stations that would recreate the site as a showroom for tires, motor oil, and other services. George Urich introduced the nation's first self-service gas station in California in 1947. By the end of the 1900s, gas stations had been further streamlined to include convenience stores and the opportunity to pay at the pump. The gas station experience would steadily become less personalized.

As cars became more familiar in everyday Americans' lives, planners and developers formalized refueling stations for the human drivers, as well. Food stands informally provided refreshment during these early days, but soon restaurants were developed that utilized marketing strategies from the motel and petroleum industries. Diners and family restaurants sought prime locations along frequently traveled roads; however, these forms did not alter dining patterns significantly. In 1921 White Castle hamburgers combined the food stand with the restaurant to create an eating place that could be put almost anywhere. Drive-in restaurants would evolve around the idea of quick service, often allowing drivers to remain in their automobile. Fast food as a concept, of course, derives specifically from Ray Kroc and the McDonald's concept that he marketed out of California beginning in 1952. Clearly the idea of providing service to automobile drivers had created an entire offshoot of the restaurant industry (Kaye, 54–59).

While most roadside building types evolved gradually, the drive-in theater was deliberately invented. Richard M. Hollingshead Jr. of New Jersey believed that entertainment needed to incorporate the automobile. Hollingshead patented the first drive-in theater in 1933, but the invention would not proliferate until the 1950s. Viewing films outdoor in one's car became a symbol of the culture of consumption that overtook the American middle class during the post-war era. Of course, it also established the automobile as a portable, private oasis where youth could express their sexuality as well as experiment with drugs and alcohol.

THE PLASTICS REVOLUTION

No discussion of the social impact of petroleum is complete, though, without acknowledging the abundant materials in our life that are made from petroleum. Since the 1950s, plastics have grown into a major industry that affects all of our lives—from providing more effective packaging of our food or other store-bought items to enabling wondrous new gadgets such as laptop computers, televisions, and cell phones. Plastics now even allow doctors to replace worn-out body parts. In fact, since 1976, plastic has been the most used material in the world, and its evolution has been called one of the top 100 news events of the century (Meikle, 12).

Plastics started well before Dustin Hoffman's character in *The Graduate* referred to them in the 1960s. The creation of synthetic materials that are related to plastics began in 1907 when a New York chemist named Leo Baekeland developed a liquid material that when cooled hardened into a replica of whatever form one chose. He called this resin material Bakelite. This new material was the first thermoset plastic, which meant that it would not lose the shape that it had taken. In fact, Bakelite would not burn, boil, melt, or dissolve in any commonly available acid or solvent.

In this same general product genre, inventors in the early 1900s developed products such as Rayon and cellophane. Very often, large chemical companies such as DuPont had researchers constantly working in labs to develop any synthetic material that might prove to be useful. DuPont developed nylon during the 1930s, but did not make the first pair of stockings until 1939. Many similar innovations also occurred in the 1930s, including polyvinyl chloride (PVC), vinyl Saran wrap, Teflon, and poly-ethylene. Although each of these items possessed well-known domestic uses, most of them were first used in other substances. For instance, during World War II, polyethylene was used first as an underwater cable coating and then as a critical insulating material for radar units. By decreasing the weight of radar units, this material made the technology more portable so that it could be placed on planes.

After World War II, many of these innovative substances found roles in the new American culture of conspicuous consumption. For instance, polyethylene became the first plastic in the United States to sell more than a billion pounds per year. It is currently used for most soda bottles, milk jugs, and grocery and dry-cleaning bags. Of course, the downside of the durability of many plastics is that now they are a major component of the solid waste being thrown away by American consumers.

WAR IN THE ATOMIC AGE: COLD WAR

Although historians speculate that U.S. President Harry Truman elected to use the atomic bomb in order to win World War II, he also clearly wished to set the stage for the next conflict. In short, Truman wanted to impress the Soviet Union, which, even as World War II ended, appeared to be moving independently in contrast to many of the Allies. It is now known that the Soviet Union was able to develop nuclear weapons in relatively short time because of its espionage activities in the United States and the United Kingdom. On August 9, 1949, the Soviet Union detonated its first atomic device, ending the United States monopoly on having nuclear bombs. Prime Minister Winston Churchill announced on February 26, 1952, that the United Kingdom also had an atomic bomb. France and China also demonstrated nuclear capability, and these five countries were considered to be the Nuclear Powers throughout the Cold War period. The technology had clearly altered global affairs.

Nuclear technology had also altered the nature of warfare. In the first major conflict of the atomic era, American led United Nations forces pressed North Koreans out of South Korea and all the way through the Korean peninsula to the border with China at the Yalu River. Led by Douglas MacArthur, the American forces were poised to move even farther. MacArthur waited for the order from President Truman; however, it never came. Truman realized that further escalation would mean a larger conflict with the enemies possessing nuclear weapons. Much to MacArthur's chagrin, atomic weapons had ushered in the need for limited warfare. Truman would send the troops no further.

Truman's successor, General Dwight D. Eisenhower, moved the nuclear era into its next phase by attempting to demilitarize the technology. In 1953, Eisenhower appeared before the United Nations and presented a speech that has become known as the "Atoms for Peace" speech, in which he clearly instructed the world on the technological stand-off that confronted it. The "two atomic colossi," he forecasted, could continue to "eye each other indefinitely across a trembling world." But eventually their failure to find peace would result in war and "the probability of civilization destroyed," forcing "mankind to begin all over again the age-old struggle upward from savagery toward decency and right, and justice."

To Eisenhower, "no sane member of the human race" could want this. In his estimation, the only way out was discourse and understanding. With exactly these battle lines, a war—referred to as cold, because it never escalated (heated) to direct conflict—unfolded over the coming decades. With ideology—communism versus capitalism—as its point of difference, the conflict was fought through economics, diplomacy, and the stockpiling of a military arsenal. With each side possessing a weapon that could annihilate not just the opponent but the entire world, the bomb defined a new philosophy of warfare referred to as a Cold War (Boyer, 22).

The Cold War was predicated on a balanced threat referred to as the doctrine of Mutually Assured Destruction (or, appropriately, MAD for short). So important was this balance to international political stability that a treaty, the Antiballistic Missile Treaty (or ABM treaty) was signed by the United States and the USSR in 1972 to curtail the development of defenses against nuclear weapons and the ballistic missiles that carry them. It was believed that such a system would upset the balance by offering one nation protection from the other.

In the United States, citizens learned to live with the threat of a nuclear attack from the Soviet Union. This threat, of course, was made possible by each nation's very advanced delivery system. Early delivery systems for nuclear devices were primarily bombers such as the American B-29 Superfortress. Later, ballistic missile systems, based on earlier designs used by Germany, were developed by both American and Soviet scientists. Similar rocket systems were also used for nonmilitary purposes, including launching satellites and space travel. Ultimately, these rocket systems were attached to nuclear missiles referred to as Intercontinental Ballistic Missiles (ICBMs) with which nuclear powers could deliver that destructive force anywhere on the globe.

Delivery technologies represented an important facet of the nuclear arms race. Each new development marked an important new chapter in the Cold War. Ultimately, when negotiations and treaties were used to defuse the Cold War, weapons systems were typically used as bargaining chips. Domestically and internationally, cultural implications emanated from the Cold War. On the domestic front, many scholars believe the logic of the Cold War began with one now-declassified document known as NSC-68.

DOCUMENT: NSC-68: LAYING THE GROUNDWORK OF THE COLD WAR

A. Nature of Conflict

The Kremlin regards the United States as the only major threat to the conflict between the idea of slavery under the grim oligarchy of the Kremlin, which has come to a crisis with the polarization of power described in Section I, and the exclusive possession of atomic weapons by the two protagonists. The idea of freedom, moreover, is peculiarly and intolerably subversive of the idea of slavery. But the converse is not true. The implacable purpose of the slave state to eliminate the challenge of freedom has placed the two great powers at opposite poles. It is this fact which gives the present polarization of power the quality of crisis. . . .

The objectives of a free society are determined by its fundamental values and by the necessity for maintaining the material environment in which they flourish. Logically and in fact, therefore, the Kremlin's challenge to the United States is directed not only to our values but to our physical capacity to protect our environment. It is a challenge which encompasses both peace and war and our objectives in peace and war must take account of it.

1. Thus we must make ourselves strong, both in the way in which we affirm our values in the conduct of our national life, and in the development of our military and economic strength.
2. We must lead in building a successfully functioning political and economic system in the free world. It is only by practical affirmation, abroad as well as at home, of our essential values, that we can preserve our own integrity, in which lies the real frustration of the Kremlin design.
3. But beyond thus affirming our values our policy and actions must be such as to foster a fundamental change in the nature of the Soviet system, a change toward which the frustration of the design is the first and perhaps the most important step. Clearly it will not only be less costly but more effective if this change occurs to a maximum extent as a result of internal forces in Soviet society.

In a shrinking world, which now faces the threat of atomic warfare, it is not an adequate objective merely to seek to check the Kremlin design, for the absence of order among nations is becoming less and less tolerable. This fact imposes on us, in our own interests, the responsibility of world leadership. It demands that we make the attempt, and accept the risks inherent in it, to bring about order and justice by means consistent with the principles of freedom and democracy. We should limit our requirement of the Soviet Union to its participation with other nations on the basis of equality and respect for the rights of others. Subject to this requirement, we must with our allies and the former subject peoples seek to create a world society based on the principle of consent. Its framework cannot be inflexible. It will consist of many national communities of great and varying abilities and resources, and hence of war potential. The seeds of conflicts will inevitably exist or will come into being. To acknowledge this is only to acknowledge the impossibility of a final solution. Not to acknowledge it can be fatally dangerous in a world in which there are no final solutions.

All these objectives of a free society are equally valid and necessary in peace and war. But every consideration of devotion to our fundamental values and to our national security demands that we seek to achieve them by the strategy of the cold war. It is only by developing the moral and material strength of the free world that the Soviet regime will become convinced of the falsity of its assumptions and that the pre-conditions for workable agreements can be created. By practically demonstrating the integrity and vitality of our system the free world widens the area of possible agreement and thus can hope gradually to bring about a Soviet acknowledgement of realities which in sum will eventually constitute a frustration of the Soviet design. Short of this, however, it might be possible to create a situation which will induce the Soviet Union to accommodate itself, with or without the conscious abandonment of its design, to coexistence on tolerable terms with the non-Soviet world. Such a development would be a triumph for the idea of freedom and democracy. It must be an immediate objective of United States policy. (NSC-68)

LIVING WITH THE BOMB

Although the nuclear bomb had shortened World War II for Americans, it was a horrific weapon that seemed to contradict nearly everything for which the United States stood. One historian describes the announcement of the bomb's use in Japan as a "psychic event of almost unprecedented proportions" (Boyer, 22). Eventually, the Soviet nuclear threat created additional anxiety for Americans. In response, some Americans constructed bomb shelters in backyards. Nearly every community confronted its mortality by creating Civil Defense plans and community bomb shelters. In schools, along with fire drills young children learned—inaccurately—to duck under their desks for safety in the event of a nuclear attack. Although it had brought an end to World War II, nuclear weapons created a kind of insecurity never before seen in human history.

From duck-and-cover drills to science fiction films, Americans learned to live with the bomb that they had created. American anxiety came from both the Soviet threat and the awareness that the United States had introduced the world to the potential of nuclear destruction. The awe that many felt upon witnessing nuclear detonations can be seen in artistic creations such as Andy Warhol's silkscreen "Atomic Bomb" (1965) and James Rosenquist's "F-111" (1964–1965). Feature films used nuclear war or the threat of it to a variety of ends. Most often, films touched the anxiety many Americans felt about their role in developing this deadly technology. *Dr. Strangelove or How I Learned to Stop Worrying and Love the Bomb* (1964), *On The Beach* (1959), *The Day After* (1983), *The War Game* (1966), *Threads* (1985), and *War Games* (1983) wove a narrative around some aspect of nuclear weapons. Another entire science-fiction genre evolved out of the unknown outcomes of radiation and nuclear testing, including the Godzilla films and 1950s B films such as *Them* (1954) that was one of many that based its narrative on the possible outcome of radiation on insects, vegetables, and humans.

On an individual basis, humans had lived before in a tenuous balance with survival as they struggled for food supplies with little technology; however, never before had such a tenuous balance derived only from man's own technological innovation. Everyday human life changed significantly with the realization that extinction could arrive at any moment. Some Americans applied the lesson by striving to live within limits of technology and resource use. Anti-nuclear activists composed some of the earliest portions of the 1960s counter-culture and the modern environmental movement, including "radical" organizations such as the Sea Shepherds and Greenpeace, each of which began by protesting nuclear tests. More mainstream Americans would also eventually question the use of such devices.

"DOMESTICATING THE ATOM"

Historian Paul Boyer writes that "Along with the shock waves of fear, one also finds exalted prophecies of the bright promise of atomic energy" (Boyer, 109–14). Many of the scientists involved in developing the bomb believed that atomic technology required controls unlike any previous innovation. Shortly after the bombings, a movement began to establish a global board of scientists who would administer the technology with no political affiliation. Wresting this new tool for global influence from the American military proved impossible. The Atomic Energy Commission (AEC), formed in 1946, would place the U.S. military and governmental authority in control of the weapons technology and other uses to which it might be put. With the "nuclear trump card," the United States catapulted to the top of global leadership.

In the 1950s, scientists turned their attention to taking the nuclear reaction and applying it to peaceful purposes, notably power generation. The reaction was a fairly simple process. Similar to fossil-fuel powered generators, nuclear plants use the heat of thermal energy to turn turbines that generate electricity. The thermal energy comes from nuclear fission, which is made when a neutron emitted by a uranium nucleus strikes another uranium nucleus, which emits more neutrons and heat as it breaks apart. If the new neutrons strike other nuclei, a chain reaction takes place. These chain reactions are the source of nuclear energy, which then heats water to power the turbines.

Soon, the AEC seized this concept as the foundation for plans for "domesticating the atom." It was quite a leap, though, to make the American public comfortable with the most destructive technology ever known. The AEC and others sponsored a barrage of popular articles concerning a future in which roads would be created through the use of atomic bombs and radiation employed to cure cancer.

The atomic future in the media included images of atomic-powered agriculture and automobiles. In one book published during this wave of technological optimism, the writer speculates that, "No baseball game will be called off on account of rain in the Era of Atomic Energy." After continuing this litany of activities no longer to be influenced by climate or nature, the author sums up the argument: "For the first time in the

"Don't touch unless told to do so." Atomic bombing survival illustration showing girl reaching toward sandwich, milk, and water fountain, as woman says, "No!" Courtesy Library of Congress.

history of the world man will have at his disposal energy in amounts sufficient to cope with the forces of Mother Nature" (Boyer, 109–15). For many Americans, this new technology meant control of everyday life. For the Eisenhower Administration, the technology meant expansion of our economic and commercial capabilities.

As the Cold War took shape around nuclear weapons, the Eisenhower administration looked for ways to define a domestic role for nuclear power even as Soviet missiles threatened each American. "Project Plowshares" grew out of the administration's effort to take the destructive weapon and make it a domestic power producer. The list of possible applications was awesome: laser-cut highways passing through mountains, nuclear-powered greenhouses built by federal funds in the Midwest to enhance crop production, and irradiating soils to simplify weed and pest management. While domestic power production, with massive federal subsidies, would be the long-term product of these actions, the atom could never fully escape its military capabilities. This was most clear when nuclear power plants experienced accidents.

NUCLEAR POWER

Begun under Project Plowshares, Eisenhower's Atoms for Peace program emphasized that it was impossible for a nuclear plant to behave as a bomb would; it could not explode. The Atomic Energy Commission, which took over the oversight of nuclear technology after World War II, worked tirelessly to encourage the commercial use of nuclear reactors for the generation of electricity. Lewis L. Strauss, chair of the AEC, proclaimed to the public that the production of nuclear power was "too cheap to meter." This was especially true if the federal government helped to finance the construction, operation, and insurance of atomic power plants (Opie, 473–74).

In 1951, the first experimental reactor went online near Idaho Falls, Idaho. Initially, it produced only enough power to light four 150-watt light bulbs. The lessons learned in Idaho, though, led to the AEC-sponsored pilot project with Duquesne Light Co. in Shippingport, Pennsylvania. This 60-megawatt breeder reactor opened in 1957 in order to serve as a model for future projects. In addition, the Westinghouse-designed plant served as a model for the navy program to develop nuclear power for submarine propulsion. Ultimately, the Shippingport reactor became the first licensed American commercial reactor.

During the ensuing decades, new reactors would be constructed throughout the United States. Although the AEC and the federal government offered assistance, these power plants were normally constructed by private utilities. The electricity that they generated was placed on the utility's grid and sold along with power made from coal, hydro-turbines, and oil.

CONCLUSION: LESSONS OF THE NUCLEAR AGE

During the 1950s and 1960s, nuclear technology symbolized the stable future that could be ensured and maintained through technological innovation. This confidence, however, shielded Americans from a more serious line of questioning about nuclear technology and other innovations. Technological progress, we would learn, was not an *automatic* good. Nuclear weapons and energy production, for instance, carried extreme health risks at each stage of their existence: production, storage, and after-life. As Americans began to consider the broader implications of nuclear testing, the arms race, and energy production, the popularity of nuclear technology would plummet over the next decades.

6

GRASSROOTS ACTIVISM AND ENVIRONMENTAL CONCERN

EVERYDAY SETTING: THE LOVE CANAL NEW YORK

The meeting was similar to any number of gatherings of concerned citizens in the late twentieth century. The subject might be the routing of a new highway, a problematic new bookstore around the corner, or a resident who failed to sufficiently manicure her gardens and lawn. However, this 1978 meeting of the Love Canal Homeowners Association (LCHA) focused the group on the concerns of one member, Lois Gibbs.

Gibbs lived in the neighborhood and her children attended the 99th Street School located in the toxic ground. She explained to the group the story that she had already told them individually. She and her family had never been told about the chemical dump that was buried before developers constructed the residential neighborhood and school. When she learned of the existence of the chemical waste from newspaper articles describing the contents of the landfill and its proximity to the 99th Street School, she grew particularly concerned, because her own sickly child attended the school. She became convinced that the waste may have poisoned her child. So, Gibbs approached the school board with notes from two physicians who recommended that her son be transferred to another school for health reasons.

The board refused on the grounds that it could not admit that the health of one child had been impacted without first admitting the possibility that the entire school population had been affected as well. Enraged, Gibbs began talking with other parents in the neighborhood to see if they were having problems with their children's health. After speaking with hundreds of people, she realized that the entire community was concerned about the potential problems from having their children interact with toxic waste. The parents wanted definitive answers.

From this start, the LCHA took shape and committed itself to alerting the entire nation, if necessary, to the dangers of chemical waste. Members of this grassroots organization came from approximately 500 families residing within a 10-block area surrounding Love Canal. Most of the members of LCHA were workers at one of the local chemical plants, with an average annual income of $10,000-$25,000. They risked job and security to better understand the issue of waste disposal in their community.

Ultimately, the LCHA became a model for countless similar organizations that gave voice to individual claims of environmental carelessness and injustice.

A STORY OF CHEMICAL PROGRESS

LCHA was one of the first examples of grass-roots action on environmental matters. Motivated activists from the middle class were products of a shift in attitudes toward the use of technology in American life. In the early twentieth century, Americans identified chemicals—like most technological innovations—almost blindly with future progress. There was very little knowledge about possible health issues related to the storage and dumping of wastes made in the production of these progressive chemicals. When, in the case of Love Canal, the Hooker Chemical Company dumped 21,800 tons of waste into an abandoned canal in New York between 1942 and 1953, it was practicing disposal methods seen throughout industrial America. It was business as usual in the United States.

The empty canal had been part of an elaborate plan to create a futuristic metropolis in the area of Niagara Falls in the late 1800s. When these plans were abandoned, the partially dug canal was left unfilled—a large hole in the ground. For the Hooker Chemical Company 50 years later, the thick clay walls of the canal provided a strong dump site for chemical waste. After disposal of their chemical wastes, Hooker covered the land with more clay. Eventually, the land was sold and developed into a small town. This became the town of Love Canal. It is likely that this residential development weakened the clay walls of the dump and allowed chemical waste to leach into the soils of the area.

In 1953, this new, growing community needed a school. The Niagara Falls Board of Education bought the land, including the dumping site, for one dollar. Although there is some debate about the builders' knowledge of the dump, the school was built without giving consideration to the possibility of ill effects from toxic waste. As early as the 1950s, residents complained of strong chemical odors; however, they were attributed to the chemical factories that were active in town. There were also some reports of children and dogs who developed skin irritations after spending time in the fields around the school. Some residents even talked about stray rocks that exploded when dropped to the ground. With these unproven stories swirling about, the *Niagara Gazette* finally took some sludge from a neighbor's sump pump and sent it to a lab for analysis. The results showed that the sludge was from Hooker's Chemical dumpings decades prior.

These results proved to be the "smoking gun"—or smoking sludge, in this case—that was necessary to attract attention and get results. This scientific evidence was publicized by the LCHA, and ultimately the Department of Environmental Conservation of New York completed additional investigations. The statistics of health problems stemming from the sludge dump were overwhelming. A few days after the report was released, the state agreed to purchase the 239 homes closest to the canal. These unprecedented actions were evidence of a new era in the American attitude toward technology and in its expectations of personal health and safety. One of the best tools for bringing about action proved to be the formation of strong, united citizens' organizations (Love Canal).

DOCUMENT: EXCERPT FROM NEW YORK STATE HEALTH ORDER

On August 2, 1978, the New York State Department of Health issued a historic finding in the following health order. It recommend that the 99th Street School be closed and that pregnant women and children under the age of two be evacuated from the areas. It also stressed that residents should not eat out of their home gardens and that they spend limited time in their basements.

The profound and devastating effects of the Love Canal tragedy, in terms of human health and suffering and environmental damage, cannot and probably will never be fully measured.

The lessons we are learning from this modern-day disaster should serve as a warning for governments at all levels and for private industry to take steps to avoid a repetition of these tragic events. They must also serve as a reminder to be ever watchful for the tell-tale signs of potential disasters and to look beyond our daily endeavors and plan for the wellbeing of future generations.

We must improve our technological capabilities, supplant ignorance with knowledge and be ever vigilant for those seemingly innocuous situations which may portend the beginning of an environmental nightmare. . . .

As we proceed, we will be continually asking ourselves if we are following the right course. Yet, history will be our judge as future scientists and government leaders, armed with better information and greater technological know-how, will assess the fruits of our endeavors, benefiting from our precursor experience, to deal more effectively with future potential Love Canals.

For the present we must continue to pursue with the same vigor and dedication that has prevailed over the last several months, the long-range health studies necessary to learn more about the risks associated with human exposure to toxic chemicals.

We cannot undo the damage that has been wrought at Love Canal but we can take appropriate preventive measures so that we are better able to anticipate and hopefully prevent future events of this kind. (Love Canal)

NATURE IN EVERYDAY LIFE: DDT

Chemicals, including some of those buried in Love Canal, were one of the greatest symbols of the modern era of technological solutions to everyday problems. In 1939 scientists were stunned when a few grains of white powder miraculously wiped out colonies of mosquito larvae. The powder had been developed years earlier but never tied to a specific purpose. With neither testing nor consideration of potential dangers, Dichlorodiphenyltrichloroethane (DDT) left the laboratory for use as an insecticide.

The chemical seemed to be one of the great examples of the ability of humans to use technology to eliminate limitations of the natural world around them. During World War II, for instance, B-25 bombers sprayed DDT prior to invasions in the Pacific to kill off insects and help reduce the possibility of disease for the American soldiers who would follow. After the war, application of DDT almost single-handedly wiped out malaria in the developed world and drastically reduced it elsewhere. Paul Müller, the chemist who first turned it on unsuspecting flies, won a Nobel Prize in 1948 for his work. And, in 1970, the National Academy of Sciences estimated that during the previous decades, DDT had likely saved more than 500 million lives from malaria (Opie, 413–15,)

DDT became a major part of the modernist view that nature could be made *pestless*. By the late 1950s, DDT production was nearly five times the production of the World War II era. Town and municipal authorities liberally sprayed DDT on American suburbs to eradicate tent caterpillars, gypsy moths, and the beetles that carried Dutch elm disease. It was an important tool in creating the suburban aesthetic of green nature composed of only what we wished. Often, residents would see the plume of spray passing through their neighborhoods and neither shield themselves nor their children and pets from possible effects from overspray. In fact, the event of the spraying rig on a truck or airplane was viewed only with relief at what the chemical would do to bothersome insects.

Slowly, though, observers began to note that DDT killed indiscriminately. It became clear that the insecticide could not be controlled or limited once it entered an ecosystem. In addition, the new lessons of ecology demonstrated that some species identified as pests actually played an important role in larger food chains and ecological webs that connected them with species that humans cared about—or even with ourselves. The connection that it had on human life, however, required that the nation be given a lesson in systems ecology.

RACHEL CARSON'S *SILENT SPRING*

Pollution composed the most frequent environmental complaint before 1950, but its nuisance derived primarily from physical discomfort more than from a scientific correlation with human illness. Scientific inquiry was required to definitively connect health problems to pollution and chemicals, but most scientists were housed in the industries that were responsible for creating such toxicity. Middle-class Americans became concerned with such information by the late 1950s. The suburban ideal had helped to create an expectation of safety in Americans. One of the first writers to take advantage of this increased interest among middle-class Americans was a government biologist named Rachel Carson. She began writing about nature for general readers in the late 1950s. Then, in 1962 Rachel Carson's *Silent Spring* erupted onto the public scene to become a bestseller after first being serialized in *The New Yorker.*

Often, literary critics compare *Silent Spring*'s impact on the American scene with that of *Uncle Tom's Cabin,* which contributed to the start of the Civil War after its publication in the 1850s. "Without this book," writes former Vice President Al Gore, "the environmental movement might have been long delayed or never have developed at all" (Carson, xix). From the day it hit bookstores, *Silent Spring* fueled a vigorous public debate about the use of chemicals—and the role of technology in our nation's future—that continues today. Carson's scientific findings brought into question basic assumptions that Americans had about their own safety and many of the chemicals that they used to create their comfortable standard of living.

At the time of the writing of *Silent Spring,* Carson had no intention of starting a large-scale public movement. Growing up in western Pennsylvania, Carson studied nature and read scientific books. She focused on marine biology and, although she began at the Pennsylvania College for Women in the mid-1920s as an English major, she graduated with a degree in biology. She earned a master's degree in marine zoology from Johns Hopkins University and went on to take a job as a junior aquatic biologist for the U.S. Bureau of Fisheries. For her first stab at writing for the general public, Carson turned to her passion for the sea. Published in 1941, *Under the Sea-Wind* sold fewer than 2,000 copies. During the next decade, though, Carson became recognized as a scientist who could write for a broader reading audience. Colleagues began alerting her to scientific issues that might make good topics for her writing—topics that would appeal to nonscientific audiences. Her second book, *The Sea Around Us* topped the best-seller list and received the prestigious National Book Award. She had achieved literary success with writing based on natural science.

She wished to use her recognition, though, to help counter specific problems in the natural environment. Carson began to consider a book that would deal with the scientific community's nagging questions about the effect of pesticides on the land and its residents. While working on this project, Carson received the diagnosis that she had breast cancer in 1960. The project became even more. important to her; however, now she was forced to contend with a mastectomy and subsequent radiation treatments that left her nauseated and bedridden. Although she did not know what

Rachel Carson, appearing before a Senate Government Operations subcommittee studying pesticides. Courtesy Library of Congress.

had caused her own cancer, her personal health problems made her more committed than ever to her book on pesticide use (Lear, 403–19).

In addition to these personal difficulties, Carson was forced to deal with harsh criticism from those that would be most effected by her findings: the chemical industry. These companies began an unparalleled assault on Carson's credibility during the early 1960s. When the *New Yorker* began serializing Carson's book, Velsicol Corporation, which manufactured the pesticide chlordane, threatened to sue the magazine for libel. Lawsuits were also threatened against Carson.

Overall, though, the cultural attitude toward chemical progress was beginning to change. In July 1962, news broke that a drug given to thousands of pregnant women in Europe for morning sickness had been proven to cause widespread birth defects. Public opinion swayed as newspapers and magazines ran photographs of malformed babies. Inadvertently, this story likely helped establish the groundswell of support for Carson's *Silent Spring*. In a single summer, chemical science had fallen from its pedestal of unchallenged confidence and progress. Here is a portion of what Carson wrote:

The "control of nature" is a phrase conceived in arrogance, born of the Neanderthal age of biology and philosophy, when it was supposed that nature exists for the convenience of man. The concepts and practices of applied entomology for the most part date from that Stone Age of science. It is our alarming misfortune that so primitive a science has armed itself with the most modern and terrible weapons, and that in turning them against the insects it has also turned them against the earth. (Carson, 12–14)

CREATING A PUBLIC REACTION

Silent Spring went on sale September 27, 1962 and quickly became a national bestseller. Its popularity remained strong throughout the fall. Although critics accused Carson of overstating the dangers of chemicals, Supreme Court Justice William O. Douglas, echoed by others. called *Silent Spring* "the most important chronicle of this century for the human race." Carson's work had struck a national nerve.

Although she was weakened by her own illness, Carson appeared on television and before Congress to answer her critics. As a result, the broad-based grassroots support for her findings grew. When she appeared on CBS television in April 1963, an estimated 15 million Americans tuned in. They heard Carson explain: "We still talk in terms of conquest. I think we're challenged, as mankind has never been challenged before, to prove our maturity and our mastery, not of nature but of ourselves." Many alarmed Americans wrote that the United States Department of Agriculture, the Public Health Service, and the Food and Drug Administration should take action to ensure their personal health safety (Lear, 450–56).

When President Kennedy's Science Advisory Committee released its report on the subject in 1963, its findings backed Carson's thesis and severely criticized the government and the chemical industry. Overall, the report called for "orderly reductions of persistent pesticides." For the first time, the connection had been forged between public concern and federal policy.

Carson died in 1964 at age 56. Her efforts brought the chemical industry under new federal oversight. More important, though, Carson's line of questioning aroused an overall awareness in the American public. "Rachel Carson's legacy has less to do with pesticides than with awakening of environmental consciousness," says biographer Linda Lear. "She changed the way we look at nature. We now know we are a part of nature, and we can't damage it without it coming back to bite us" (Carson).

GENERATING A POPULAR ENVIRONMENTAL MOVEMENT

Carson's descriptions were based in the science of ecology that had emerged in the 1930s. Combined with her skills as a writer and storyteller, though, the ecological principles were welcomed by a general public more interested than ever in understanding its place in the natural environment. Her scientific findings added credibility and meaning to students involved in "back to nature" movements. As students grew willing to question nearly every aspect of their existence, the human role in nature came under increasing scrutiny. Was our lifestyle sustainable? Did we take more than we gave to the environment? Were we good stewards of the world around us? Many Americans started local recycling projects or became active in local politics. Others checked out completely. Such disenfranchised people would become known as hippies, but the intent behind their actions was often based around forming what became known as a " counter-culture."

Of course, a counter-culture movement is organized around ideas of a cultural norm to which discontented individuals react. Many youth in the 1960s rejected government, the organization of society, and the war in Vietnam. Similar to the ethic of Carson's writing, the counter-culture that they created rejected the assumption of new technologies as an automatic good. Young people in particular rejected the stable patterns of middle-class life that their parents had created in the decades after World War II. Some disenchanted youth plunged into radical political activity; many more embraced new standards of dress and sexual behavior.

Although not a cohesive cultural movement with manifestos and leaders, hippies expressed their desire for change with communal or nomadic lifestyles and by renouncing the symbols of middle-class American life such as labor-saving household technologies and mass-produced, packaged food products. These types of products became known as symbols of the "establishment." Instead of the preferences of mass American culture, hippies strove for simplicity and self-sufficiency. They sought the opportunity to entirely disengage from the "establishment." The most successful hippies were likely those who took up residence on one of many communes that sprang up around the nation. Modeled after the transcendental farms and camps of the early 1800s, communes grew their own food organically and allowed residents to live a life totally outside of American culture.

CREATING MECHANISMS FOR GRASSROOTS ACTION

The counter-culture contributed to the development of institutions that would change the relationship with nature nationwide. Much of what became known as the modern environmental movement was organized around groups and organizations that prospered with the influence of 1960s radicalism; however, the real impact of these organizations came during the later 1960s and 1970s when their membership skyrocketed with members of the concerned middle class, such as Lois Gibbs and members of the LCHA.

During the late 1900s, many of these environmental special-interest groups would evolve into major political players through lobbying. Nongovernmental organizations (NGOs) broadened the grassroots influence of environmental thought; however they also created a niche for more radical environmentalists. The broad appeal as well as the number of special-interest portions of environmental thought stood in stark contrast to nineteenth-century environmentalism. Whereas early conservationists were almost entirely members of the upper economic classes of American society, the new environmentalists came most from the middle class that grew rapidly after World War II (Opie, 418–25).

During the 1970s and 1980s, these NGOs helped to bring environmental concern into mainstream American culture. Some critics argue that American living patterns changed little; however, the awareness and concern over human society's impact on nature had reached an all-time high in American history. These organizations often initiated the call for specific policies and then lobbied members of congress to create legislation. By the 1980s, NGOs had created a new political battlefield as each side of environmental arguments lobbied lawmakers.

Often, the American public financially supported organizations that argued for their particular perspectives. Even traditional environmental organizations such as the Sierra Club (1892), National Audubon Society (1905), National Parks and Conservation Society (1919), Wilderness Society (1935), National Wildlife Federation (1936), and Nature Conservancy (1951) took much more active roles in policy making. The interest of such organizations in appealing to mainstream, middle-class Americans helped to broaden the base of environmental activists. However, it also contributed to the formation of more radical-thinking environmental NGOs that disliked the mainstream interests of the larger organizations. In fact, many devout environmentalists argued that some of these NGOs were part of the "establishment" that they wished to fight.

NGOs' ability to attract middle-class membership, though, significantly changed the environmental movement, resulting in a popular, middle-class effort often referred to as the modern environmental movement (Hays, *Beauty*, 32–39). Here are descriptions of some of the most successful NGOs of this new social and political movement:

Sierra Club: Originally established by John Muir and others, the Sierra Club remains the preeminent environmental organization in the United States. David Brower led the group through much of the late twentieth century as it emerged to play an important role in many different issues. Often, the Sierra Club proved willing to take the lead role on issues such as Hetch Hetchy, Echo Park, and other western issues.

Audubon Society: Viewed as more moderate than the Sierra Club, the Audubon Society is a much more comfortable fit for many Americans who call themselves environmentalists. The group prioritizes work with public information, particularly in American media. Of course, most Americans assume that Audubon emphasizes bird preservation; however, the organization is founded on a broad selection of environmental issues.

National Parks and Conservation Association: Focusing on national park land, this organization prioritizes management and land use within parks. Throughout the twentieth century, the NPCA has argued most for careful use of these areas and has not always been willing to get involved in larger environmental issues.

The Wilderness Society: After its founding in 1935, the Wilderness Society used the influence of Bob Marshall and Aldo Leopold to alter policies within the National Park Service and Forest Service. In each case, the organization stressed the importance of maintaining unspoiled, unused areas as pristine. The Wilderness Society was influential in the passage of the Wilderness Act during the 1960s.

Nature Conservancy: Founded in 1951 with the primary mission to buy environmentally significant tracts of land that it will manage itself or hand over to the federal government. With a foundation in preserving unique locales that can potentially be turned over to the federal government, the Nature Conservancy is the nation's wealthiest environmental NGO.

Environmental Defense Fund (EDF): Established in 1967, EDF and a few similar NGOs grew from the scientific understanding of environmentalism. Picking up where Rachel Carson left off, EDF sought to fight pollution and empower the powerless to make their communities more environmentally safe.

National Resources Defense Council (NRDC): Similar to EDF, the NRDC was founded in 1970 to emphasize legal tools in the fight against environmental exploitation. The NRDC proved willing to bring suit against private individuals, corporations, or the federal government in order to demand enforcement of the new environmental laws that grew out of the 1970s.

NATURE GUIDE: DAVE FOREMAN, EARTH FIRST! AND ECO-RADICALISM

Mainstream environmental NGOs helped to clear the way for more extreme organizations that held ideas unpalatable to most middle-class Americans. In addition to holding extreme philosophical stands, many of these organizations also went about their activities in a much more confrontational manner. The best known of these extreme environmental organizations was Earth First!, which was led by Dave Foreman. These activists argued that protests and writing letters was not sufficient. Earth Firsters sought out more active methods of action, which became known as "eco-radicalism" or "eco-terrorism" (Foreman, 5–9).

Carrying the banner of antiestablishment direct action, Earth First! claimed the slogan "no compromise in defense of Mother Earth." Initially, the organization adopted many of the tactics of the American Civil Rights movement. They were inspired by the writing of Edward Abbey, who, in his 1975 book *The Monkey Wrench Gang*, wrote of a band of activists wreaking havoc on development efforts in the American West. Earth Firsters swiftly intensified their actions to include ecotage (environmental terrorism), which became standard fare, particularly in the American West. Tree spiking, tree sitting, equipment damaging, and even resort burning became part of the radicals' arsenal. Some organizations continue these practices today.

Earth First! acquired a national image for environmentalists with one of its most famous acts, which took place on March 31, 1981. Earth First! unfurled a black plastic tarp with a 300-foot painted crack over the Glen Canyon Dam in Arizona. In a very public act, Earth First! had introduced guerilla theater to the wilderness movement (Opie, 427).

Intellectually, Earth Firsters and other extreme environmentalists also introduced ideas more extreme than those broadly entertained by environmentalists of previous eras. In the past, an individual such as Thoreau or Muir presented an extreme philosophical stance and interested Americans steered their minds in that general direction. Now, however, fairly large groups of Americans were willing to entertain concepts such as the need to focus less on human needs and more on those of other portions of nature.

One of the best-known of these philosophical stances is referred to as "deep ecology." Subscribers to deep ecology argue that nature contains its own purposes, energy, and matter, and its own self-validating ethics and aesthetics. Calling themselves defenders of wilderness, such thinkers included Arne Ness, David Rothenberg, William Duvall, and George Sessions. For these deep ecologists, even preservation was based on science that grew from values that remained committed to the control of nature by industrial society. Deep ecologists urged environmentalists to turn their backs on society and adopt a radical new position for humans within nature. All decisions begin by asking the question of what benefits the entire natural system. This holistic perspective prioritizes wildness over any utilitarian view of the environment.

Of course, perspectives such as deep ecology made it impossible for subscribers to also support middle-class, American ideas. Therefore, quite inadvertently, the radical end of environmentalism functioned to make the mainstream movement seem more reasonable. In 1992, for instance, some members of Earth First! grew frustrated that their organization had become too mainstream and then formed the international group known as the Earth Liberation Front (ELF). ELF's uncompromising goal was to "inflict economic damage on those profiting from the destruction and exploitation of the natural environment."

NIMBY: NOT IN MY BACKYARD

Serious environmental concerns fueled grassroots movements, such as that in Love Canal, to demand governmental or industrial action. Social movements such as the one initiated by Lois Gibbs were often linked together under the term: "Not in my Backyard" or NIMBY. At the root of this movement was a change in Americans' expectations of their own safety and health.

One of the issues most scrutinized by NIMBY concerns in the 1970s was the nuclear power industry that the federal government had helped to develop throughout the nation. Americans' accepted federal assurances of the safety of nuclear energy plants during the late 1960s and early 1970s, and most plants were placed in close proximity to densely residential areas; however, many environmental groups began to question these assurances by the mid-1970s. Nuclear power soon came under attack from NIMBY groups all over the country. The antinuclear effort became a lightening rod for many other environmental concerns as well.

The criticism of nuclear power and the NIMBY movement more generally received a significant boost from one of the most important events in the history of American technology. When things went bad at the Three Mile Island Nuclear Power Plant, nearly every American began a chorus of "Not in My Backyard."

Although it had been introduced during the war years, recycling quickly became an important expression of environmental commitment in the 1970s. Courtesy Library of Congress.

NATURE AT WORK: THREE MILE ISLAND

Located within a working-class neighborhood outside a major population center, the Three Mile Island (TMI) nuclear power plant experienced a partial core meltdown in 1979. As pregnant women and children were evacuated from Pennsylvania's nearby capital, Harrisburg, the American public learned through the media about potential hazards of this technology as well as about many other sources. More than the potential danger specifically from nuclear power, though, TMI marked a watershed in the expression of NIMBY ideas in American life.

The accident at the Three Mile Island Unit 2 nuclear power plant is still recognized as the most serious accident at a U.S. commercial nuclear power plant. Although it led immediately to no deaths or injuries, the publicity that it stirred instigated sweeping changes in emergency response planning, reactor operator training, and almost every other area of nuclear power plant operations. It also caused the U.S. Nuclear Regulatory Commission to tighten and heighten its regulatory oversight (Rothman, *Greening,* 146–48)

Although the sequence of events at TMI led to a partial meltdown of the TMI-2 reactor core, only very small off-site releases of radioactivity occurred. The accident, however, revealed a massive lack of knowledge about the technology of atomic power production. The lack of information about the impact of the accident led to a fearful few days and, ultimately, the demise of the industry.

The actual events of the accident began at about 4:00 A.M. on March 28, 1979, when the plant experienced a failure in the secondary, non-nuclear section of the plant. A mechanical failure stopped the flow of feedwater to the reactor, and therefore the reactor automatically shut down. This led to an increase in the pressure within the reactor (Opie, 447).

In order to prevent that pressure from becoming excessive, the pilot-operated relief valve (a valve located at the top of the pressurizer) opened and released water and pressure. Unknown to the pilot, however, the valve stuck open and cooling water poured out of the stuck-open valve and caused the core of the reactor to overheat. Plant operators then took a series of actions that made conditions worse by simply reducing the flow of coolant through the core. It was later found that about one-half of the core melted during the early stages of the accident.

In short, the accident caught federal and state authorities off-guard in a dramatic, public moment. On March 30, a significant release of radiation from the plant's auxiliary building caused a great deal of confusion. In an atmosphere of growing uncertainty about the condition of the plant, the governor of Pennsylvania, Richard L. Thornburgh, consulted with the NRC about evacuating the population near the plant. Eventually, Thornburgh advised pregnant women and pre-school-age children within a five-mile radius of the plant to leave the area.

Soon, observers began discussing a large hydrogen bubble in the dome of the pressure vessel. Speculation suggested that the bubble might burn or even explode and rupture. Of course, the public very quickly undid all that Eisenhower and others had done to distance atomic power from atomic weapons. The bubble bursting became the equivalent in the popular imagination of an atomic explosion. On April 1, experts established that the bubble could not do any damage and the panic passed.

Although there has been considerable debate about the health impact of TMI, the Nuclear Regulatory Commission studies estimated that 2 million people in the area received about 1 millirem of radiation (chest x-rays expose patients to approximately 6 millirem). The real impact of TMI came through the public's lesson that technical answers were not always the best answers.

Events at Three Mile Island effectively squelched further development of nuclear reactors not yet planned in 1979. While the number of nuclear units increased through 1990, most of the contracts had been drawn up many years before. By 1990, most Americans refused to help finance new reactors. Most communities lobbied to remove or shut down reactors near residential areas. While the dangers of radiation were now more widely understood, Americans also had an expectation of physical safety that is unique in human history. In short, Americans expected to live in uncontaminated safety. Responsibility for ensuring this safety would fall to the federal government.

TIMELINE: THE STIRRING OF ENVIRONMENTAL ACTION IN THE 1960s–1970s

- 1962: Rachel Carson writes *Silent Spring*
- 1964: Barry Commoner's group, formed in the 1950s to oppose development of atomic energy, begins publishing the journal that will become known as *Environment.*
- 1965: Commoner and Ralph Nader lead a critique of the American economic system and the ability of science to question development.
- 1965: The Sierra Club files a lawsuit to protect Storm King Mountain in New York from a power project. The U.S. Supreme Court rules in favor of the club and of noneconomic interests in a conservation case.
- 1966: The Sierra Club opposes building two dams that would have flooded the Grand Canyon and publishes newspaper ads that say "This time it's the Grand Canyon they want to flood. The Grand Canyon." The dam plan is defeated. Congress passes the Endangered Species Act.
- 1968: Apollo 8 sends back the earth-rise pictures from space (see Chapter 10).
- 1969: The Santa Barbara oil spill attracts public attention to polluted beaches.
- 1969: Congress passes the National Environmental Policy Act (NEPA) to mandate consideration of environmental issues prior to major public decisions.
- 1970: The first Earth Day is April 22.
- 1972: Congress passes the Clean Water Act, Coastal Zone Management Act, Federal Environmental Pesticide Control Act, Marine Mammal Protection Act, Ocean Dumping Act, and Federal Advisory Committee Act to require representation of public interest advocates on committees.
- 1972: Oregon passes the first bottle-recycling law.
- 1972: The Club of Rome publishes Limits to Growth in 1972.
- 1973: Congress passes the Endangered Species Act.
- 1974: Congress passes the Safe Drinking Water Act.
- 1977: Love Canal, New York, identified as a chemical waste site requiring evacuation of all inhabitants.
- 1979: Three Mile Island nuclear reactor near-meltdown in Pennsylvania.
- 1980: Congress passes the Superfund bill to help identify and pay for cleaning up abandoned toxic waste sites.

CONCLUSION: DEFINING ENVIRONMENTAL RACISM AND ECOFEMINISM

From the efforts of Rachel Carson and middle-class women such as Lois Gibbs, the modern environmental movement emerged. Clearly, humans thought of their role in the world quite differently than previous generations. Primarily, human change to the environment was no longer assumed to be acceptable. Although it would slow the American march toward development, a new intellectual paradigm demanded that changes in the environment be analyzed in what would eventually come to be called "cost-benefit analysis."

This new intellectual paradigm was fairly simple to connect to symbolic patterns in American history. Thinkers in the 1970s drew patterns in the historical use of nature in the United States and found similar trends emanating specifically from issues of gender and race. In the movement that became known as modern environmentalism, the role of women and the importance of racial issues remained part of American environmentalism for years to come. In each case, each of these portions of the movement acquired a specific term: environmental racism and ecofeminism.

The combination of grassroots activism and the clearer scientific understanding of the connection between human health and environmental pollution forged a clear link between human and environmental rights after 1970. The NIMBY concerns that grew out of events of the 1970s helped to empower new expectations of social equality. Linking this idea to environmental concerns, proponents used the term "environmental racism" to describe environmental injustices that adversely effected minority populations. By the 1980s, social activists realized the problem was even more insidious in some parts of the United States.

In 1983 the National Association for the Advancement of Colored People (NAACP) protested the positioning of a hazardous waste landfill in a predominantly black neighborhood. In 1987 Benjamin Chavis, executive director of the United Church of Christ (UCC) Commission for Racism and Justice and later the Executive Director of the NAACP called it "environmental racism" that such facilities were placed near populations that lacked the political and economic voice to protest it. He stated publicly that "race is the most significant factor in determining the location of hazardous waste facilities" (Barbalace).

Expressing a different ideological perspective, ecofeminists argue that the exploitation of natural resources is part of a male-dominated human society. With women making decisions and leading the species, ecofeminists argue, humans could achieve a much more cooperative and sustainable relationship with nature. Ecofeminists want to eradicate all oppressive conceptual frameworks and create a world in which differences do not lead to domination. Ecofeminism argues that there are important connections between the domination of women and the domination of nature. A main project of ecofeminism is to make visible these "woman-nature connections" and, where harmful to women and nature, to dismantle them (Zimmerman, 253–67).

Each of these categories of thought demonstrates that modern environmentalism had brought the human dimension of environmental thought to the fore. Of course, this marked an important watershed in nature in everyday American life. In short, ecology had demonstrated to us that misdeeds against the environment effect our own and future generations.

7

CREATING A POLITICAL FRAMEWORK FOR ENVIRONMENTAL ACTION

EVERYDAY SETTING: FROM THE *WASHINGTON POST*, APRIL 23, 1970

Richard Harwood, "Earth Day Stirs the Nation"

A great outpouring of Americans—several million in all likelihood—demonstrated yesterday their practical concern for a livable environment on this earth.

School children by the hundreds of thousands roamed through parks, city streets, and suburban neighborhoods in communities across the land collecting tons of litter cast off by a consumption-oriented society.

The academic community—ranging from the Smithsonian Institution in Washington to the Mesa Community in Arizona—lectured the old and the young on the fragility of the world they inhabit.

Within 200 years, said Dr. J. Murray Mitchell of the Federal Environmental Science Services Administration, air pollutants—mainly carbon dioxide—may cause the earth's temperature to rise to levels that will threaten life itself. . . .

The American business community, ordinarily indifferent to hostile mass demonstrations, endorsed Earth Day and announced some practical actions of its own to deal with environmental problems. . . .

There were other pragmatic responses yesterday to the growing environmental movement. Gov. Nelson Rockefeller of New York, wearing a button that said "Save the Earth," established a new Environment Department in the state government. . . .

So many politicians, in fact, took part in yesterday's Earth Day activities that the United States Congress shut down. Scores of senators and congressmen fanned out across the country to appear at rallies, teach-ins and street demonstrations.

The oratory, one of the wire services observed, was "as thick as the smog at rush-hour;" that was hardly an exaggeration, for Earth Day attracted enthusiastic support from all bands on the political spectrum—the New Left, the Old Right, the continuous Center. . . .

Besides the oratory, the teach-ins and the clean-up brigades, many street theatricals were staged to dramatize environmental issues.

In Washington, 1700 college students and school children marched to the Interior Department. A couple of quarts of oil were poured out on the sidewalk as a protest to oil spills in the ocean. Government workers later cleaned up the puddles.

At Indiana University, one of the stops on Sen. Nelson's transcontinental speaking tour yesterday, 20 girls tossed birth control pills at the Earth Day crowd. They dressed as witches, danced in a circle and chanted: "Free our bodies, free our minds." . . .

New Yorkers blocked off Fifth Avenue for two hours while 100,000 people strolled in the sun, listened to guitar players and watched Mayor John V. Lindsay drive by in an electric bus. . . .

In Birmingham, Ala., where a pall of smoke from heavy industry hangs over the city, an organization called Greater Birmingham Alliance to Stop Pollution, or GASP, sponsored a "right to live" rally at the municipal auditorium. . . .

At the University of Texas in Austin, the campus newspaper came out with a make-believe inside page dated April 20, 1990. The headline said: "Noxious Smog Hits Houston; 6000 Dead." . . .

Overall, however, the Earth Day activities were placid and energetically constructive. One of the few non-participants among public figures was President Nixon who sent word through a press secretary that he "feels the activities show the concern of people of all walks of life over the dangers to our environment."

The White House statement assessed no blame. New York's Mayor Lindsay, however, had an opinion: "People are the real polluters. It's a matter of habit for they have been littering for years."

SETTING THE POLITICAL INFRASTRUCTURE

Grassroots environmentalism relied on the expansion of the middle class after World War II. Of course, it is ironic that this society based on conspicuous consumption and the production to supply it fueled new interest in the environment. The conservative impulse proclaimed by Pinchot and others at the turn of the twentieth century had little bearing on a post-1950 America that will likely be recalled as one of the most wasteful civilizations in world history. At the root of this type of modern environmentalism was more advanced scientific knowledge on the public's part and a much higher degree of expectation for personal safety. Samuel P. Hays writes that this era "displayed demands from the grass-roots, demands that are well charted by the innumerable citizen organizations . . . " that grew out of such public interest. Within growing suburbanization, middle-class Americans expected health and home safety, as well as economic expansion. These versions of the American dream were not seen to be mutually exclusive in the late twentieth century (Hays, *Beauty*, 30).

While there was as yet little regulative authority available, grass-roots environmentalists would demand that their government intercede and insure community safety. As we saw in Chapter 6, a groundswell of interest in the environment mobilized with the counter-culture movements of the 1960s. As Americans rethought the ethics of everyday human existence, some explored a more ecologically sustainable way of life. Alternative fuels, whole grain, natural foods, and communal living are only a few examples of life-changing options that Americans chose to pursue. Most importantly, a national stage linked scientific data with environmental concern. National parks, which had begun without much controversy, became a major forum in which this debate would play out throughout the late twentieth century. As a national symbol, these parks also represented the nation's environmental ethic during a time of reappraisal and open contest.

And, of course, at the outset, we also must consider the problem of definitions. Historian Hal Rothman observes that in 1968 when the Brookings Institute surveyed the nation about which issues most concerned them, their list did not even include any environmental issues. Only a year later, however, "environmental crisis" was the top issue in the same survey (Rothman, *Greening*, 125–30). This is a dramatic shift, but what exactly did the term "environmental" and "crisis" mean to each American? When considering nature's role in his or her everyday life, would each American *really* be willing to alter their preferences and choices?

DEFINING NATIONAL PARKS

The mainstay within environmental politics was the ideal—the national park. As was discussed in Chapter 2, the earliest national parks possessed little if any unifying philosophy or ethic. A remedy to this began with the Hetch Hetchy episode and then with passage of the National Park Service Act in 1916.

This act created the National Park Service (NPS) as a unit of the Department of the Interior, staffed no longer by military personnel but now specially trained rangers (although this change would not be truly noticeable until later in the century). In his popular 1917 book on the parks, Enos Mills stated their mission as: "A national park is an island of safety in this riotous world. Within national parks is room—glorious room—room in which to find ourselves, in which to think and hope, to dream and plan, to rest, and resolve" (Nash, 189).

Stephan T. Mather, a businessman, was made the first NPS director. In addition to creating a unifying mission based in preservation, Mather also sought to develop parks as certifiable tourist attractions. By mid-century some critics had even come to criticize overcrowding in the parks. Preservationist organizations such as Muir's Sierra Club and the Land Conservancy would argue for as little use as possible; others argued that national parks were a trust open for the use of any citizen. This, of course, meant Americans had every right to use the sites as they saw fit.

Environmental policy also continued to move forward from 1950 through the 1960s. The initial interest of the public in the 1940s and 1950s was garnered through an event similar to Hetch Hetchy. The Bureau of Reclamation, an agency developed by applying Pinchot's idea of conservation to waterways of the American West, set out to construct the Echo Park Dam along the Utah-Colorado border, and within a little used national monument, named Dinosaur—even though most of its fossils and bones had been stolen. As Congress neared a vote on the issue in 1950, 78 national and 236 state conservation organizations expressed their belief that national parks and monuments were sacred areas.

David Brower, executive director of the Sierra Club, and Howard Zahniser of the Wilderness Society used the opportunity to create a model for environmental lobbyists to follow. Direct-mail pamphlets asked: "What is Your Stake in Dinosaur?" and "Will You DAM the Scenic Wildlands of Our National Park System?" Additionally, a color motion picture and a book of lush photos, each depicting the Echo Park Valley's natural splendor, were widely viewed by the public. Such images and sentiments forced Americans to react. With mail to Congress late in 1954 running at 80 to 1 against the dam, the bill's vote was suspended and the project eventually abandoned. The issues had been packaged by environmentalists to connect concerns with romantic images of the American past. Americans loved this idea and reacted more positively than ever before (Gottleib, 36–41).

Built on this example, National Parks became the nation's greatest tourist attractions during the 20th century. The 80 million acres of National Park in the year 2000, though, was just one segment of the federally-owned lands in the U.S. In 2000, acreage for the Bureau of Land Management was 270 million acres, the U.S. Forest Service held 191 million acres, and the Fish and Wildlife Service administered 91 million acres. In each case, the administration of these federally-owned lands could be guided and controlled through federal legislation. This opportunity offered the environmental movement a unique opportunity to express a new ethic for the entire nation.

BASING POLICY IN ECOLOGY

After experiencing success at Dinosaur National Monument, Zahniser identified this moment as the best to press for the environmental movement's greatest goal: a national system of wilderness lands. Based on the idealistic notion of pristine wilderness espoused by Theodore Roosevelt and others, such a system had been called for beginning with Aldo Leopold in the 1910s. and envisioned by the wilderness Society after 1935. With increased recreation in parks and public lands, argued Zahniser, it had become even more crucial that some of the land be set aside completely (Gottleib, 41–44).

The ideal of wilderness had received scientific definition through the growing science of ecology and the related development of the concept of ecosystems, which was discussed in Chapter 4. Building on the ideas of Clements and others, scientists developed a much deeper understanding of human impact on the natural environment. The term *ecosystem* is credited to Arthur George Tansley, who in the 1940s argued that nature occurred in self-sufficient (except for solar energy), ecological systems. He would go on to add that such systems could overlap and interrelate. The existence of such systems, of course, began to suggest that the human agent existed as the interloper in any system (Worster, *Nature's Economy*, 307–11).

This concept of the human surrounded by biological systems independent from it became a basic realization to the modern environmental movement. The concept used by environmentalists to link together high-level ecological theories for the general public was wilderness. By the early 1960s, when many Americans had begun to be aware of the fact that many human activities were injuring the environment, wilderness became the term used to describe a nature free from human influence.

Zahniser's bill, which was introduced to Congress in the 1950s, precluded land development and offered recreational opportunities only for a few rather than for the great mass of travelers. Such an ideal goal required great salesmanship, and Zahniser was perfect for the job. As the political climate shifted in the early 1960s, lawmakers became more interested in wilderness. Finally, in 1964, President Lyndon Johnson signed the Wilderness Act into law. The United States had taken one of the most idealistic plunges in the history of environmentalism: nearly 10 million acres were immediately set aside as "an area where the earth and its community of life are untrammeled by man, where man himself is a visitor who does not remain." Additional lands would be preserved in similar fashion by the end of the decade (Harvey, 23).

While the concept of wilderness forced the general American public to begin to understand ecosystems and the webs of reliance operating within natural systems, the application of scientific understanding to environmentalism occurred most often in other realms. Defeating the dam at Echo Park and the passage of the Wilderness Act set the stage for a 1960s shift in environmental thought that combined with NIMBY culture of the 1970s to create a federal mandate for policy action. From a vague ideal, wilderness became a structuring agent for the administration of federal lands (Gottleib, 41–48).

DOCUMENT: WILDERNESS ACT, SEPTEMBER 3, 1964

In order to assure that an increasing population, accompanied by expanding settlement and growing mechanization, does not occupy and modify all areas within the United States and its possessions, leaving no lands designated for preservation and protection in their natural condition, it is hereby declared to be the policy of the Congress to secure for the American people of present and future generations the benefits of an enduring resource of wilderness. For this purpose there is hereby established a National Wilderness Preservation System to be composed of federally owned areas designated by Congress as "wilderness areas", and these shall be administered for the use and enjoyment of the American people in such manner as will leave them unimpaired for future use and enjoyment as wilderness; and no Federal lands shall be designated as "wilderness areas" except as provided for in this Act or by a subsequent Act. . . .

Definition of Wilderness

(c) A wilderness, in contrast with those areas where man and his own works dominate the landscape, is hereby recognized as an area where the earth and its community of life are untrammeled by man, where man himself is a visitor who does not remain. An area of wilderness is further defined to mean in this Act an area of undeveloped Federal land retaining its primeval character and influence, without permanent improvements or human habitation, which is protected and managed so as to preserve its natural conditions and which (1) generally appears to have been affected primarily by the forces of nature, with the imprint of man's work substantially unnoticeable; (2) has outstanding opportunities for solitude or a primitive and unconfined type of recreation; (3) has at least five thousand acres of land or is of sufficient size as to make practicable its preservation and use in an unimpaired condition; and (4) may also contain ecological, geological, or other features of scientific, educational, scenic, or historical value.

PRIORITIZING SPECIES

If the Wilderness Act marks the beginning of the political expressions of America's new environmental sensibility, the high point of this new legislative push came in the early 1970s, particularly in 1973 with the passage of the Endangered Species Act. This act illustrated how far the ecosystem realization might carry Americans in reconfiguring their view of humans' role in nature: this act prioritized keystone or endangered species over the wants and needs of human society.

Such a concept would have been unthinkable a century before—or even during the early years of progressive environmentalism. The concept of biological integrity, enforced by scientific understanding, presented a revolution to human life on Earth. Ecology had come to demonstrate that humans were not the most important species on Earth (Rothman, *Greening*, 126–28).

DOCUMENT: ENDANGERED SPECIES ACT, 1973

(a) FINDINGS-.The Congress finds and declares that-

   (1) various species of fish, wildlife, and plants in the United States have been rendered extinct as a consequence of economic growth and development untempered by adequate concern and conservation;
   (2) other species of fish, wildlife, and plants have been so depleted in numbers that they are in danger of or threatened with extinction;

    (3) these species of fish, wildlife, and plants are of aesthetic, ecological, educational, historical, recreational, and scientific value to the Nation and its people;

    (4) the United States has pledged itself as a sovereign state in the international community to conserve to the extent practicable the various species of fish or wildlife and plants facing extinction. . . .

(b) PURPOSES-.The purposes of this Act are to provide a means whereby the ecosystems upon which endangered species and threatened species depend may be conserved, to provide a program for the conservation of such endangered species and threatened species, and to take such steps as may be appropriate to achieve the purposes of the treaties and conventions set forth in subsection (a) of this section.

(c) POLICY.-

    (1) It Is further declared to be the policy of Congress that all Federal departments and agencies shall seek to conserve endangered species and threatened species and shall utilize their authorities in furtherance of the purposes of this Act.

    (2) It is further declared to be the policy of Congress that Federal agencies shall cooperate with State and local agencies to resolve water resource issues in concert with conservation of endangered species.

NATURE AT WORK: TENNESSEE VALLEY AUTHORITY V. HILL, 437 U.S. 153 (1978) (THE SNAIL DARTER CASE)

With laws such as the Endangered Species Act now enforced, how would the courts react when the needs of nature conflicted with those of human development? One of the first public controversies along these lines occurred when the Tennessee Valley Authority (TVA) began construction on the Tellico Dam on the Little Tennessee River in 1967. Initially it appeared that the project would proceed smoothly. Typical of most TVA projects, the goal was multi-use, including the creation of hydroelectric power, shoreline, and recreational opportunities, as well as flood control. During much of the twentieth century, such projects were considered progressive improvements—even called conservation. In the new era of environmental consciousness, though, such projects endured new scrutiny (Stine, 20–32)

    In 1973, an ichthyologist conducting sampling in the area that would be flooded by the Tellico Dam discovered a previously unknown species of fish: a three-inch, tannish-colored perch called the snail darter. Studies of this small fish showed that its entire population lived in one small part of the Little Tennessee River, an area, of course, that was destined to be turned into the Tellico Dam Reservoir. To protect the Snail Darter and its habitat, the secretary of the interior used the new environmental legislation and listed it as an endangered species.

    This lawsuit then was brought against TVA in an effort to force a halt to construction on the Tellico Dam. While the courts debated the issue, the project approached 80 percent completion. Despite this stage of near completion, the Supreme Court ruled that the construction must be halted. However, just as environmental activists were learning exactly how to use these new legal tools, other interests were perfecting ways to thwart them.

In mid-1979, Senator Howard Baker, who was also the Republican Senate minority leader, and Congressman John Duncan, both from Tennessee, buried a small provision into a larger piece of legislation pending before the Congress. This provision undid the Supreme Court's decision in *TVA v. Hill* and provided that the Tellico Dam project could be completed without further legal delay. The project was completed in late-1979 (Rothman, *Greening*, 127–28).

The case at once represented a success and a failure for the nascent environmental movement. No snail darters survived in the specified portion of the Little Tennessee River impacted by the Tellico Dam project. Small populations of the snail darter, however, were subsequently discovered. As a result, the Department of Interior now lists the species as "threatened" rather than "endangered."

NATURE IN FULL REBELLION

Many Americans favored the establishment of environmental regulation because they felt that the American ethic for development had pushed nature too far. If any additional evidence were needed to prove the need for such legislation, nature seemed to be in open rebellion against humans in 1969. These events, which became large-scale media events, functioned to radically change the role of nature in everyday American life. For that reason, they are discussed below as a series of "Nature at Work" entries.

Together, these environmental catastrophes changed the American conscience. Each of the following events cycled directly into the new concern for the environment and became prominent headlines in American newspapers and news media (Rothman, *Greening*, 96–99).

NATURE AT WORK: LAKE ERIE

In the 1960s, with little visible life in its waters, Lake Erie was declared "dead." Scientists quickly learned that the opposite was true; the lake was full of life but not a correct balance of life forms. Primarily, an excessive amount of algae, created by pollution and excessive nutrients, had led to eutrophication in Lake Erie. As the algae expanded, it soaked up the lake's supply of oxygen, making it impossible for other species to survive.

Lake Erie's situation was particularly acute because it is the shallowest and warmest of the five Great Lakes. It had been used extensively for decades, enduring runoff from agriculture, urban areas, industries, and sewage treatment plants along its shores. The worst of the pollutants coming into the lake was phosphorous, which entered from agricultural fields. Unfortunately, the phosphorous did just what the farmers intended when they spread the fertilizer on their fields—only it also stimulated vegetative growth in the lake. This phosphorous was one of the primary reasons for the growth of the algae.

In response to Lake Erie's "death," the Great Lakes Water Quality Agreement (GLQWA) was signed by the United States and Canada in 1972. The agreement emphasized the reduction of phosphorous entering Lakes Erie and Ontario. Coupled with the U.S. and Canadian Clean Water acts, the GLQWA made significant progress toward reducing the phosphorus levels in Lake Erie. Through

GLQWA two nations for the first time committed themselves to creating common water quality goals. (Ashworth, 130–37).

NATURE AT WORK: CUYAHOGA RIVER

Throughout American industrialization, many rivers were exploited and left heavily laden with pollutants. Rivers near industrial centers such as Pittsburgh and Cleveland became symbols of this degradation. This legacy attracted national attention in 1969 when the Cuyahoga River did something that it had done many times before: it caught on fire. This time, however, the American public viewed the occasion as a profound statement about the impact of pollution on our natural environment (Steinberg, *Earth*, 239–40).

The fire was actually very brief in duration. It began at 11:56 A.M. and lasted for approximately 20 minutes. The area of the river that caught fire was fairly out of the way, just southeast of downtown Cleveland. The flames damaged two railway bridges and were estimated to reach heights of roughly five stories. The cause was nothing out of the ordinary for the Cuyahoga: a slick of highly volatile petroleum derivatives had leaked from one of the refineries located along the river. That commonness turned out to be the real issue; it generated great national disdain that such an event was fairly routine for such industrial locales.

The river fire served as a reminder of the importance of continued support for cleanup of Lake Erie and the Cuyahoga River. On the day after the fire, Cleveland Mayor Carl Stokes stood on the damaged Norfolk and Western bridge and called for the public to support an effort to cleanup the Cuyahoga and promised to sue the state of Ohio and the individual polluters. Stokes referred to the polluted state of the river as "a long-standing condition that must be brought to an end."

The Cuyahoga fire was most important as a symbol for a new era. The river fire received major national media attention with a *Time* Magazine article on August 1, 1969 (approximately one month after the fire). In October of 1969, federal officials passed a bill that would grant states more assurances that projects aimed at improving water quality would receive federal support.

NATURE AT WORK: OIL SPILL, CALIFORNIA

On the afternoon of January 29, 1969, a Union Oil Company platform stationed six miles off the coast of Summerland suffered what is referred to as a blowout. Oil workers had drilled a well down 3,500 feet below the ocean floor. Riggers began to retrieve the pipe in order to replace a drill bit when the "mud" used to maintain pressure became dangerously low. Natural gas blew out the pipe, sending oil into the surrounding water. When the drillers successfully capped the well, pressure built up and five breaks appeared in an east-west fault on the ocean floor, releasing oil and gas from deep beneath the earth (Rothman, *Greening*, 101–5).

For 11 days, oil workers struggled to cap the rupture. During that time, 200,000 gallons of crude oil bubbled to the surface to form an 800- square-mile slick. Incoming tides brought the thick tar to beaches from Rincon Point to Goleta, covering 35 miles of coastline and coastal life. The slick also moved south, tarring Anacapa Island's Frenchy's Cove, and beaches on Santa Cruz, Santa Rosa, and San Miguel Islands.

Many lessons were learned on this first oil spill of the environmental era. Rapid cleanup was crucial. In this spill, it took oil workers 11½ days to control the leaking oil well. The cleanup had to be multifaceted: skimmers scooped oil from the surface of the ocean while airplanes dumped detergents on the spill to try and break up the slick. Meanwhile, on the beaches and harbors, volunteers spread straw to soak up the tar and oil, and rocks were steam cleaned.

Just days after the spill occurred, activists founded Get Oil Out (GOO) in Santa Barbara. Founder Bud Bottoms urged the public to cut down on driving, burn oil company credit cards, and boycott gas stations associated with offshore drilling companies. Volunteers also helped the organization to gather 100,000 signatures on a petition calling for the ban of offshore oil drilling. Although drilling was only halted temporarily, new laws eventually tightened regulations a bit more on offshore drilling.

THE ERA OF ENVIRONMENTAL PROTECTION

Many Americans had simply had enough. Others very clearly felt shameful at the present state of America's natural environment. During the next decade the social and cultural change initiated by the 1960s and fed by a barrage of demonstrations of environmental degradation (see Chapter 6) and the need for conservation created a deluge of environmental legislation.

The public outcry would be so severe that even a conservative such as Richard Nixon might be deemed "the environmental President" as he signed the National Environmental Protection Act in 1969, creating the Environmental Protection Agency (EPA). The public entrusted the EPA as its environmental regulator to enforce ensuing legislation monitoring air and water purity, limiting noise and other kinds of pollution, and monitoring species in order to discern which required federal protection. The public soon realized just how great the stakes were (Rothman, *Greening*, 115–21).

During the 1970s, oil spills, river fires, nuclear accidents, and petroleum shortages made it appear as if nature were in open rebellion. In short, nearly every industrial process was seen to have environmental costs associated with it. From chemicals to atomic power, long-believed technological "fixes" came to have long-term impacts in the form of wastes and residue. Synthetic chemicals, for instance, were long thought to be advantageous because they resist biological deterioration. In the 1970s, this inability to deteriorate made chemical and toxic waste the bane of many communities near industrial or dump sites.

Among the assorted catastrophes, Love Canal stood out as a new model for federal action. The connection between health and environmental hazards became obvious throughout the nation. Scientists were able to connect radiation, pollution, and toxic waste to a variety of human ailments. The "smoking gun," of course, contributed to a new era of litigation in environmentalism. Legal battles armed with scientific data provided individuals armed with only NIMBY convictions with the ability to take on the largest corporations in the nation.

Rapidly, this decade instructed Americans, already possessing a growing environmental sensibility, that humans—just as Carson had instructed—needed to live within limits. A watershed shift in human consciousness could be witnessed in the popular culture as green philosophies infiltrated companies wishing to create products that appealed to the public's environmental priority. Recycling, requiring the use of daylight savings time, car-pooling, and environmental impact statements became part of everyday life after the 1970s.

DOCUMENT: NATIONAL ENVIRONMENTAL PROTECTION ACT (NEPA), 1969

(a) The Congress, recognizing the profound impact of man's activity on the interrelations of all components of the natural environment, particularly the profound influences of population growth, high-density urbanization, industrial expansion, resource exploitation, and new and expanding technological advances and recognizing further the critical importance of restoring and maintaining environmental quality to the overall welfare and development of man, declares that it is the continuing policy of the Federal Government, in cooperation with State and local governments, and other concerned public and private organizations, to use all practicable means and measures, including financial and technical assistance, in a manner calculated to foster and promote the general welfare, to create and maintain conditions under which man and nature can exist in productive harmony, and fulfill the social, economic, and other requirements of present and future generations of Americans.

(b) In order to carry out the policy set forth in this Act, it is the continuing responsibility of the Federal Government to use all practicable means, consistent with other essential considerations of national policy, to improve and coordinate Federal plans, functions, programs, and resources to the end that the Nation may—

1. fulfill the responsibilities of each generation as trustee of the environment for succeeding generations;
2. assure for all Americans safe, healthful, productive, and aesthetically and culturally pleasing surroundings;
3. attain the widest range of beneficial uses of the environment without degradation, risk to health or safety, or other undesirable and unintended consequences;
4. preserve important historic, cultural, and natural aspects of our national heritage, and maintain, wherever possible, an environment which supports diversity, and variety of individual choice;
5. achieve a balance between population and resource use which will permit high standards of living and a wide sharing of life's amenities; and
6. enhance the quality of renewable resources and approach the maximum attainable recycling of depletable resources.

(c) The Congress recognizes that each person should enjoy a healthful environment and that each person has a responsibility to contribute to the preservation and enhancement of the environment. . . .

The Congress authorizes and directs that, to the fullest extent possible: (1) the policies, regulations, and public laws of the United States shall be interpreted and administered in accordance with the policies set forth in this Act, and (2) all agencies of the Federal Government shall—

(A) utilize a systematic, interdisciplinary approach which will insure the integrated use of the natural and social sciences and the environmental design arts in planning and in decisionmaking which may have an impact on man's environment;

(B) identify and develop methods and procedures, in consultation with the Council on Environmental Quality established by title II of this Act, which will insure that presently unquantified environmental amenities and values may be given appropriate consideration in decisionmaking along with economic and technical considerations;

(C) include in every recommendation or report on proposals for legislation and other major Federal actions significantly affecting the quality of the human environment, a detailed statement by the responsible official on—

(i) the environmental impact of the proposed action,
(ii) any adverse environmental effects which cannot be avoided should the proposal be implemented,
(iii) alternatives to the proposed action,
(iv) the relationship between local short-term uses of man's environment and the maintenance and enhancement of long-term productivity, and
(v) any irreversible and irretrievable commitments of resources which would be involved in the proposed action should it be implemented.

DEVELOPMENT OF THE SUPERFUND AND THE LEGACY OF INDUSTRIALIZATION

NEPA was a watershed change in the role of nature in American life. Although the degree of its involvement would continue to vacillate, the federal government was now entrusted with the responsibility of enforcing and maintaining the health of American citizens. Overnight, for instance, government projects in nearly all branches required an "Environmental Impact Statement." These reports required that *prior* to any construction or natural disruption, federal agencies needed to first have consultants assess the project's impact on the natural ecosystem (Opie, 452–56).

As a reaction to environmental catastrophes and to NEPA, environmental legislation became of interest to nearly all legislators during the 1970s. One of the most interesting pieces of legislation considered the unwieldy problem that began this chapter. After it had been made clear that Love Canal was a serious health threat, actions were taken to create a program that would fund the cleanup of this and similar sites. Chemical companies resisted new legislation that forced them to clean up their own wastes.

The original bill created a $1.6 billion fund and allowed participating companies to escape liability from private citizens who wished to sue for property and personal damage due to the dumps or spills. Owners and operators of disposal sites and producers or transporters of hazardous wastes were made liable for up to $50 million in cleanup costs. The financial costs proved too great for the Superfund to succeed. In addition, different presidential administrations fluctuated the political and financial support for this project (Opie, 458–60).

MANAGING FORESTS UNDER NEW REGULATION

The environmental ethic of this new era could also be seen in some holdovers from previous eras in the history of conservation. For instance, forests have also been impacted by related environmental legislation. The 1964 Wilderness Act verified many years of Forest Service reservations of such lands. Under the Land and Water Fund Conservation Act of 1965 the agency has been able to acquire land specifically for public outdoor recreation in national forests. This land by the mid-1970s approached 200 million visitor-days of use. Under the Endangered Species Preservation Act of 1966 the Forest Service expanded its protection of rare wildlife and under the Environmental Quality Act of 1969 took special steps to minimize undesirable impacts of forest uses on land, water, wildlife, recreation, and aesthetics. In the Job Corps and other manpower programs, the Forest Service trained and rehabilitated thousands of underprivileged youths for meaningful careers and lives and accomplished considerable forest conservation work (Rothman, *Greening*, 63–69).

Some scholars argue that the Forest Service fell victim to its own propaganda. In its earlier campaigns to attain legislation to regulate private practices, the agency portrayed logging as wasteful and even bad. As more and more recreationists came to the national forests, the agency's own activities as a logger and road builder became well-known. Clearcutting was one of the debates begun in the 1960s by protestors who had viewed national forest practices. By the 1970s, the Forest Service had become convinced of its need to pursue "balance." By mid-1973 the Forest Service was overseeing more than 187 million acres of public lands in 155 national forests and 19 national grasslands—including 14.5 million acres of reserved wilderness and primitive areas-in 44 states and Puerto Rico (Hirt, 156–59).

CHANGING OUR MINDS ABOUT LEAD

As one indicator of the cultural climate, recall that in Chapter 3 Americans had decided that the impacts on our health were less important than the way our auto engines responded when we accelerated with leaded gasoline running through them. By the 1960s, the amount of lead added to a gallon of gasoline hovered in the vicinity of 2.4 grams. The Department of Health, Education and Welfare, which was home to the surgeon general starting with the Kennedy administration, had authority over lead emissions under the Clean Air Act of 1963. The criteria mandated by this statute were still in the draft stage when the act was reauthorized in 1970 and a new agency, the EPA, came into existence.

By the 1970s, the adverse effects of America's addiction to fossil fuel laced with lead were becoming obvious. In January 1971, EPA's first administrator, William D. Ruckelshaus, declared that "an extensive body of information exists which indicates that the addition of alkyl lead to gasoline . . . results in lead particles that pose a threat to public health." The resulting EPA study was released on November 28, 1973. In this study, scientists confirmed that lead from automobile exhaust posed a direct threat to public health. As a result, the EPA issued regulations calling for a gradual reduction in the lead content of the total gasoline supply, which includes all grades of gasoline.

Ultimately, though, this marked the shift of the gasoline market to domination by unleaded. With the 1975 model year, autos made in the United States were equipped with pollution-reducing catalytic converters designed to run only on unleaded fuel (Lead).

RALPH NADER AND DESIGNING CARS FOR EVERYTHING BUT SAFETY

Beginning in the 1920s, auto manufacturers achieved a nearly untouchable status in the corporate world. For many years, this allowed these massive corporations to disregard innovation that did not help their profits. This was most glaring in the area of vehicle safety; however, it also relates to gas mileage and the environmental impact of emissions. The effort to allow consumers to balance this playing field begins with a single individual: Ralph Nader.

As a student at Harvard Law School in the late 1950s, Nader researched unconventional issues. In 1959, Nader took research that he had conducted about the rationale for specific automotive designs and turned it into an article in the *Nation* magazine. Titled "The Safe Car You Can't Buy," Nader's article asked hard questions about the choices driving Detroit's design of automobiles. Specifically, he wrote that "It is clear Detroit today is designing automobiles for style, cost, performance, and calculated obsolescence, but not—despite the 5,000,000 reported accidents, nearly 40,000 fatalities, 110,000 permanent disabilities, and 1,500,000 injuries yearly—for safety."

With his knowledgeable concern, Nader carved himself a niche in Washington, DC as a consumer advocate. His consulting and research asked the simple question: "why shouldn't American consumers expect to be safe and healthy?" Obviously, the primary mechanism that could help Nader implement new ethics in American corporations was the federal government. He went to work for Daniel Patrick Moynihan in the Department of Labor and volunteered as an adviser to the U.S. Senate.

Having continued his research about automotive design, Nader in 1965 published *Unsafe at Any Speed.* This best-selling book was an indictment of the auto industry in general for its poor safety standards. However, Nader specifically targeted General Motors' Corvair for its faulty design. Largely because of his influence, Congress passed the 1966 National Traffic and Motor Vehicle Safety Act.

Activists flocked to Nader's causes. Referred to as "Nader's Raiders," activists involved in the modern consumer movement demanded that the federal government enforce corporate responsibility. They pressed for protections for workers, taxpayers, and the environment. In 1969 Nader established the Center for the Study of Responsive Law, which exposed corporate irresponsibility and the federal government's failure to enforce regulation of business. He founded Public Citizen and U.S. Public Interest Research Group in 1971, an umbrella for many groups of concerned citizens.

From the use of seat belts to product labeling, the influence of Nader's efforts can be seen throughout everyday American life. Crash tests and other consumer information became more and more available as public awareness grew. In addition, environmentally motivated standards for clean air were forcing auto manufacturers to change the way that they did business (Kay, 250).

AUTOMOBILES' CONTRIBUTION TO AIR POLLUTION

As scientists began to understand the complexities of air pollution in the late 1960s, it became increasingly apparent that in addition to specific toxic emissions such as lead, the internal combustion engine was a primary contributor to air pollution, which in cities is usually referred to as smog. Emissions from the nation's nearly 200 million cars and trucks account for about half of all air pollution in the United States and more than 80 percent of air pollution in cities. The American Lung Association estimates that America spends more than $60 billion each year on health care as a direct result of air pollution (Doyle, 134).

When the engines of automobiles and other vehicles burn gasoline, they create pollution. These emissions have a significant impact on the air, particularly in congested urban areas. This is hard to track or trace, though, because the sources are moving. The pollutants included in these emissions are carbon monoxide, hydrocarbons, nitrogen oxides, and particulate matter. Nationwide, mobile sources represent the largest contributor to air toxins, which are pollutants known or suspected to cause cancer or other serious health effects. These are not the only problems, though. Internal combustion engines also emit greenhouse gases, which scientists believe are responsible for trapping heat in the Earth's atmosphere. These gases are credited by many scientists for intensifying global climate change.

Table 7.1   U.S. Emissions of Carbon Monoxide by Sector
(in million tons)

Year	Industrial Processing	On-road Vehicles
1940	10.905	30.121
1950	16.353	45.196
1960	15.873	64.266
1970	16.899	88.034
1980	9.25	78.049
1990	5.852	57.848
1998	4.86	50.383

Source: U.S. Dept. of Commerce.

In each state, clean air acts have spurred regulations on vehicle emissions, but these levels and policies vary with each state. For instance, California, which has one of the nation's most severe smog problems in Los Angeles, is a national leader in smog regulation. In 1982, California began a vehicle inspection and maintenance (Smog Check) program. The state's Smog Check program has achieved an overall tailpipe emissions reduction of 17 percent in hydrocarbons and carbon monoxide from vehicles repaired after failing a Smog Check test (Doyle, 200). Beginning in 1994, California's Smog Check II took smog regulation to the next step. By using remote sensing devices that are placed on the side of the freeways, state regulators could trace gross polluters (vehicles that pollute at least two times the emissions allowed for that particular model). These vehicles account for 10–15 percent of California vehicles but create more than 50 percent of the vehicular smog

REDUCING GREENHOUSE GAS EMISSIONS

The difficulties caused by this air pollution are not limited to local environmental impacts. Cars and light trucks, which include sport utility vehicles, pickups, and most minivans, emit more than 300 million tons of carbon into the atmosphere each year in the United States. The transportation sector alone is responsible for about one-third of our nation's total production of carbon dioxide, the greenhouse gas that contributes in a big way to global warming. In response to burgeoning consumer demand over the past decade, auto makers have shifted their fleets to sport utility vehicles (SUVs) and other light trucks—popular vehicles whose fuel economy standards are lower than those of cars (Gelbspan, 9–13).

An ever-growing concern among government, industry, and environmental organizations is global climate change. A buildup of carbon dioxide in the atmosphere over the last century has been identified as a possible contributor to climate change. Auto companies are working on a number of initiatives to improve vehicle fuel economy in order to reduce carbon dioxide emissions.

Although automobile engines have been made more efficient than ever before, Americans continue to use more gasoline than ever. Since 1980, the miles-per-gallon rating of passenger cars has improved 39 percent, yet fuel consumption is up 19 percent. On average, Americans are driving about 50 percent more miles than they did in 1980. In addition, some vehicles have been made heavier, and traffic has gotten more congested. That means less gasoline than ever is actually being used to propel vehicles forward. (Gelbspan, 40–45).

FUEL CONSERVATION AND ENSURING AMERICAN AUTOMOBILITY

Given the significant problems associated with the emissions generated by vehicles, common sense, then follows that every effort be made to increase automobiles' efficiency. Known as the CAFE program, the Corporate Average Fuel Economy started in 1978 in an effort to stimulate the manufacture of more efficient autos and thereby reduce American dependence on foreign oil. Each auto manufacturer was required to attain government-set mileage targets (CAFE standards) for all its car and light trucks sold in the United States. In a compromise with manufacturers, the complex standards were calculated as a total for the entire fleet of autos and trucks made by each company. Thus, the manufacture of a few fuel-efficient models could off-set an entire line of light trucks that fell below the standards (Doyle, 240).

Originally passed in 1975, the Energy Policy and Conservation Act was a reaction to the Arab oil embargo of the early 1970s. The public demanded that the federal government force auto manufacturers to offer them some assistance in managing the rising price of petroleum. The act quickly influenced many aspects of the industry, including petroleum mixes, automobile design, and vehicle safety.

As a supplement to this original act, the 1978 CAFE standards required 18 miles per gallon (mpg) for cars. In order to spur innovation, the standard increased each year until 1985. With the automobile standard at 27.5 mpg in 1985, lawmakers expected that manufacturers would willingly surpass this goal. Instead, the 1990s saw manufacturers increase the size of most vehicles, particularly in the area of light trucks, including pickup trucks and SUVs—arguably the most popular type of vehicle at the close of the twentieth century. With the fleet standards based on vehicular weight, manufacturers have found ways to sell vehicles such as Hummers if they offset them with enough fuel-efficient products to allow the overall fleet to meet the CAFE standards.

One other initiative begun in the 1970s was a federally mandated speed limit. In the 1970s, federal safety and fuel conservation measures included a national speed limit of 55 miles per hour. Today, consumers have led states to loosen such restrictions; however, concern over fuel conservation continues (Doyle, 251–62).

FEDERALIZING PUBLIC HEALTH

Throughout American life in the 1970s, new expectations were placed on the federal government. In some cases, though, new legislation simply picked up on trends begun in an earlier generation. When progressive reformers demanded that the federal government become more involved in Americans' health, for instance, the Public Health Service (PHS) was established in the early 1900s as part of the Department of Health and Human Services. By the end of the twentieth century, the PHS had grown to be the major health agency in the federal government, with more than 51,000 Civil Service employees and a budget of over $20 billion.

NIMBY expectations significantly altered the expectations placed on the PHS. With a broad mission to protect and advance the nation's health, today the PHS creates programs to help control and prevent diseases, fund biomedical research, protect Americans against unsafe food and drugs, and try to make new technologies and medicines available to as many Americans as possible. The major changes for PHS began in the 1950s, when President Dwight D. Eisenhower reorganized the federal health agencies to ensure that the important areas of health, education, and social security be represented in the president's cabinet. The newly created Department of Health, Education, and Welfare eventually gave way in 1979 to the Department of Health and Human Services.

The eight major agencies that make up the PHS and that do this work are the Centers for Disease Control and Prevention (CDC), the Agency for Toxic Substances and Disease Registry (ATSDR), the National Institutes of Health (NIH), the Food and Drug Administration (FDA), the Substance Abuse and Mental Health Services Administration (SAMHSA), the Health Resources and Services Administration (URSA), the Agency for Health Care Policy and Research (AUCPR), and the Indian Health Service (IHS).

Recent events and debates have involved the agency in some of the most controversial issues of our age, including national security, abortion rights, and the morality of bioengineering. A similar effort to call into question the basic values of Post World War II American consumption came from a genre of writing known as consumer advocacy. Ralph Nader helped define a field known as consumer rights with the publication of *Unsafe at Any Speed* in 1965. In 2002, similar titles including *High and Mighty* and *Fast Food Nation* criticized the SUV and American nutrition. *Fast Food Nation* suggested that restaurant chains such as

McDonald's contributed to Americans becoming the most obese people in world history.

THE CONTESTED REALM OF FEDERAL HEALTH CARE

The federal role in citizens' health care was the source of great debate at the end of the twentieth century. Although most Americans wished good health on other citizens, paying for such services became enmeshed in political philosophy. For instance, in the 1990s, the administration of President William Clinton placed the federal government at the forefront of research to explore the use of DNA in medical procedures and, especially, to map the human genome. Similar to space travel, such scientific frontiers were often considered to merit the organization and funding of the federal government. In addition, many scientists believed the project was best kept in the public sector. The administration of George W. Bush, by contrast, took a stand against medical research related to stem cells and human cloning and argued that the federal government should not be involved in such scientific efforts.

In efforts such as food labeling, the federal government has been consistently involved in helping to give Americans nutritional information about what they eat and drink. Responding to reports of nutritional deficiencies, the FDA in 1973 adopted voluntary labeling that emphasized vitamins, minerals, and proteins. While nutritional deficiencies are now uncommon, problems with labeling became apparent. As consumers became concerned about the link between diet and disease, the food industry began adding phrases such as "light" and "healthy" or "low fat" to labels. What these phrases meant was unclear. The Nutrition Labeling and Education Act of 1990 required food labels and the FDA set standard serving sizes. In 1994 requirements for a standardized food label took effect, making it easier for consumers to check the nutritional content of packaged foods. The nutrition pyramid released by the FDA is part of a national effort to reduce obesity, particularly among younger Americans.

One of the major controversies of the 1980s and 1990s was over the government's response to the AIDS crisis. When AIDS emerged in the 1980s, gays and lesbians were already a well-organized political force. Their experiences had often led them to be skeptical of the medical and scientific communities. AIDS activist groups, such as the New York-based ACT UP (AIDS Coalition to Unleash Power) and the San Francisco-based Project Inform, pressured the FDA to provide promising but still experimental drugs to people with AIDS on a parallel track with standard clinical trials required before FDA approval of drugs.

Despite resistance, the FDA moved toward such a policy and established accelerated approval procedures in 1992. Accelerated approval is intended to get promising but still unproven drugs for life-threatening diseases to patients as quickly as possible. The drugs must still be shown to be safe but the usual standards of efficacy are relaxed. While drug companies have long resisted increasing regulation, this particular case did not meet with resistance. Unlike other consumer groups, AIDS activists had an interest in less stringent regulations, and by the late 1980s prominent researchers became convinced that there was a moral obligation to provide promising therapies as early as possible.

The public expected protection and action from the federal government. These NIMBY expectations stimulated federal action on a number of issues related to public health by the end of the 1970s. Although these initiatives varied with each presidential administration, the expectations of middle-class Americans have made certain that they never are lost entirely.

NATURE AT WORK: BALD EAGLE, A SYMBOL OF PROTECTION AND RECOVERY

By the 1990s, there were examples that the initiatives of the 1960s and 1970s had made changes in the nature of everyday American life. Possibly the best example of the capabilities of modern environmentalism was the bald eagle. By the 1990s, our nation's symbol had also become a symbol of the possibilities of environmental regulation.

In the early 1900s, eagles inhabited every large river and concentration of lakes in the interior United States. It was estimated that eagles nested in 45 of the lower 48 states. Within a few decades, though, the population of eagles had plummeted. Scientific explanations for this decline are complex and include a number of different factors.

Essentially, eagles and humans were in competition for the same food, and humans, with guns and traps at their disposal, had the upper hand. By the 1930s, public awareness of bald eagles and their plight began to increase, and in 1940 the Bald Eagle Act was passed. This act reduced the direct pressures caused by humans (such as hunting), and eagle populations began to rebound. However, this was also the era when American agriculture began to rely more than ever on DDT and other pesticides. Part of Rachel Carson's research for *Silent Spring* directly discussed the effect of these chemicals on eagle populations. Primarily, the chemicals ran off the land and into waterways where they infected fish that would eventually be eaten by eagles and other birds of prey.

Scientific research demonstrated definitively that the chemicals caused a softening of eagles' eggs, which caused them to break prematurely and not reach birth. With their population plummeting, bald eagles were officially declared an endangered species in 1967 in all areas of the United States south of the 40th parallel. This law was then followed by the Endangered Species Act of 1973. Federal and state government agencies, along with private organizations, successfully sought to alert the public about the eagle's plight and to protect its habitat.

Although only a handful of species have fought their way back from the United States's endangered species list, the eagle regained its population stability in the 1990s. Once endangered in all of the lower 48 states, the bald eagle's status was upgraded to "threatened" in 1994, two decades after the banning of DDT and the passing of laws to protect both eagles and their nesting trees. Clearly, Americans had learned valuable lessons about their role in managing the natural environment.

CONCLUSION: EARTH DAY 1990

How far could the influence of environmental thought come in 20 years? April 22, 1990 may have seemed like an ordinary day; however, instead of the regular television schedule listings, the *New York Times* listed "TV and the Environment." Most impressive, there were a host of programs to delineate! However, many Americans were not taking time to watch TV; instead, they performed cleanup enterprises on behalf of Mother Earth. Internationally, more than 40 million humans marked some kind of celebration on Earth Day 1990.

For American culture, though, Earth Day 1990 marked a day of broader recognition. American society celebrated a new relationship with the natural world surrounding it. Today, polls reveal that nearly 70 percent of Americans refer to themselves as "environmentalists." Such developments are simply the latest in a watershed shift in Americans' awareness of the human impact on the natural environment. The 1990s marked a maturing period for the environmental movement, which had been evolving in the United States since the nineteenth century.

8

GREEN CULTURE

Something looks incongruous at 555 Bottonfield Lane. The single-level home is nearly identical to the two dozen homes on either side of the block. However, each of the other homes is cast on the typical American setting: a backdrop of green. Number 555, though, has no green. It is surrounded by pebbles and packed dirt. Where other residents have placed trees that must be watered twice a day, 555 has cacti, sagebrush, and other plants indigenous to the Colorado area. None of these require water or extra care.

Here, in the arid lands of western North America, though, that backdrop of green relies on the region's precious supply of water. Nationally, communities have been faced with increased demands on existing water supplies. Consequently, there is a greater focus on water conservation, not just in times of drought, but in anticipation of future population growth. Water can no longer be considered a limitless resource. A philosophy of conservation of water through creative landscaping has engendered the new term, xeriscape.

Early on, a landscape such as that at 555 Bottonfield often resulted in complaints from neighborhood associations. But with Americans' increasing understanding of the limits of arid environments, xeriscape was seen as a form of environmental planning. The term xeriscape derives from the Greek word xeros, meaning dry, combined with landscaping. Therefore, xeriscaping is an aesthetically pleasing landscape planned for arid conditions. The term is said to have been used first by the Front Range Xeriscape Task Force of the Denver Water Department in 1981. The stated goal of a xeriscape is to achieve visual appeal with plants selected for their water efficiency. Properly maintained, a xeriscape can easily use less than one-half the water of a traditional landscape. Once established, a xeriscape should require less maintenance than turf landscape.

In many of these areas, homeowners have implemented other ideas while still maintaining a public outdoor buffer. One of the most interesting gardening methods is xeriscaping in which one uses species native to the natural surroundings. Instead of turf grass, the use of cacti and scrub or prairie grasses reduces maintenance significantly.

Clearly, the lawn of green grass is a social and cultural product of the age of conspicuous consumption. Its roots, though, fall within the realm of gardening. Ideas such as xeriscaping reintroduce the ethic of gardening, while requiring that such a human-managed environment still function within the natural ecosystem.

GREEN CULTURE SETS NEW STANDARDS

As policy makers reacted to grassroots demand for environmental reform in the 1970s and 1980s, many Americans sought out ways to integrate their new-found environmental ethics into their everyday lives. More than at any other time in American history, then, the living patterns of everyday American life in the 1980s included a thought or awareness of humans' impact on the world around them.

Once this environmental awareness made it into basic patterns of American mass culture, it often held little identifiable connection to its roots in the ecological principles of Cowles, Clements, Leopold, and Carson. However, many Americans clearly had added impact on the environment to their list of considerations when they made choices about which product to buy, where to eat, and what to do in their free time. When these choices reflected a bit of environmental conscience or reflection, it can be grouped with a cultural pattern termed "green culture." Often, this change was marked by alterations to tradition and practices already ingrained in American life, including residential patterns, leisure culture, and film preferences. In terms of nature in everyday life, therefore, the late 1970s and the 1980s mark a period of applied cultural change in American ideas about nature.

Once one begins to study green culture, one finds, of course, that there are examples of this form throughout the twentieth century. In certain cases, green culture can derive from forms that seem incongruous with the environment. However, there are also plenty of clear patterns within American mass culture that suggest a growing interest in the environment, possibly even a more widespread environmental ethic.

IMAGING CONSERVATION: SMOKEY AND WOODSY

Smokey Bear, the guardian of our forests, has been a part of the American popular culture for over 60 years. Although Smokey's story is interesting for a variety of reasons, it especially symbolizes an era when resource conservation issues could be taken directly to an interested and educated American public. Today, Smokey

Bear is one of the most famous advertising symbols in the world and is protected by federal law. He has his own private zip code, his own legal council, and his own private committee to insure that his name is used properly. Smokey Bear is much more than a make-believe paper image; he exists as an actual symbol of forest fire prevention (Pyne, 170–75).

Smokey Bear and the interest in bringing fire prevention to the public actually relates directly to events of World War II. As one historian explains: "In the Spring of 1942, a Japanese submarine surfaced near the coast of Southern California and fired a salvo of shells that exploded on an oil field near Santa Barbara, very close to the Los Padres National Forest. Americans throughout the country were shocked by the news that the war had now been brought directly to the American mainland. There was concern that further attacks could bring a disastrous loss of life and destruction of property. One of the areas that seemed ripe for destruction were valuable forests on the Pacific Coast. With experienced firefighters and other able-bodied men engaged in the armed forces, the home communities had to deal with the forest fires as best they could. Protection of these forests became a matter of national importance, and a new idea was born. If people could be urged to be more careful, perhaps some of the fires could be prevented" (Smokey). This very genuine security concern eventually combined with the emerging American interest in the environment.

During World War II, the Forest Service worked with the Wartime Advertising Council to create a marketing campaign in which posters and slogans proclaimed "Forest Fires Aid the Enemy," and "Our Carelessness, Their Secret Weapon." Throughout the campaign, the suggestion was clear: more careful practices by humans could prevent many forest fires. Indirectly, fewer fires could help the war effort by maintaining timber supplies and minimizing necessary expenditures of manpower.

Disney also got into the act when it released the motion picture "Bambi" in 1944. The company allowed the character to be used in the forest fire prevention campaign for one year. The "Bambi" poster was a success. Although the Forest Service was contractually bound not to use a fawn following Bambi's one year run, they did feel certain that an animal mascot had helped to raise public interest in fire prevention. After internal debates, the Forest Service settled on using a bear as its new mascot.

The first Smokey Bear poster was released later in August 1944. The poster, which depicted a bear pouring a bucket of water on a campfire, was a hit. Within a decade, Smokey Bear was a money-maker for the federal government. His character was officially moved from the public domain and placed under the Secretary of Agriculture's control. Whether Smokey was a stuffed toy or a poster, the federal government could now collect fees and royalties while also publicizing fire safety (Pyne, 178–80).

Smokey was joined a few decades later by Woodsy Owl. Created by the USDA's National Forest Service in celebration of Earth Day 1970, Woodsy Owl told Americans: "Give a Hoot! . . . Don't Pollute!" These ad campaigns were especially effective with school children, and Woodsy was used in many informational programs that were developed to educate American children about these environmental issues.

INTERPRETING GREEN CULTURE

Green culture did not only emanate from conservation agencies. The dissemination of greener ethics has also greatly impacted the popular culture created by mass media. This development seems to have occurred at a pace with the growing interest of Americans in the environment; therefore, one can argue that the popular images fed the evolving desire of many Americans to be environmentally aware.

Most prevalent might be the genre of culture that seeks to give television viewers access to the natural world, which lay quite distant from the professional worlds of most viewers. Mutual of Omaha's *Wild Kingdom* began this tradition in the 1970s. In the tradition of *National Geographic,* Marlon Perkins created adventure from far-off locations that was based in the unknown secrets of the natural world. Breeding an entire genre of television—even an entire network—*Wild Kingdom* continues production but has spawned a great many programs, particularly for young viewers. Finally, Perkins's search for showing animals in their natural surroundings contributed to the interest in " ecotourism," in which the very wealthy now travel to various portions of the world not to shoot big game but only to view it.

Zoos and wildlife parks have also seized on this interest and attempted to manufacture similar experiences for visitors. Possibly the most well-known cultural manifestation of environmental themes is Sea World, the marine theme park that first opened in 1964 and now includes parks in Florida, California, and Ohio. Unlike Disneyland and other amusement parks, Sea World carries a full-blown theme: the effort to bring visitors into closer contact with the marine world. As this agenda has become more routine since 1980, performing mammals have taken center stage. The most famous of these performers is Shamu the killer whale. In the highly competitive amusement industry, Sea World has exploited its niche by focusing since 1990 on environmental themes deriving from threats to marine life (Davis, 68–69).

Such cultural interest in natural history and science is most clearly evident for children. While entire school curricula have been altered to include environmental perspectives, juvenile popular culture has guided such interest. From Disney's *Bambi* to Dr. Seuss's *The Lorax,* artists have clearly identified a sensitivity in juveniles. Each of these tales stresses overuse, mismanagement, or cruelty toward the natural world. The typical use of easily recognizable examples of good and evil that support children's media have been radically expanded.

Mixing science with action, environmentalism proved to be excellent fodder for American educators. More importantly, though, the philosophy of fairness and living within limits merged with cultural forms to become mainstays in entertainment for young people, including feature films such as *Lion King, Free Willie,* and *Fern Gully,* environmental music, and even clothing styles. Contemporary films such as *Lion King* bring complex ecological principles of balance between species to the child's level.

Many parents find children acting as environmental regulators within a household. Shaped by green culture, a child's mindset is often entirely utopian, whereas parents possess more real-world stress and knowledge.

Even so, many adults long for such simplicity and idealism, and scholars say that children awaken these convictions in many adults. In fact, a growing number of adults hold jobs involved with the environment. Environmental regulation and green culture created a mandate for a new segment of the workforce: technically trained individuals to carry out new ways of managing waste and consumption.

IMAGING ENVIRONMENTAL CATACLYSM: *THE LATE, GREAT PLANET EARTH*

Throughout the history of mass and popular culture, creators of popular reading material and film—especially science fiction—have sought to strike American anxieties by choosing topics about which the public has great trepidation. During the 1970s, one of the most popular paradigms revolved around human exploitation of natural resources that then resulted in widespread human suffering. This form of tragic environmental drama continues to be popular in the twenty-first century.

One of the first examples of this line of thought was Hal Lindsey's *The Late, Great Planet Earth*, which was originally published in 1970. In this text, Lindsey offered readers a guide to finding the future in the text of the Bible. With 15 million copies in print, this bestseller obviously struck a nerve in the modern world. Specifically, Lindsey offered order to the chaotic close of the twentieth century by arguing that many of the predictions of the Old and New Testament have come true. Such a connection offered hope to many Judeo-Christians that the Bible and the morality that it imposes had resonance in contemporary life. It also made many readers turn to the Bible in order to prophesy future events.

In this fashion, Lindsey spurred contemporary readers to read the Bible with care and helped to reenergize Christianity. Many critics, however, suggest that few of his predictions for the 1980s came true and that he preyed on readers' hopes and fears. Regardless, the prophetic rhetoric of the *Late, Great Planet Earth* made it one of the most popular books of the 1970s.

Although there have been many science fiction films designed to depict cataclysm and the end of the world, one of the most recent blockbusters was more specific than all of the others. *The Day After Tomorrow* (2003) marked a new approach and a new awareness of the potential impact of human living patterns.

WHOLE EARTH CATALOGUE AND GREEN CONSUMPTION

Aspects of the early environmental movement's roots in the 1960s counter-culture persisted in alternate forms of consumption during the late twentieth century. The roots of this movement reach back to 1968 when Stewart Brand's *Whole Earth Catalogue* (TWEC) introduced Americans to green consumerism. Winner of the National Book Award and a national bestseller, TWEC quickly became the unofficial handbook of the 1960s counter-culture. The book contained philosophical ideas based in science, holistic living, and metaphysics as well as listings of products that functioned within these confines. As many Americans sought to turn their backs on America's culture of consumption, TWEC offered an alternative paradigm based in values extending across the counter-culture. Even if Americans did not choose these values, they garnered a valuable lesson in discerning consumption.

As many of the participants in the 1960s counter-culture entered communes or "returned to the land" in other fashions, Brand's book became an instruction manual. The first page declared that "the establishment" had failed and that the catalogue aimed to supply tools to help an individual "conduct his own education, find his own inspiration, shape his own environment , and share his adventure with whoever is interested." The text offered advice about organic gardening, massaging, meditation, and do-it-yourself burial: "Human bodies are an organic part of the whole earth and at death must return to the ongoing stream of life." Many Americans found the resources and rationale within TWEC to live as rebels against the American "establishment." Interestingly, though, Brand did not urge readers to reject consumption altogether. TWEC's enlightened philosophy had a significant impact on patterns in American mass culture.

In particular, TWEC helped to create the consumptive niche known today as green consumerism, which seeks to resist products contributing to or deriving from waste or abuse of resources, applications of intrusive technologies, or use of nonnatural raw materials. The *Whole Earth Catalogue* sought to appeal to this niche by offering products such as recycled paper, and the rationale for its use. As the trend-setting publication of green consumption, TWEC is viewed by many Americans as having started the movement toward whole grains, healthy living, and environmentally friendly products. Today, these products make up a significant portion of all consumer goods and entire national chains have based themselves around the sale of such goods.

The original catalogue combines the best qualities of the *Farmer's Almanac* and a Sears catalogue, while merging wisdom and consumption with environmental activism and expression. Today, even though green culture has even infiltrated mass society, Whole Earth continues as a network of experts who gather information and tools in order to live a better life, and, for some, to construct "practical utopias." The *Millennium Whole Earth Catalog*, for instance, claims to integrate the best ideas of the past 25 years with the best for the next, based around the TWEC standards, such as environmental restoration, community building, whole systems thinking, and medical self-care. Despite the increased environmental awareness of the American public, TWEC continues to find a niche for its unique ideas about soft-living and careful consuming. It has also led to the growth of organic products and markets.

NATURE COMPANY

As with many aspects of green culture, some of the forms appear to be false attempts to exploit consumer interest in the environment.

A revealing example of this green culture occurred during the 1980s when the American shopping mall—the quintessential example of artifice—played host to green consumerism. The Nature Company, which sold scientific and naturalistic gadgets as well as holistic and third-world crafts, had originally been founded in Berkeley, California in 1973 by Tom and Priscilla Wrubel, who had been members of the Peace Corps in the 1960s.

By 1994, the Wrubels had sold their interest to a corporation that specialized in newer models of consumption targeting "yuppie" consumers. Now, there were 124 stores in the United States, and approximately 20 more worldwide. Since then, Nature Company's fortunes have declined. However, the interest in this type of green consumption has not diminished. The niche that the Nature Company identified has now become part of mainstream consumption and can be found in many different types of stores (Price, 195–200). In this niche, Americans unapologetically mix consumptive practices with symbols and forms of the natural environment.

WHAT IS THE ENVIRONMENTAL ETHIC OF THE PLASTIC PINK FLAMINGO?

Can a pink, artificial, plastic decoration actually connect the everyday life of Americans to the natural forms around them? Some scholars argue that the pink flamingo placed in many American lawns does just that.

The pink flamingo was first sold to the public in 1957. By the 1970s, the flamingos became a prevalent part of the landscape of middle-class suburbs. For suburbanites, the plastic bird signaled a hint of disconformity in the homogeneous world of suburbia. Jenny Price, however, writes that the flamingo swiftly came to also signal definitions of nature. She writes:

The baby boomers didn't invent the bird. But as with television, we were born with it and grew up with it. And we appropriated it for ourselves. Through the 1970s, we used the pink flamingo as a ubiquitous signpost for crossing the various, overlapping boundaries of class, taste, propriety, art, sexuality, and Nature. (Price, 146)

During the 1980s and 1990s, the flamingo became more popular than ever before. Price adds that during this ever more fluid era of boundaries and definition, the flamingo became a symbol of the connection between nature and art or artifice (Price, 161).

It was these types of consumers that by the end of the century would be considering xeriscaping, such as that found on Bottonfield Lane. When selecting the aesthetic for their home, Americans could have gone many directions. Time and again, however, Americans chose natural symbols. Possibly the best example of this is the green lawn on which the flamingo is placed. The tastes of today's American homeowners took shape during the twentieth century. To understand this change in consumers, one must first understand what traditions brought the desire for turf grass and yard spaces with the typical American home. This quest begins on the links.

NATURE AT WORK: GOLF COURSE HISTORY

Although turf grass is not indigenous to most of North America, its presence marks a complicated portion of the American connection to the natural environment. Part of this tradition includes a leisure activity not normally identified with environmentalists: golfing.

With roots in Europe, particularly Great Britain and Scotland, golf was first a hobby of royalty and the very wealthy. The United States broadened this interest to the middle classes but still clearly linked golfing to social and economic status. The most enduring link grew between golf and the new American suburbs of the upper middle class that began to be seen in the late nineteenth century. Today, with nearly 60 percent of Americans living in suburbs, golf's popularity has also increased significantly. No other aspect of the American landscape is as responsible as golf courses for creating an aesthetic bond between twentieth-century Americans and turf grass.

Golf made its appearance in the United States in 1888 and was initially played in close-cropped cow pastures. Despite its appeal to women, golfing was largely limited to a tiny minority of primarily affluent white men who could afford to support the large expanse of carefully managed and highly maintained acreage needed for a golf course. Public links were established in parks in New York City, Boston, Cincinnati, Philadelphia, and Providence, Rhode Island, in the 1890s, with 80 courses in place by 1894 and 982 by 1900. Many of these courses were less than picturesque though. As American courses became more competitive, the best lured greens keepers from Europe to recreate the American courses as beautiful parks. Of these newer courses, the most influential were Myopia, north of Boston, the Garden City Golf Course, and National Golf Links of America, each on New York's Long Island.

More public courses followed in the 1920s, and a few elite suburbs were laid out around golf courses so that the fairways seemed to flow into the lawns around the houses. Charles Hugh Alison, the first course architect to be recognized internationally, was the most active of around 12 architects presiding over this golden era. Construction costs, real estate values, and interest rates were low and the public was prioritizing leisure. Six hundred new courses were opened each year between 1923 and 1929! By 1929 there were nearly 6,000 courses in the United States. Only long-established courses were able to weather the Depression and war years, though the post-war years, then, would bring significant changes to golf course design and use (Jenkins, 34–40).

The greatest revolution in course construction after 1945 was technology—particularly the availability of massive earth-moving machines. The appearance of courses now could include cultivating and carefully smoothing fairway seed beds. Robert Trent Jones and other well-known designers combined such methods with the expansion of the middle class to recreate golf as a male standard through the late twentieth century. By 1980 there were over 400 Trent Jones courses located in 42 states. Additionally, many suburban communities included courses in their overall designs. Clearly, golf was a part of life for many Americans.

The growth in golf's popularity during the latter half of the twentieth century includes strategic marketing through the mass media. As types of labor gave way to service and management, middle-class men had a bit more leisure time as well as an automobile to carry them where they wished. Historian Virginia Scott Jenkins finds that a connection was firmly made between the aesthetic of the golf courses and the suburbs in which players lived. One advertisement urged homeowners to "ask the Greens-keeper at your own Club what he thinks of TORO Equipment." Golfers such as Sam Sneed and Jack Nicklaus were used in advertisements to instill the connection between homeownership and lawn care (Jenkins, 61–64).

GIDDY OVER GRASS

Golf courses helped to shape the aesthetic with which Americans measured and defined their preferred environments. By association, creating better species of turf grass became an interest of many Americans. The agriculture departments of state land-grant colleges and universities studied turf-grass growing with subsidies from the Golf Association of America. The most significant developments came from the combined forces of the U.S. Golf Association and the U.S. Department of Agriculture to create a heat-, drought-, and disease-resistant grass for use on the modern American landscape. Specifically, the American aesthetic required a grass that could be green year round. Such priorities also extended to the American home, where the golf course aesthetic contributed to the American idealization of the lawn surrounding most homes (Teysott, 121–22).

The popularity of golf and the use of turf grass in urban parks linked it into the American aesthetic. This portion of American taste combined with home-building technology of the twentieth century to make green grass the context for nearly every American home. The lawn can often seem more closely related to an artificial area than to an organic creation such as a garden; however, placed within its historical context, this landscape form can be viewed for its "natural" significance in the lives of many Americans.

A greensward generally surrounds nearly 60 per cent of American homes, offering a border between public and private space. While there are certainly utilitarian purposes for the lawn, particularly for children's play, it remains largely an aesthetic creation. Imported from France and England, the lawn was normally a transitional zone into manicured gardens. While lawns were not uncommon in the United States at the turn of the eighteenth century, the more purposeful design was not devised until the mid 1800s. Starting with the rural cemetery movement of the 1830s, Andrew Jackson Downing and other landscape architects created a general aesthetic that relied on the green space as a multipurpose setting that helped to civilize the wild vista beyond one's property. This was particularly important in the country estates that Downing normally designed (Teysott, 44–49).

More than a century later, when Arthur Levitt and other builders streamlined the suburban model of construction, the lawn remained an integral part of the American landscape. As nondescript housing developments swept the nation after World War II, the lawn became one of the few aesthetic staples of the design. Today, many homeowners parcel their lawn into different zones depending on patterns of use, including a front lawn that is most heavily manicured and managed, intended most to frame the home's presentation, and the back yard, which is less manicured and chemically managed and is more of a personal space.

MAKING A BETTER BLADE

The evolution of the lawn has not been without a scientific presence. The lawn industry got its start in 1901 when the U.S. Congress allotted $17,000 to ascertain best turf grass species for lawns and pleasure grounds. In 1920, the U.S. Golf Association began working with the USDA to devise a species of grass that would remain green all year round. Today, grass research centers are available at most agricultural universities. The industry now mixes science, aesthetics, and marketing. Interestingly, advertising is most often carried out by successful golfers who represent lawn-care companies. Also composed of elements such as a garden, the lawn has clearly become a social landscape for Americans—one that provides important statements about one's standing in society. In many communities, the pursuit of the perfect lawn is reinforced by peer pressure. The physical aesthetic is relatively simple: the space contains only healthy, green grass and few weeds and is consistently cut so that it maintains a low, even height (Jenkins, 160–65).

Of course, such a lawn is not attuned to particularities of place. Significant technology is required to insert such a garden site in areas of varied climate and rainfall. Using marketing skills and advertising, lawn and garden companies were able to sell their products and gradually shape the concept of the lawn to meet their desire for increased profit. Michael Pollan writes that the artificial green space that he refers to as the "industrial lawn" also has become a significant symbol in American life. He writes, "Since we have traditionally eschewed fences and hedges in America, the suburban vista can be marred by the negligence—or dissent—of a single property owner. This is why lawn care is regarded as such an important civic responsibility in the suburbs" (Pollan 10–11).

The industrial lawn has also spurred the exportation of the lawn mystique to other parts of the world. While many nations included gardens and pasture near homes, the standardized lawn is considered an American creation. Today, the image of American prosperity has aided the dissemination of the lawn aesthetic globally, particularly into wealthier homes. This is also demonstrated by the popularity of other, related forms, such as golf courses in Asia and elsewhere. Regardless of the nation's garden preferences, such lawn design is directly modeled after the American form.

The lawn is considered so uniquely American that Canadian scholars created a museum exhibit in 1998 titled "The American Lawn," which contained historical developments as well as design replicas. Although Americans may prefer that other nations acknowledge our natural wonders or technological developments, for many international observers the lawn has become a symbol of America's successful era of consumption. To many Americans, caring for and maintaining the aesthetic of the lawn may be their closest relationship to the natural world. Clearly, though, grass forms an aesthetic preference for Americans whether in their own home space or in the sporting events they choose to patronize.

NATURE AT WORK: SPORTS FIELDS

One of the most ubiquitous versions of our pastoral ideal is the tradition of American sports fields. Of course, athletic stadiums are utilitarian structures that also offer major cities the opportunity to possess a cutting-edge stadium that will earmark a city on the move. The precedent for such structures differs significantly from the private, corporate development of contemporary stadium planning.

The earliest modern stadiums emphasized utility and monumentality. Olympic stadiums, including the White City stadium in London for the 1908 games and the Berlin Olympic stadium for the 1936 games, carried on these traditions while also stressing flexibility in the facility's use. After World War I, the United States broke new ground with a series of pioneering stadiums, including: the Yale Bowl at New Haven in 1914, the Rose Bowl at Pasadena, and Ann Arbor stadium. Using grass playing fields as their setting, these and other stadiums built before 1950 simply organized and systematized an audience's ability to watch sports. The nature of stadiums, however, changed dramatically after 1950. Multipurpose facilities became the rage for modernist planners who created urban designs that allowed for stadiums to be surrounded by massive parking lots so that fans could arrive by automobile.

The multipurpose form was extended by a development that seemed foreboding for the American commitment to turf grass: the enclosed dome. The originator of this form was the Houston Astrodome, which opened in 1964. Judge Roy Hofheinz, with the quirky idea to combine attending a sports event with going to a cocktail party, designed the dome around the idea of skyboxes. These private boxes allowed high-paying clients to attend games without interacting with other fans. A young pitcher for the Houston Astros bounded into the stadium in April 1965, taking in the miracles of the dome: air conditioning, grass growing indoors (artificial turf would be laid in 1966), the translucent roof (greenhouse by day, a planetarium by night), and seating for 66,000. "It was," he says, "like walking into the next century" (Jenkins, 143–44).

Many traditionalists viewed attending baseball in air-conditioned splendor as a travesty. The players, though, were most critical of the roof, the panels of which created a glare that made it impossible to see the ball. The league tried changing the color of the ball but to no avail. The team painted over the roof panels, banishing the sun and killing the grass—Tifway 419 Bermuda, which had been specially developed by scientists in Georgia. For the rest of the season, the Astros simply painted over the dead grass. Following the season, Monsanto's new artificial turf, renamed AstroTurf, was installed. By 1973 five more stadiums would have synthetic surfaces and many others would follow.

Turf proved the highpoint of the artificial stadium. Other domes would follow, including the Louisiana Superdome, the largest dome when it was built in 1975 with a seating capacity of 95,000. While traditionalists would wage war against domes and turf, there was practical value to the controlled environment. Particularly when sports became more concerned with money making, these technologies reduced the dependence on weather and made the games more appealing for family and business groups. The effort to reconcile these needs led to a few innovations, including the retractable roof, which was first installed in the Toronto Skydome in 1989. On the whole, though, the domes have fueled a return to a more traditional model of stadiums seen in the early 1900s.

Many current stadium projects have followed the model of Camden Yards, Baltimore and the new Comiskey Park, Chicago. Returning to the one-dimensional parks, these forms fuse modern convenience with nostalgic detail. The postmodern fusion has been a universal success, even functioning to attract entire families to baseball games. Many stadiums have built on this to include amusement and shopping facilities within the park for those less enamored with sports. Among the nostalgic detail is also a return to turf. Natural grass has been found to be much kinder on athletes' bodies. Today, very little artificial turf is installed at the professional level.

From being viewed as a utilitarian structure, stadiums appear now to be viewed as an attraction of their own. The mixture of traditional nostalgia and business concerns created a great stadium boom in the final years of the twentieth century.

A NEARLY GREEN ERA IN SUBURBAN DEVELOPMENT

By 1970, most Americans lived in suburbs. These developments were often designed around the aesthetic of the lawn, which meant that for most Americans, their section of turf grass represented their most consistent nature/human relationship. The homes themselves also reflected new preferences for many Americans.

When the United States went through one of the largest sweeps of new home construction in history after World War II, it fed the movement toward prefabrication and homogeneous suburbs. However, many builders actually argued for green technology well before it was prevalent in other parts of American life. In the 1950s, writes historian Adam Rome, solar and atomic technologies vied for the home heating market in a way that would never be seen again in the twentieth century (Rome, 53). The September, 1943 *Newsweek* offered readers a postwar dream house that would "hedge against future fuel shortages" by describing a tour through a solar house in Chicago, Illinois.

In fact, the 1950s marked the high point for research into creating an American home that did not rely on oil or gas for heating. This research sector interest, however, could not compete in the marketplace. Rome writes: "The predictions of a bright new day in housing proved false, however. From 1945 to 1970, the energy consumption of the average American household increased precipitously." In the 1960s alone household energy consumption jumped by 30 percent (Rome, 46).

The housing market, of course, was governed by the interest in this era to make homes as inexpensive as possible. In the end, the price of the mortgage was more important than that of utilities. Another influence on this outcome was a specific technical innovation: air conditioning.

The efficiency of the home became unnecessary with the sale of inexpensive air conditioning by the end of the 1940s. Sales of room air conditioners rose from a few thousand during World War II to 43,000 in 1947 and over one million in 1953. Thoughts of energy conservation literally went out the window with the window air conditioner (Cooper, , 24–34).

Ironically, during this era of peaked interest for solar and other green designs, the home-building industry produced a vast new demand for energy consumption. Rome suggests that the spread of air conditioning, for instance, became a symbol of American abundance during the Cold War. But the implications to home construction held long-term significance. In order to keep prices low and to still install central air conditioning, writes Rome, "builders eliminated traditional ways of providing shade and ventilation" (Rome, 85).

When President Richard Nixon's Council for Environmental Quality took a look at criticism of the lack of energy efficiency in American tract housing during 1970s, they emphasized zoning and land-use. The primary outcome would be state and federal regulations designed to regulate home building in order to minimize erosion, runoff, and the like; however, no regulations considered the energy conservation of the design.

RECYCLING EXPRESSES GREENNESS

During World War II, Americans experimented with conservation and recycling as a matter of national security. Afterward, 1950s middle-class life unapologetically adopted the ethics of expansion and newness. As more and more middle-class Americans began to express environmental attitudes, the wastefulness of modern consumption became obvious to more and more consumers. More Americans than ever before became willing to integrate such practices into their lives as part of a commitment to the environment. For instance, most children born after the 1980s assume the "recycle, reduce, and reuse" mantra has been part of the United States since its founding. In actuality, it serves as a continuing ripple of the cultural and social impact of Earth Day 1970 and the effort of Americans to begin to live within limits—albeit at its most conservative roots.

Earth Day 1970 suggested to millions of Americans that environmental concern could be expressed locally. Through organized activities, many

Americans found that they could actively improve the environment with their own hands. Many communities responded by organizing ongoing efforts to alter wasteful patterns. Recycling has proven to be the most persistent of these grassroots efforts. Though the effort is trivialized by extremist environmentalists, trash and waste recycling now stands as the ultimate symbol of the American environmental consciousness.

Recycling, of course, did not begin as an expression of environmentalism; instead, it grows out of a conservative impulse to reduce waste. The effort to make worthwhile materials from waste can be traced throughout human society as an application of common sense rationality. The term became part of the American lexicon during war-time rationing, particularly in World War II. Scrap metals and other materials became a resource to be collected and recycled into weaponry and other materials to support

The view made possible by space travel brought a valuable new prop to environmentally-oriented advertising. Courtesy Library of Congress.

fighting overseas. Ironically, it is also World War II that aids Americans in disavowing such an effort during times of peace.

Historians point to the climactic conclusion of World War II and its commensurate growth in the American middle class as defining points in the American "culture of consumption," which became prevalent in the 1950s, but certainly extended in some form through the 1980s. The prodigious scale of American consumption quickly made the nation at once the most advanced and the most wasteful civilization in the world. It was only a matter of time before a backlash brought American patterns of consumption into question. As the 1960s counter-culture imposed doubt on much of the American "establishment," many Americans began to consider more carefully the patterns with which they lived everyday life.

Belittled by many environmentalists, recycling often seems like busy-work for kids with little actual environmental benefit. However, such a minor shift in human behavior suggests the significant alteration made to many humans' view of their place in nature. This change in worldview, caused by many political, social, and intellectual shifts in the 1960s, forced Americans to question their lack of restraint. The culture of consumption of post-World War II America reinforced carelessness, waste, and a drive for newness. Environmental concerns contributed to a new ethic within American culture that began to value restraint, reuse, and living within limits. This ethic of restraint, fed by over-used landfills and excessive litter, gave communities a new mandate to restrain the wasteful practices of their population. Reusing products or creating useful byproducts from waste offered application of this new ethic while also offering new opportunity for economic profit and development.

Green, or environmental, industries have taken form to facilitate and profit from this impulse, creating a significant growth portion of the American economy. Even more impressively, the grassroots desire to express an environmental commitment has compelled middle-class Americans to make recycling part of an everyday effort to reduce and better manage waste.

MODELING GREEN CORPORATIONS

The culture of consumption of post-World War II America reinforced carelessness, waste, and a drive for newness by prioritizing plastics and other materials that were used once and disposed. After the move toward environmental awareness, the business world picked up on the new ethic. Most often referred to as industrial ecology, businesses such as DuPont, 3M, and Dow Chemical have used cost-benefit analysis to restructure their production in order to minimize environmental costs and also waste.

After 1990, green or environmental industries grew quickly in an effort to profit from the nation's growing environmental awareness. Consultants also advised existing companies on ways to make their processes more environmentally friendly. One well-known company had its own, built-in environmental consultant: Bill Ford, the great-grandson of the founder of Ford Motors. When the younger Ford took over the car manufacturing giant, he set out to lead the company into the next, greener era of manufacturing.

Ford's Rouge Plant led the move to mass production in the late 1920s. Bill Ford hopes that his re-vamped Rouge Plant will lead other manufacturers to consider greener methods and facilities. With a price tag of more than $2 billion, the new Rouge Plant attempts to marry natural and industrial systems.

To oversee the greening of the plant, Ford hired Virginia architect William McDonough, who was well known for his environmentally sensitive designs in offices such as those used as the headquarters for Gap. Atop the new truck factory, McDonough designed a 10.4-acre "living roof." On the roof, sedum plants act as a filter, absorbing water from rain and snow. They absorb the carbon dioxide generated by the factory and give off oxygen. In the winter, the plant-covered roof keeps the factory warm. In the summer, the roof does the opposite. Another roof, atop the visitors' center, holds photovoltaic panels to turn sunlight into electricity that can help to power the building. Other solar collectors heat water for the building.

McDonough used the surrounding land to create natural filters to help neutralize the pollution that the factory gives off. Approximately 85,000 flowering perennials were planted along a new greenbelt parkway, along with 20,000 shrubs and hundreds of new trees. In other surrounding areas, planners created natural water-treatment wetlands and wildlife habitat. His effort was to remake the surrounding acreage as a habitat for animals. Of course, it is not easy to make a site that has endured more than 80 years of industrial pollution into an inviting habitat.

By viewing the surrounding site as a buffer for the industrial enterprise, McDonough and Ford offered manufacturing a radical new model of green business.

NATURE GUIDE: IAN MCHARG

How did planners and architects apply the ethics of modern environmentalism and move Americans from Levittown toward xeriscaping? One of the most important guides in this intellectual progression was Ian McHarg, who was one of the true pioneers of the environmental movement, but in a very applied fashion. Whereas many activists argued for "green" methods of constructing or laying out towns, McHarg took the idea of planning and reconfigured the entire process to reflect ecological considerations.

In terms of spreading his ideas, McHarg was responsible for the creation of the department of landscape architecture at the University of Pennsylvania. In addition, though, McHarg sought to tell the public about his ideas of green planning. In 1960, McHarg hosted his own CBS television program, "The House We

Live In," in which he discussed ways of creating inviting landscapes for humans that do not overlook the surrounding environment. McHarg argued that well-designed architecture and landscape helped to define humans' relationship with the natural world. Therefore, the planning process of designing such spaces required knowledge about ecology and the nature of the site. In 1969, McHarg published his ideas in a landmark book, *Design With Nature*. He specifically called for urban planners to consider an environmentally conscious approach to land use and provided a new method for evaluating and implementing it.

According to Ian McHarg, "the task [of design] was given to those who, by instinct and training, were especially suited to gouge and scar landscape and city without remorse—the engineers." He urged those trained in design to demand control over such projects from the earliest points. "[The engineer's] competence is not the design of highways," McHarg explained, "merely of the structures that compose them—but only after they have been designed by persons more knowing of man and the land" (McHarg, 1–5).

NEW URBANISM TRIES TO CONTROL SPRAWL

McHarg's ideas moved through the architecture community for a few decades before coalescing into a new philosophy of planning and land use. Clearly, the automobile had radically reorganized American society and its landscape after 1950. Certain aspects of this structure are undeniable: license plates, drivers licenses, and parking meters and lots, just to name a few. The auto landscape culminated in the shopping mall, which quickly became a necessary portion of developers' plans for the roadside strips that would connect housing with shopping areas. By the 1970s, developers' initiative clearly included regional economic development for a newly evolving service and retail world. Incorporating suburbs into such development plans, designs for these pseudo-communities were held together by the automobile. The marketplace for this culture quickly became the shopping mall. Strip malls, which open on to roadways and parking lots, were installed near residential areas as suburbs extended further from the city center. Developers then perfected the self-sustained, enclosed shopping mall.

Try as they might, such artificial environments could never recreate the culture of local communities. Beginning in the 1960s, Ralph Nader and other critics would begin to ask hard questions of the auto's restructuring of American society. Shopping malls became the symbol of a culture of conspicuous consumption that many Americans began to criticize during the 1990s.

Critics such as Jane Jacobs and Jim Kunstler identified an intrinsic bias on the American landscape in the 1970s. Kunstler writes, "Americans have been living car-centered lives for so long that the collective memory of what used to make a landscape or a townscape or even a suburb humanly rewarding has nearly been erased" (Kunstler, 21). The 1990s closed with the unfolding of the new politics of urban sprawl. "I've come to the conclusion," explained Vice President Al Gore on the campaign trail in 1999, "that what we really are faced with here is a systematic change from a pattern of uncontrolled sprawl toward a brand new path that makes quality of life the goal of all our urban, suburban, and farmland policies." One form these new plans took became known as "new urbanism" as designers attempted to design for humans and not just for automobiles.

MAKING A BETTER AUTOMOBILE

New urbanists saw the automobile as the greatest symbol of American waste by the end of the 1970s. However, for the American public, the lesson of oil shortage of the 1970s did *not* radically alter energy use. Americans increased their use of electricity even more than oil, and utilities struggled to meet the new demand. Rejecting initiatives under the Carter administration, utilities dismissed energy conservation. Eventually, utility companies even managed to defeat efforts at cleaner generation of power that were initiated during the Clinton administration. As the twenty-first century began, though, high oil prices at last appeared to force Americans to give serious consideration to devising a greener automobile.

Just as in the 1960s technological innovation helped guide Americans away from homes that helped to conserve energy, automobiles during the twentieth century helped to increase consumption of energy. At the close of the twentieth century, when Americans began to more fully consider more efficient autos, one of the proposals, ironically, was the path not taken in the 1890s: electric cars.

Electric or hybrid cars were introduced to the United States in 1905 when H. Piper applied for a patent on a vehicular power-train that used electricity to augment a gasoline engine. Piper's technology actually followed the work of French inventors. From 1897 to 1907, the Compagnie Parisienne des Voitures Electriques (Paris Electric Car Company) built a series of electric and hybrid vehicles, including the fairly well-known 1903 Krieger. Although these vehicles used electric power, some also ran on alcohol (Motavalli, 9–14).

General Electric even dabbled in the vehicle business after 1900. The GE lab built a hybrid with a four-cylinder gasoline engine. In Chicago, the Woods Motor Vehicle Company produced the 1917 Woods Dual Power, which was a parallel hybrid engine that could use its electrical and gasoline-burning sources of power simultaneously. Another Chicago firm, the Walker Vehicle Company, built both electric and gasoline-electric trucks, from around 1918 to the early 1940s. These examples show us that it was not at all a foregone conclusion that automobiles must run on gasoline when early manufacturing began in the 1900s.

However, during the early 1900s, great new supplies of petroleum transformed gasoline into an abundant and inexpensive source of energy. This spurred inventors to focus on perfecting gasoline-powered engines. In addition, Rockefeller and other titans of American business lobbied hard for the use of the internal combustion engine in American automobiles. Under this influence, the path to take was clear, and we have burned petroleum in our cars ever since. However, that could be changing.

The new surge in hybrid development began in 1993 when the Clinton administration announced the formation of the Partnership for a New Generation of Vehicles consortium. This group consisted of the "Big Three" automobile manufacturers (General Motors, Ford, and Chrysler) and about 350 smaller technical firms. Their goal was to create operating prototypes by 2004. Later, high gasoline prices further stimulated new hybrid designs (Motavalli, 109–17).

HYBRIDS OF THE FUTURE

In the early twenty-first century, the electric car has reemerged as a possible supplement to the internal combustion engine. Similar to the first designs in the 1890s, these hybrid autos combine gas power with the use of an electric battery that allows the vehicle to use much less petroleum. New designs look for opportunities to minimize power and shift off the gasoline engine. For instance, most vehicles require their full wheel power for only very short bursts. While the maximum power for most new cars sold in the United States today is more than 100 kilowatts, the average power actually used during city and highway driving is only about 7.5 kilowatts. During these lulls, the hybrid runs on battery power and burns no gasoline (Motavalli, 154–57).

The hybrid rebirth began when the Toyota Prius went on sale in Japan in 1997, making it the world's first volume-production hybrid car. Today, the five-passenger Prius is the world's most popular hybrid. The Prius utilizes a separate generator to keep the electric battery pack charged. For this reason, owners never need to plug in their cars for recharging. During braking, the electric motor also acts as a generator to recapture energy and further charge the batteries. That means that even in stop-and-go city driving, the Prius can travel on approximately 52 miles per gallon of gas.

Other hybrids include the Honda Insight, first sold in the United States as a 2000 model, and the Honda Civic Hybrid, which came to market in the United States as a 2003 model. A variation of the Civic sedan, the Civic Hybrid is a mild hybrid, meaning that the electric motor assists the gasoline engine during acceleration or times of heavy load but doesn't move the car on its own.

Honda and Toyota are leading the movement toward hybrids, but both Mitsubishi and the Nissan Corporation will release hybrids in 2006. Of the "Big Three" American manufacturers, only Ford has moved into the hybrid sector with vigor (Motavalli, 159–70).

THE END OF THE ROAD: THE AMERICAN JUNKYARD AND "LIFECYCLE ANALYSIS"

Hybridization will not defeat one of the automobiles most pesky legacies: junkyards. Old cars simply will not disappear. An eyesore around the nation, junkyards have been the typical conclusion to the life of each auto. Whether the car has been totaled in a collision or worn out from use, the end of the road for each automobile in the United States is an ill-prepared and often ill-managed site. Through a combination of federal regulation, industrial shifts, and consumer awareness, there may soon be some new developments in this regard.

With an eye toward the ecological sciences, some manufacturers have required their products be subjected to a "life-cycle assessment." Used by many European nations, this form of product accounting considers its impact from cradle to grave. Life-cycle analysis quantifies the environmental impact of a vehicle, beginning with its production and continuing through the end of its useful life and through the recycling of vehicle materials back into use. Considerations include:

- price of purchase, insurance, and maintenance
- fuel economy
- environmental impact of manufacture, operation, and disposal
- hazardous substance content
- transportation of components and cars
- road construction and maintenance
- storage and packaging
- recycling
- health and safety of workers

When accounted for in this manner, portions of the production process such as the use of environmentally hazardous substances appear very different than they do when one is simply concerned with the bottom line. In this example, the use of hazardous substances tends to lower a vehicle's initial purchase price; however, if one instead includes the associated costs of using the hazardous substances (such as management, disposal, and liability), the price increases considerably. When viewed through life cycle assessment, alternatives to hazardous substances wind up saving money in the long run, in addition to being the right thing for the environment.

For instance, in 1995, USCAR, a research arm of DaimlerChrysler, Ford, and General Motors, requested that the aluminum industry conduct a life-cycle inventory for the North American aluminum industry, with the objective of generating a resource consumption and environmental profile of the industry as a whole. This study demonstrated that only five percent of the energy required to produce primary aluminum (from ore to finished product) is required to produce product from recycled aluminum. Accordingly, recycling drastically reduces the emissions that would otherwise result from the production of primary aluminum.

Toyota has started its own system of assessment that it calls Eco-VAS (Eco-Vehicle Assessment System). Under Eco-Vas, the assessment process begins at the very start of planning. The vehicle designer must first prove that his project would fall within environmental impact reduction targets. These figures also consider fuel efficiency, emissions, and noise during vehicle use, the disposal recovery rate, the reduction of substances of environmental concern, and carbon dioxide emissions throughout the entire life cycle of the vehicle from production to disposal.

Although each of these programs is in its infancy, together they represent a new ethic for the future of automobile design.

CONCLUSION: GREENWASHING

While many corporations have attempted to implement environmentally friendly measures, others sought to appeal to green culture while doing business as usual. The term "greenwashing" is the term used for corporations who try to present an image of being environmentally friendly without necessarily making any changes in their actual business practices.

In response to retail demand and partly in an effort to placate environmentally minded consumers, green goods and financial services have been offered since the early 1970s. One of the most notable efforts in this arena has been that of the giant oil company BP. Formally known as British Petroleum, in 2000 BP Amoco officially made its initials stand for "Beyond Petroleum."

To combat what it viewed as misleading corporate practices, Greenpeace USA began publishing the *Book of Greenwash* during the 1990s. Some critics even argue that community recycling programs also should be grouped under the heading of greenwash because they prevent calls for reducing consumption and economic growth.

Regardless, the admission by nonenvironmental political and corporate actors that greenness appeals to the general public has contributed to a confusing era in environmental politics and marketing. By obscuring the connection between corporations or policies and environmental degradation, the public often is misled about the primary agenda of such practices.

For instance, some environmentalists would look at 555 Bottonfield Lane and see a dramatic improvement from the water-intensive green spaces surrounding many American homes. However, others would clearly see xeriscaping as only "lip service": The owner of 555 Bottonfield Lane continues to reside in a suburban development that requires the expansion of fossil fuels to do almost anything. These variations in thought demonstrate how the nature of environmentalism had changed dramatically by the end of the twentieth century. Regardless of one's perspective, though, environmentalism had clearly gained a new connection to everyday patterns of living instead of being restricted to the annual dues sent to conservation organizations.

9

GOING GLOBAL

As humans traveled to space for the first time in history during the 1960s, their view of the universe changed, but so did the view of their role in it. During each of the early trips, astronauts photographed Earth from space. In snapping these photos, they achieved a perspective no human had ever before seen. The first photo made public in 1968 was referred to as "Earthrise." "Whole Earth" followed on December 7, 1972, during the Apollo 17 mission. Together, these images profoundly altered human ideas of Earth. "Whole Earth" reached an American public ready to reconsider its place in the world and led to the environmental campaign: "Think Globally, Act Locally."

"Whole Earth" put a biological face on the planet. The view from space revealed identifiable environments without differentiating by border, politics, or economics. In this "Whole Earth" view, the globe, more than ever before in human history, emerged as much greater than the humans who resided on it. Some geographers specifically noted that by centralizing the view of locations such as Africa, the Middle East, and Antarctica, the Apollo 17 photograph "upsets conventional Western cartographic conventions." Instead of a United States-centered view for Americans, "Whole Earth" revealed a global natural environment.

"Whole Earth" offered a view of Earth that played directly into the growing culture of environmentalism. The organic Earth portrayed in this photo appeared as an environmentally threatened home. Activists such as Stewart Brand, who was discussed in Chapter 9, embraced this profoundly new perspective of Earth. Space travel, in fact, offered a type of technological middle ground: a perspective brought by new technology that afforded us a better understanding of the world around us. Clearly, this technology was a tool for global good, unlike the nuclear possibilities of the Cold War.

In fact, "Whole Earth" marked a new approach for NASA's use of technology. In addition to the initiatives that would make space the next frontier for American society, NASA increasingly used its research to examine and understand nature back on Earth. Soon after Apollo 17 took the "Whole Earth" picture, NASA launched its first Landsat satellite to help examine ecological changes from soil erosion and deforestation to ocean dumping, air pollution, and urban sprawl (Maher).

GOING GLOBAL IN A VIEW OF NATURE

Earth Day 1990 continued environmental traditions of the past but also marked an important change in environmentalism's scope. Worldwide, 14 nations participated in this celebration. While a global perspective seemed inherent in the web of life put forward by Rachel Carson and others, it would take global issues such as the Chernobyl nuclear accident in 1986

Similar to the realization that Earth was round during the 1400s, the view from space showed humans a living, organic Earth.

and shared problems such as greenhouse gasses and global warming to bind the world into a common perspective. Organizations, including Greenpeace and the United Nations, assisted members from many nations to shape a common stand on issues.

The UN presented the leading tool for facilitating global environmental efforts. With its first meeting on the environment in 1972, the global organization created its Environmental Program, which was referred to as UNEP. This organization would sponsor the historic Rio Conference on the Environment in 1992 and the conference on global warming in 1997. UNEP would also be the primary institution moving the UN's environmental agenda into the areas that were most in need of assistance, primarily developing nations. In response to such activities, the U.S. federal government declared the environment a genuine diplomatic risk in global affairs by creating a State Department undersecretary for the environment in 1996.

What began as an intellectual philosophy in the early 1800s had so impacted the human worldview that it would now influence global relations. Of course, a primary portion of this environmental worldview was scientific understandings that were communicated to the public after the 1960s. During the 1990s, a global agenda for action took shape that was organized around environmental improvement. Such an agenda, though, was not without its difficulties.

The most difficult portion of this global debate may be the fairness of each nation to be allowed to develop economically. Many less-developed nations resent the environmental efforts of nations that have already industrialized, including many European nations and the United States. Such nations believe they are being denied their own opportunity to develop economically simply because of problems created by industrial nations. This sentiment has been part of major demonstrations in recent meetings of global organizations, such as the World Trade Organization. Any global agreements will need to balance the basic differences of these constituencies.

THE GREEN REVOLUTION AND THE START OF INTERNATIONAL COOPERATION

Most scholars date the interest in globalization to the world wars and the Cold War. In addition, the world's worst recorded food disaster occurred in 1943 in British-ruled India. Known as the Bengal Famine, an estimated four million people died of hunger that year alone in eastern India (that included today's Bangladesh). The international community blamed poor food production for the shortage and began to consider ways of helping India and other less-developed nations. The gap separating developed and less-developed nations had become most pronounced by 1950, when modern conveniences and technologies made the standard of living in the United States and many other developed countries leap forward, while other nations lagged further behind.

When British occupiers left India in 1947, the Indian government set about to try to close this gap in terms of food production. However, two decades later, India realized that its efforts at achieving food self-sufficiency were not entirely successful. This awareness led to the importation of new agricultural technology from around the world. Referred to as the "Green Revolution," the effort to bring new agricultural know-how to developing nations radically altered the possibility of famine while also attacking the primary issue dividing developed nations, such as the United States, and less-developed nations, such as India and much of Africa.

Headed by Norman Borlaug, a plant breeder from the University of Minnesota, American agricultural technology was given to many Third World nations. Although there were many successful examples, Borlaug was awarded the Nobel Prize for his work on a high-yielding wheat plant. Work on this wheat had begun in the mid-1940s in Mexico as Borlaug and others developed broadly adapted, short-stemmed, disease-resistant wheats that excelled at converting fertilizer and water into high yields.

The "winter wheat," as it was called, could be grown much more easily in areas such as Mexico and India. The impact of this plant was monumental. While in 1944 Mexico imported half its wheat, by 1956 it was self-sufficient in wheat production and by 1964 it was growing enough of a surplus that it exported approximately one-half million tons of wheat. In India, wheat production increased four times in 20 years (from 12 million tons in 1966 to 47 million tons in 1986). This success inspired rice experiments in the Philippines and elsewhere.

The agricultural assistance system grew during the late 20th century and by 1992 it included 18 centers. Most were located in developing nations and staffed by scientists from all over the world. The funding for such centers comes from a consortium of foundations, national governments, and international agencies. Although the spread of agricultural technology has helped many less-developed nations better feed their populations, the Green Revolution is not without its critics. For instance, some critics argue that new techniques in agriculture are too dependent on fertilizers, irrigation, and other factors that poor farmers cannot afford and that may be ecologically harmful. Critics also argue that many techniques promote monoculture, which is of little help to areas in need of self-sufficiency. Some critics argue that the Green Revolution depends on fertilizers, irrigation, and other factors that poor farmers cannot afford and that may be ecologically harmful; and that it promotes monocultures and loss of genetic diversity. Clearly, though, the spread of agricultural technology has greatly assisted less-developed nations in feeding their populations.

NATURE GUIDE: "THE TRAGEDY OF THE COMMONS."

After 1960, Americans' worldview changed considerably, whether influenced by photos from the moon or scientific concepts. Our lives, it became clear, were tied to many other creatures and systems. Therefore, our choices and actions had broad impacts.

Following Rachel Carson, in 1968 Garrett Hardin wrote an article that developed the ecological idea of the commons. This concept and his argument of its tragic (undeniable) outcome in depletion, gave humans new rationale with which to view common resources such as the air and the ocean. He wrote:

> The tragedy of the commons develops in this way. Picture a pasture open to all. It is to be expected that each herdsman will try to keep as many cattle as possible on the commons. Such an arrangement may work reasonably satisfactorily for centuries because tribal wars, poaching, and disease keep the numbers of both man and beast well below the carrying capacity of the land. Finally, however, comes the day of reckoning, that is, the day when the long-desired goal of social stability becomes a reality. At this point, the inherent logic of the commons remorselessly generates tragedy.
>
> As a rational being, each herdsman seeks to maximize his gain. Explicitly or implicitly, more or less consciously, he asks, "What is the utility to me of adding one more animal to my herd?" This utility has one negative and one positive component. . . .
>
> Adding together the components . . . the rational herdsman concludes that the only sensible course for him to pursue is to add another animal to his herd. And another. . . . But this is the conclusion reached by each and every rational herdsman sharing a commons. Therein is the tragedy. Each man is locked into a system that compels him to increase his herd without limit—in a world that is limited. Ruin is the destination toward which all men rush, each pursuing his own best interest in a society that believes in the freedom of the commons. Freedom in a commons brings ruin to all. (Hardin, 243–48)

NATURE AT WORK: "GODZILLA" AND UNDERSEA CHIMNEYS

Global cooperation, particularly in scientific research, blossomed with the freedom of the end of the Cold War in 1990. One example of this research also demonstrates the shared nature of one of Earth's greatest commons, the ocean. The exploration of the deep ocean has contributed to new understanding about the Earth and the origin of life, particularly at the close of the twentieth century.

After the Cold War concluded in the early 1990s, scientists were able to access deep ocean and the hardware—submarines, microphones, and so on—necessary to study it. What had been the realm of science fiction became more real than at any time in human history. In the deep ocean environment, of course, Robert Ballard in mid-1980s located the wreck of the Titanic. Although this discovery helped to form one portion of Americans' new relationship with the deep sea, it was the scientific discoveries that followed that proved to be truly revolutionary.

Beginning in the early 1990s, submersibles began investigating seismic activity on the ocean bottom, particularly off Central America and off Oregon in the Pacific Ocean. Scientists were most interested in what they thought were undersea volcanoes. In 1991, diving off Seattle to depths of more than one mile, scientists found towering chimneys of percolating heat in what they expected to be Earth's deepest, darkest, and coldest areas. The world of submarine hot springs bubbling with sulfide minerals and gases from Earth's interior and crawling with exotic life was unknown until 1977, when the first such site was discovered off the Galapagos Islands. Two years later, off Mexico, the first pinnacle-shaped black smokers were observed. They appeared to be a common phenomenon along the volcanically active ridges under the Pacific.

The early discoveries showed chimneys rising like a city of skyscrapers, with "Godzilla," the most impressive, rising to approximately 15 stories high. Although these structures were impressive enough, the creatures living around them have forced scientists to rewrite textbooks. Discovering many creatures for the first time, scientists slowly deduced that they were watching at least one portion of the creation of life on Earth play out before their eyes. Instead of being powered by sunlight, as is everything on Earth's surface and much of what lives in the sea, these areas were powered by the planet's inner heat and energy (Broad, 110).

The ocean's status as a commons fueled further exploration by members of the scientific community from many different nations. In recent years, Korean and Chinese teams have exhumed large portions of the rock chimneys to the surface. Two of the largest chimneys were recovered while still hot and teeming with small worms, sea spiders, and limpets. Countless worms inside tiny tubes, although dead on arrival at the surface, clung to the chimney surfaces like a fringe. Still alive inside were microbes that may be among the most primitive forms of life ever found by scientists. These efforts suggest a few of the many lessons to be learned by studying the sea in joint efforts with other nations.

THE GLOBAL AIR COMMONS: FIGHTING TO SAVE THE BRAZILIAN RAINFOREST

The awareness of Earth's air commons has altered global environmental policy more than any other issue. Although pollution was discussed by the 1970s, the linked impact of massive deforestation in tropical regions was first brought to the public by a book called *The Sinking Ark* by Norman Myers, which was published in 1979.

In this book, Myers argued that of the original 6.2 million square miles of tropical moist forests, only about 3.6 million square miles remained. He estimated that the world had already lost approximately 44 percent of its rainforest. These losses were most concentrated in Central America, Brazil, Africa, and Southeast Asia. Scientists already knew that in addition to producing oxygen, trees are generally helpful in cleaning Earth's polluted air. The loss of these great forests seemed a dire forecast for what was to come.

Springing to action, American environmental activists set out to stop deforestation in the Brazilian Amazon. Experts estimate that each year 5 million acres of forest is lost in Brazil Primarily, these forests are felled by farmers clearing land to grow crops. In addition, though, companies from all over the world felled trees or sold products made from the timber. Ironically, many of these products were sold in the United States, Europe, and Japan, where protesters demanded the forest be left alone.

Efforts to raise funds to stop the loss of rainforests became one of the first global issues in popular American environmentalism. Although the impact of the movement is impossible to determine, the discourse about rainforests was obvious in the United States after the 1980s. These efforts are also linked to green consumerism, with many cities now offering diners a Rainforest Café. While dining on products considered to be rainforest-friendly, customers are surrounded by a living example of the South American rainforest—much like one can find today at major zoos.

NATURE AT WORK: SAVE THE WHALES!

While the commons idea fueled new ideas about global policies in the late 20th century, the sea commons had already been responsible for bringing nations together for the sake of one of its most well-known beings: the whale. By the early 1900s, the international whaling fleet had become one of the world's most efficient industries. With whale products used in many manufactured goods (including explosives), whalers from Britain, Norway, and Japan perfected the location and processing of whales in the international waters of both polar areas. By the 1920s, the League of Nations urged the international community to begin monitoring whale populations before they had dropped too far to repair.

In 1930, the Bureau of International Whaling Statistics was created to monitor the number of whales taken. This led to the first international regulatory agreement signed by 22 nations in 1931. Without signatures from Germany and Japan, though, whalers still killed 43,000 whales in 1931. In 1948, the International Convention for the Regulation of Whaling recognized that many whale species neared extinction. As a result, the International Whaling Commission (IWC) was established by fourteen member nations. Today, 61 nations are members of the IWC and whales are only hunted for purposes of scientific or cultural tradition.

Although these early initiatives were largely carried out by the whaling industry, the IWC took advantage of the interest in environment after the 1960s. Similar to rain forests, whales became one of the first venues through which many people came to know ideas such as extinction and sustainable management. Groups such as Greenpeace carried out "direct action" against whalers from remaining nations in order to publicize the issue during the 1970s.

FORMING A DISCOURSE OF INTERNATIONAL COOPERATION

During the 1980s and 1990s, the international discourse on environmental issues took a more organized and systematic form. On the twentieth anniversary of the first UNEP meeting in Stockholm, the United Nations hosted the 1992 Rio Conference on Environment and Development, the "Earth Summit," in which world leaders agreed on Agenda 21 and the Rio Declaration.

The summit brought environment and development issues firmly into the public arena. Along with the Rio Declaration and Agenda 21 it led to agreement on two legally binding conventions: Biological Diversity and the Framework Convention on Climate Change (FCCC).

Agenda 21, in particular, functioned to place an important new idea into mainstream international environmentalism: sustainable development. Agenda 21 was a 300-page plan for achieving sustainable development in the twenty-first century. The United Nations Commission on Sustainable

Development (CSD) was created in December 1992 to ensure effective follow-up of UNCED and to monitor and report on implementation of the Earth Summit agreements at the local, national, regional and international levels. The CSD is a functional commission of the UN Economic and Social Council (ECOSOC), with 53 members. For such international policies to be successful, the U.N. must be free to assess nations' efforts and to enforce political regulations. At this point, the U.N. primarily emphasizes assessment. A five-year review of Earth Summit progress took place in 1997 by the United Nations General Assembly meeting in special session, followed in 2002 by a 10-year review by the World Summit on Sustainable Development.

The CSD now focuses on assessment and education. Most important, it must contain representatives from the nations that most need assistance with development strategies. In 2005, the membership of the CSD includes: thirteen members are elected from Africa, 11 from Asia, 10 from Latin America and the Caribbean, 6 from Eastern Europe, and 13 from Western Europe and other areas. Such a balanced membership is a priority of most U.N. efforts; however, on CSD it may be even more important because representation can ensure that nations receive the help that they need most.

Global environmental initiatives remain just that. There remains no authority that can enforce environmental policies and regulations across political lines everywhere in the world. However, great strides have been made in creating regional, cooperative initiatives.

NAFTA AND REGIONAL AGREEMENTS

Outside of the United Nations, the new international connections that were inherent in globalization altered relations between nations. For the United States, global free trade remained a priority but regional development required new agreements with neighbors. The 1993 North American Free Trade Agreement (NAFTA) defined a vast new region for free trade. Organizations such as the World Trade Organization (WTO) also helped to prioritize free trade over environmental protection.

Opposed to such agreements, public interest activist Ralph Nader argued that such deals would erode environmental and social legislation. The Clinton administration negotiated at least two environmental side agreements. One of these created the North American Commission for Environmental Cooperation, which emphasized cross-border initiatives. The second agreement specifically focused on the Mexican border.

The success of such efforts to limit the environmental impact of such initiatives and agreements has been limited by factors including a difficulty in regulating users and accessing documents that would allow investigators to bring suit. Most observers believe that the environmental problems along the United States-Mexico border have intensified under NAFTA. Green

NGOs have joined with American labor organizations to call for the United States to renegotiate or pull out altogether from the 1993 agreement.

THE SCIENCE OF GLOBAL WARMING

In the late twentieth century, the environmental issue referred to as global warming seemed to be the next great issue in the global unification of efforts to diminish the impact of humans on the Earth. However, by the beginning of the twenty-first century, it was obvious that instead of bringing the world together, global warming was going to cause even more division. Unlike the issues behind the Green Revolution, the science behind global warming was difficult to verify. And, most important, acting on global warming could potentially hurt the U.S. economic dominance of the globe.

What scientists refer to as the greenhouse effect is actually essential to human existence: The sun warms the earth, and certain gases (including carbon dioxide and water vapor) act like the glass of a greenhouse, trapping heat and keeping the planet's surface warm enough to support life. However, measuring humanity's effect on the concentration of greenhouse gases is a key issue in understanding global climate change. Industry and other human activity add carbon dioxide to the atmosphere. This strengthens the greenhouse effect and may cause a significant warming trend. During the 1990s, the issue of global warming received attention worldwide.

For nations to attempt to confront this issue, researchers needed to ascertain a reliable method for tracing temperatures and gas levels in the near and distant past. Ice core sampling made this possible. In the ices found on the Earth's frozen poles, scientists drilled core samples from water that hadn't been thawed for thousands of years. The ice offered snapshots of the air and water from long ago—long before humans began to burn fossil fuels.

Actually, the ice cores contained remnants from snow from long ago. The snow carried with it compounds including sulfate, nitrate, and even dust, radioactive fallout, and trace metals. In polar areas, this snow falls on top of the previous year's snow without either melting. As this happens repeatedly over many years, the snow compresses to form ice. This is the ice, then, that scientists can use to provide a record of changes in air composition and temperature. This record has suggested the warming trend in Earth's temperature since humans began burning fossil fuels.

NATURE GUIDE: PINE ISLAND GLACIER

In search of other ways to demonstrate that global warming was in fact taking place, scientists have carefully tracked patterns of existing glacial formations on either pole. In 2001–2002, western Antarctic's Pine Island Glacier convinced many scientists that global warming was taking place at a pace even greater than feared. The information came from scientists at the University College London and the

British Antarctic Survey who showed that the Pine Island Glacier was thinning at a rapid rate that could cause it to break off within 600 years.

This is particularly significant because Pine Island Glacier is the largest glacier in west Antarctica and the largest ice stream feeding the ocean. Therefore, its thinning could likely be significant enough to raise global sea levels. Such a rise in the sea, of course, could inundate areas of inhabited land and force changes to many living patterns.

The most alarmed scientists predict that up to a quarter of the mountain glacier mass around the globe could disappear by 2050, and up to half by 2100—leaving large patches only in Alaska, Patagonia, and the Himalayas. Other scientists, of course, deny that any melting is taking place at all.

THE KYOTO PROTOCOL

Currently, global warming and the emissions of greenhouse gasses have fueled international debate over the ratification of the Kyoto Protocol. Such legislation would place caps on emissions from all nations. The Kyoto Protocol is a document signed by about 141 countries at Kyoto, Japan, in December 1997. The protocol commits 38 industrialized countries to cut their emissions of greenhouse gases between 2008 and 2012 to levels that are 5.2 per cent below 1990 levels. According to one estimate, global warming could cause the world about $5 trillion of damage. Developing countries are expected to be the hardest hit.

Advocates see it as a baby step along the necessary road to reducing human impact on climate before the oceans rise and prairie songbirds emigrate to the Arctic. Some opponents of Kyoto refuse to believe the scientific findings. Armed with contrary findings, other scientists have claimed to disprove global warming altogether. Other opponents admit that the science proves global warming, but Kyoto is simply too costly to the standing of developed nations such as the U.S.

The reality, though, is that since 1990 the United States has increased its release of greenhouse damaging emissions, including carbon dioxide, methane, nitrous oxide, and other pollutants. Build-up of such gasses contributes to rising temperatures as well as to an increase in skin cancer. It also appears unlikely that American leaders will accept limitations on emissions that may impact American productivity—even in the short term. Philosophically opposed to any effort to limit its own development, the United States under the administration of President George W. Bush has rejected the protocol.

DOCUMENT: LETTER FROM PRESIDENT
GEORGE W. BUSH TO U.S. SENATORS

I oppose the Kyoto Protocol because it exempts 80 percent of the world, including major population centers such as China and India, from compliance, and would cause serious harm to the U.S. economy. The Senate's vote,

95–0, shows that there is a clear consensus that the Kyoto Protocol is an unfair and ineffective means of addressing global climate change concerns.

As you also know, I support a comprehensive and balanced national energy policy that takes into account the importance of improving air quality. . . .

At a time when California has already experienced energy shortages, and other Western states are worried about price and availability of energy . . . , we must be very careful not to take actions that could harm consumers. This is especially true given the incomplete state of scientific knowledge of the causes of, and solutions to, global climate change and the lack of commercially available technologies for removing and storing carbon dioxide.

Consistent with these concerns, we will continue to fully examine global climate change issues—including the science, technologies, market-based systems, and innovative options for addressing concentrations of greenhouse gases in the atmosphere. I am very optimistic that, with the proper focus and working with our friends and allies, we will be able to develop technologies, market incentives, and other creative ways to address global climate change.

I look forward to working with you and others to address global climate change issues in the context of a national energy policy that protects our environment, consumers, and economy.

Sincerely,

George W. Bush (Bush)

CONCLUSION: PROTESTING THE WTO AND GLOBALIZATION

A policy infrastructure for globalization had taken shape by the mid-1990s. The nature of the American worldview expanded to consider the interests of other nations as well as other ecological entities. However, just as many proponents began to think that they had created the agencies and initiatives to close the gap separating developed and less-developed nations, activists—many of them associated with environmental causes—altered their view of initiatives such as the WTO and the World Bank.

Whereas instruments of change such as the World Bank, WTO, and even the United Nations had been created to promote global peace and stability, critics began to argue that such organizations exerted the will of powerful nations on those of the less powerful and less developed nations. Many American environmentalists argued that not only were the agencies' actions heavy handed, but they also fueled less developed nations to follow the less sustainable paths to progress used and favored by Western nations.

By the end of the 1990s, every meeting of the WTO became a gathering for activists denouncing its activities. In only a few short years the attitude toward international assistance had undergone a radical shift. Although there was a clear history of cooperation on some global environmental issues, consensus seemed to shatter at the start of the twenty-first century.

10

ENVIRONMENTAL BACKLASH AND GROWING ENERGY NEEDS

EVERYDAY SETTING: PETER MATTHIESSEN, "FOOTPRINTS IN THE LAST WILD PLACE"

This return to the Alaskan Arctic was my first visit since May of 1957, when I accompanied a U.S. Fish and Wildlife Service representative:

The 22-year battle is far from over. With the Republican takeover of Congress came the stated intention to resurrect the Bush energy agenda, including oil development in the Arctic Refuge. The future of North America's last great stronghold of wildlife will depend on a few key votes. . . .

The Carter administration's monumental Alaska National Interest Lands Conservation Act of 1980, a farsighted triumph for conservation, virtually doubled the refuge area to nearly 20 million acres, setting aside an inviolable wilderness of 8.9 million acres. Unfortunately, most of the designated wilderness lay in the barren mountains, leaving the coastal region containing the Porcupine calving ground entirely vulnerable. The relevant fine print in the Lands Act was Section 1002 (known as the "Ten-Oh-Two"), which directed that this critical 1.5-million-acre coastal area be placed in an "undecided" category while being assessed for its fossil fuel potential and biological significance.

Oil drilling in the 1002 seemed inevitable until the night of March 23, 1989, when the oil tanker Exxon Valdez went aground on an offshore reef in Prince William Sound, leaking 11 million gallons of oil and destroying the ecology of well over a thousand miles of Alaska's coast. Though the oil industry lay low during the ensuing investigations, the first President Bush would make drilling in the Arctic Refuge a plank of his energy policy. However, his 1991 attempt to forward drilling stalled in Congress, and his successor, President Clinton, vetoed a draft of the *national budget that contained a drilling provision. Undaunted, the second Bush administration has been promoting an "energy initiative" that includes an estimated $27 billion in subsidies for fossil-fuelers, with a special provision that would permit drilling in the refuge—what the oilmen refer to as "the AN-war."*

Though the Bush energy bill was approved by the House in August 2001, the inclusion of the drilling provision was rejected by the Senate in March 2002. However, the 22-year battle is far from over. (Matthiessen)

ANTI-ENVIRONMENTALISM COMES OF AGE

By the 1970s and 1980s, environmental concerns had emerged as a major player in local and federal politics. Although many global issues brought nations together on matters of the environment, acting locally proved to be terrain fraught with legal fights and political disagreements. In short, by the end of the twentieth century, the nature of Americans' view of the environment had altered to the point where there truly was an additional paradigm to economic development. Regulations and laws required that many additional issues be considered in determining a project's economic viability. Efforts of modern environmentalists to tie this ethic into the nation's legal framework altered the way Americans could live; however, it also set the stage for an era of political backlash against environmental initiatives.

By tying environmental ethics to politics and regulations, federal regulation and policy initiatives were destined to fluctuate with the political winds of the time. Contentious issues such as the preservation of wilderness areas and petroleum development on federal lands have created political division throughout the late 1900s. In addition, though, by 1980 there existed significant political division about what exactly should be the role of the federal government in managing and regulating environmental health and safety.

The politicization of environmental concerns meant that legislative initiatives would ultimately also become part of the political playing field. Specific locales, such as the uninhabited portions of Alaska, would change with on-going public discourse and provide historians with a type of "weather vane" with which to gauge the winds of environmental concern. Although this antienvironmental effort became a widespread movement during the late twentieth century, it took shape in the 1970s when a group of 11 western states rallied to gain control of the development of the resources on their public lands.

THE SAGEBRUSH REBELLION AND THE REAGAN BACKLASH

In what become known as the "Sagebrush Rebellion" and the "Wise Use Movement," antienvironmental groups gained national attention in their efforts to bypass the 1976 Federal Land Policy and Management Act

(FLPMA) and other government regulations. When this rebellion became an organized effort in the late 1970s, it rose with the financial support of Adolph Coors and other westerners. Prominent in this legal effort, the Rocky Mountain Defense Fund employed talented lawyers James Watt and Ann Gorsuch. Declaring FLPMA unconstitutional, the group requested that all Bureau of Land Management (BLM) lands in Nevada be turned over to the state. In 1980, many other western states followed suit. Each of the suits was defeated on the state level, but the Sagebrush rebels had reached a national audience with their antifederalism message.

On the national level, the primary example of such fluctuation in environmental thought is the presidency of Ronald Reagan, who was first elected in 1980. Prior to his election, Ronald Reagan espoused support for the Sagebrush Rebellion. When he was elected, Reagan wasted no time in appointing Watt the secretary of the interior and Gorsuch to head the Environmental Protection Agency. Watt and Gorsuch had worked together in Colorado to dismantle federal policies controlling the use of federal lands.

Watt pressed his ideas forward and was able to open thousands of acres of public land to coal mining. However, with his forced resignation in 1983, the movement lost a great deal of its support from the White House. Reagan and his successor George H. W. Bush each demanded that the EPA become not an advocate agency but a "neutral broker," which might actually foster development. Personnel in the EPA dropped by 25 percent and its budget was sliced by more than half. Policies and limitations were put in place to limit the number of lawsuits that could be brought and most other EPA cases were mired to inactivity (Opie, 448–49).

And these ideas have found new life in the administration of George W. Bush. Guided by leaders such as the Assistant Secretary of the Interior J. Steven Griles, who served under Watt and then spent years as a consultant to the energy industry, the Bush administration pushed to open up vast new tracts of federal land to oil, gas, and coal development.

"WISE USE" ADOPTS ENVIRONMENTAL TERMINOLOGY

One of the long-term implications of the rebellion was a national movement organized around the name and idea of wise use, which was borrowed from conservationists such as Gifford Pinchot. This is a well-financed right-wing movement that blossomed in the 1980s, and most observers agree that the use of the conservation terminology derived more from greenwashing than from any genuine ethic. Wise users sought to use public frustration with government interference to attract the support of middle-class voters.

Wise use became one of the first organized responses to environmentalism. Prioritizing use, particularly of federally owned resources, wise users fought against federal regulation and environmental limitations.

Some support came from property rights advocates. Other supporters of wise use argued that environmentalists were antihumans. Wise use continues to have an active influence on efforts to mitigate or abolish environmental regulations.

NATURE GUIDE: SPOTTED OWLS AND THE LIMITS OF THE ENDANGERED SPECIES ACT

When President Richard Nixon signed the Endangered Species Act (ESA) into law in 1973, it was intended to conserve plant and animal species in danger of extinction. Specifically, the ESA sought to ensure the species in question access to a significant portion of their range within their typical ecosystem. In the late 1980s and early 1990s, the ESA was the focus of a series of public, political, and legal controversies. One of the most memorable was the northern spotted owl on national forest lands in Washington and Oregon.

The debate over the spotted owl played across newspapers across the country and led to hostilities in many of the Pacific Northwest's small towns. Although the issues were in fact far more complex, many reports pitched the controversy as a struggle between loggers' jobs and protection of the owls' ancient forest habitat.

The debate began in June of 1989 when the U.S. Fish and Wildlife Service advised the spotted owl be placed on the threatened list and protected under the Endangered Species Act. With the prospect of a halt in cutting and lost jobs, the timber industry reacted quickly. "Save Timber" groups started in many places in the Pacific Northwest. Towns united to fight the listing of the spotted owl, urging that a single species was not worth the disruption to countless families. Some logging companies responded with their own "threatened" listing for the jobs, towns, and lives that saving the spotted owl would alter. By 1989, the government had begun to loosen its stand and allow cutting. This resulted in a suit filed by the Seattle Audubon Society against the Forest Service.

On March 7, 1991, U.S. Federal District Court Judge William L. Dwyer ruled on this lawsuit and directed the Forest Service to revise its standards in order to protect owls and their habitat. In his March ruling, the judge ordered the Forest Service to revise its standards and guidelines "to ensure the northern spotted owl's viability." Such victories for environmentalists, though, seem to have often helped anti-environmental groups learn how to better present their future arguments to the public.

ENERGY DEPENDENCE IN AN ERA OF LIMITS

As energy supplies became a more significant topic after the 1970s Arab oil embargo, each side of the environmental argument staked out its claim on the issue. Environmentalists used the 1973 oil shortage to argue that Americans needed to learn "living within limits." This lesson would be demonstrated again in 1990 when the nation went to war against Iraq largely to maintain control of oil supplies. Additional concerns came with an increasing awareness of the effects of air pollution and particularly auto emissions' relationship to global warming. The Clean Air Act of 1991 began a process requiring automobile makers to prioritize increased mileage and also to investigate alternative fuels.

Of course, the argument for a conservation ethic to govern American consumers' use of energy was a radical departure from the post-war American urge to resist limits and to flaunt the nation's decadent standard of living. Although this ethical shift did not take over the minds of all Americans in the 1970s, a large segment of the population began to consider a new paradigm of energy accounting. They became interested in energy-saving technologies, such as insulation materials and low wattage light bulbs. As a product of the 1970s, some Americans were ready and willing to consider less convenient ideas of power generation such as alternative fuels.

NATURE GUIDE: AMORY LOVINS, *SOFT ENERGY PATHS*

In a 1976 *Foreign Affairs* article entitled "Soft Energy Paths," Amory Lovins became spokesman for the small but vocal American movement for alternative fuels. In his subsequent book, Lovins contrasted the "hard energy path," as forecast at that time by most electrical utilities, and the "soft energy path," as advocated by Lovins and other utility critics.

> The energy problem, according to conventional wisdom, is how to increase energy supplies . . . to meet projected demands. . . . But how much energy we use to accomplish our social goals could instead be considered a measure less of our success than of our failure. . . . [A] soft [energy] path simultaneously offers jobs for the unemployed, capital for businesspeople, environmental protection for conservationists, enhanced national security for the military, opportunities for small business to innovate and for big business to recycle itself, exciting technologies for the secular, a rebirth of spiritual values for the religious, traditional virtues for the old, radical reforms for the young, world order and equity for globalists, energy independence for isolationists. . . . Thus, though present policy is consistent with the perceived short-term interests of a few powerful institutions, a soft path is consistent with far more strands of convergent social change at the grass roots (Lovins, 121–22).

ALTERNATIVES AND THOUGHTS OF CONSERVATION

How did Americans react to the energy crisis of the 1970s? With heightened environmental awareness following the first Earth Day in 1970, public calls for change found many receptive ears. This especially became the case following the oil embargo of the early 1970s. One set of receptive ears resided in the White House after the 1976 election (Horowitz, 20–25).

President Jimmy Carter's administration would be remembered for events such as the Iranian hostage crisis; however, when he controlled the agenda he steered American discourse to issues of energy. In a 1977 speech, Carter urged the nation:

Tonight I want to have an unpleasant talk with you about a problem unprecedented in our history. With the exception of preventing war, this is the greatest challenge our country will face during our lifetimes. The energy crisis has not yet overwhelmed us, but it will if we do not act quickly.

It is a problem we will not solve in the next few years, and it is likely to get progressively worse through the rest of this century.

We must not be selfish or timid if we hope to have a decent world for our children and grandchildren.

We simply must balance our demand for energy with our rapidly shrinking resources. By acting now, we can control our future instead of letting the future control us. . . .

Our decision about energy will test the character of the American people and the ability of the President and the Congress to govern. This difficult effort will be the "moral equivalent of war"—except that we will be uniting our efforts to build and not destroy.

Carter would introduce wide-reaching policy initiatives mainly aimed at energy conservation. Although he offered a clear vision of our limited future based on extracted energy resources, by the 1980s many Americans were returning to business as usual (Horowitz, 43–46).

A GREEN NATION?

Reagan and Carter each demonstrated the ways that each president possesses the ability to alter the intensity with which federal regulation of environmental factors is carried out. In the 2000 presidential election, Ralph Nader ran as a member of the Green Party with a platform against development, large corporations, and in support of environmental causes. Even though 70 percent of Americans call themselves environmentalists, Nader's campaign garnered less than five percent of the national vote. However, genuine pockets of such sentiments were seen in states such as Wisconsin, Florida, Oregon, and California. It seems a growing percentage of Americans are willing to entertain radical political change in the best interests of environmental causes.

Under the Bill Clinton administration, many new national monuments were set aside in western states. The EPA and other agencies monitored industrial effects on air and water pollution. The nation began discussing ways of controlling sprawl development and maintaining green spaces in the 1990s and gave serious consideration to energy conservation ideas in the early twenty-first century.

With suburbanization has come a preponderance of NIMBY concerns. The federal regulations that such public support brings have ushered in a new era for heavy industry. While no industry is untouched by

Office of Safety and Health Administration (OSHA) or EPA regulation, many have now reached beyond these minimal standards to radically change policies.

In the national parks, recent years have also seen a growth in the use of ecosystem management to control development within and around parks, including Yellowstone. In 2000, Congress approved the largest management plan in its history for the restoration of Everglades National Park. Possibly the nation's most threatened national park—if only because wetlands are particularly affected by the living patterns of their surroundings—Everglades National Park has been dammed, diked, and drained to the point that it can no longer support the web of life that depends on it. Federal initiatives will spend billions to restore the natural hydrologic conditions over the next 10 to 20 years.

In the western United States, a grassroots movement of the late 1990s made states seriously consider dismantling some of the hydroelectric dams that were designed to "reclaim" the arid western lands. Environmentalists' most urgent argument against such dams is the restoration of salmon spawning runs. By 2000–2001, however, energy shortages throughout the Northwest made such environmental hopes seem unlikely. For most Americans, maintaining everyday American living patterns still outweighs ecologically based environmental arguments.

A SYMBOLIC DEBATE: ALASKA AND ENERGY DEVELOPMENT

By the close of the twentieth century, most observers had admitted that changes needed to be made in energy management in the United States. The primary debate grew from what role the federal government would play in any new structure. Environmentalists and those prioritizing conservation argued for federal stimulants, like those during the Carter administration, to force auto producers and electricity producers to develop alternative technologies for generation. The energy industry, with the backing of the George W. Bush administration, argued for federally aided growth in existing supplies. Alaska has been a flashpoint for debate over energy development for more than a half century.

In the National Energy Policy put forward by the Bush administration in 2001, the mandate was placed on the construction of new power plants using existing fossil fuels (primarily coal and natural gas), emphasis on nuclear technologies, and an effort to harvest existing U.S. petroleum supplies. Public debate grew from the latter point, which specifically called for the drilling for oil in the Alaskan National Wildlife Reserve, which Carter created in 1980.

In authorizing the drilling for oil in northern Alaska and the construction of a Trans-Alaska pipeline to Valdez in 1977, Carter vowed to also preserve the remaining Alaska wilderness. From 1978–1980, President Jimmy Carter established Alaska National Wildlife Refuge (ANWR) and set aside 28 percent of Alaska as wilderness. Carter announced this watershed legislation as follows: "We have the imagination and the will as a people to both develop our last great natural frontier and also preserve its priceless beauty for our children" (Nash, 296–307). With the passage of the Alaska National Interest Lands Conservation Act in 1980, the BLM was ordered to oversee 11 million acres of Alaska as wilderness, including ANWR. The symbolic role of Alaska for environmentalists and friends of wilderness was clear to Carter.

After the construction of the trans-Alaska pipeline and Carter's designation of ANWR in the late 1970s, this symbolic role took on the appearance of a tragic drama in 1989 when the Exxon tanker *Valdez* ran aground and created a vast oil spill in the pristine Prince William Sound. As Americans witnessed the impact of spilled oil on the water fowl and environment of Alaska, they seemed to collectively re-evaluate whether crude oil supplies were worth threatening what many people began to call "America's last wilderness."

This same symbolism, however, was clear to the Republican-dominated Congress when it voted to open ANWR (estimated to create enough oil to satisfy American use for approximately three months—after ten years to prepare and drill the site) to development in 2005. The place that Peter Mathiessen referred to as the "Last Wild Place" seems destined for development in the twenty-first century. Such a change in destiny, of course, suggests a significant shift in the role of oil in everyday American life, which, by association, suggests expansive changes in the role of nature in everyday American life.

CONCLUSION: THE NATURE OF AN OWNERSHIP SOCIETY

Increasingly a matter of individual definitions, many Americans move into the twenty-first century unclear about what it means to be an environmentalist. In the presidential election of 2004, when a questioner asked President Bush to assess his view on the environment, the president responded simply: "I'd say that I am a good steward of the land." Many environmental organizations would never say this about the Bush administration. In short, though, history will most certainly show that Bush policies introduced an entirely new phase in the American use of policy to administer and enforce adherence of environmental legislation. Part of this new phase in legislation is a lack of clarity in presenting this agenda to the American people.

The Bush administration stresses an effort to achieve quantifiable results when discussing its no-nonsense approach to overseeing America's natural environment. A brief list of accomplishments claimed by the administration includes: "Clear Skies Initiative," cuts in mercury emissions, a "growth-oriented" approach to climate change, tax incentives for renewable energy and hybrid and fuel-cell vehicles and the development of domestic energy sources, including hydrogen. In each of the cases, however, initiatives and even the names of the policies demonstrate little about the ethical intent of the policy and are more an example of greenwashing. Are Americans being misled? Many critics say so.

One of the Bush administration's most vocal critics is attorney and business consultant Robert F. Kennedy, Jr. In his book *Crimes Against Nature,* Kennedy writes: "You simply can't talk honestly about the environment today without criticizing this president. George W. Bush will go down as the worst environmental president in our nation's history" (Kennedy).

Clearly, though, Americans continue to be able to agree that nature has played a tremendously important role in the development of the nation during the twentieth century.

Epilogue: Sifting Through the Debris of Hurricane Katrina

The overall theme of this volume has been the tenuous path that twentieth-century Americans chose by relying on their own technology alone, instead of searching for a compromise, middle ground, such as that symbolized by Frank Lloyd Wright's seminal structure, *Fallingwater*. This understanding leads to a catalogue of how we lived and the choices we made in the twentieth century. In this relationship with nature, the alternate paradigm is represented by the impulses of the environmental movement, which sought to find a place for human life within natural constraints and limitations. But such cultural change occurs less quickly than many Americans would like.

When the warnings went out in September, 2005 that Hurricane Katrina had risen to the status of category five as it prepared to slam into the Gulf Coast just east of New Orleans, Louisiana, it was too late to flee for most remaining residents. It was too late for many to prepare their home for any potentiality. And it was certainly too late to steady the levees or move the entire historic city to a safe, dry location. The story behind this event, of course, was a parable of the role that nature played in most Americans' lives during the 20th century. As the nation recovered from serious flooding along the Mississippi in the late 1920s, it made a fateful choice: to invest in levees and rely on the contrivances of the U.S. Corps of Engineers to stave off natural calamity. Ultimately, the 2005 flooding was inevitable and expected by many engineers and planners.

The U.S. southern central coast will be recovering for a generation. Katrina has brought critical lessons for American society about race and poverty as well as about emergency response. Clearly, though, this event of the twenty-first century offers us an essential lesson about decisions of the twentieth century. The visionary architect who gazed on the limited site in Pennsylvania's Laurel Highlands could have stopped the stream to make room for a trophy home. Or he could have flattened out the forest and hillside in order to create an ideal upon which to construct a typical mansion.

Instead, Frank Lloyd Wright became the genius of the place: he measured the site's limits and conditioned his activities and plans around them. By doing so, he wedded humans and nature at *Fallingwater* and created a landscape that stands simultaneously as a symbol of our success in finding ways to live with nature and of our many failures to do so. His actions seemed to say: let our paths wind with nature whenever possible in a sign of mutual respect.

BIBLIOGRAPHY

Adams, Judith A. *The American Amusement Park Industry.* Boston: Twayne Publishers, 1991.

Albright, Horace M., and Robert Cahn. *The Birth of the National Park Service: The Founding Years, 1913–33.* Salt Lake City, Utah: Howe Brothers, 1985.

Albright, Horace M, and Marian Albright Schenck. *Creating the National Park Service: The Missing Years.* Norman: University of Oklahoma Press, 1999.

Anderson, Oscar E. Jr. *The Health of a Nation: Harvey W. Wiley and the Fight for Pure Food.* Chicago: University of Chicago Press, 1958.

Anderson, Terry H. *The Movement and the Sixties.* New York: Oxford University Press, 1995.

Annis, S. "Evolving Connectedness among Environmental Groups and Grassroots Organizations in Protected Areas of Central America." *World Development* 20, no. 4 (1992): 587–95.

Ashworth, William. *The Late, Great Lakes: An Environmental History.* New York: Knopf, 1986.

Athansiou, Tom. *Divided Planet: The Ecology of Rich and Poor.* Athens: University of Georgia Press, 1998.

Bailey, Anne J. *The Chessboard of War: Sherman and Hood in the Autumn Campaigns of 1864.* Lincoln: University of Nebraska Press, 2000.

———. *War and Ruin: William T. Sherman and the Savannah Campaign.* Wilmington, Del.: Scholarly Resources, 2003.

Ballard, Joe N., ed. *The History of the U.S. Army Corps of Engineers.* New York: Diane Publishers, 1998.

Barbalace is available on-line at: http://environmentalchemistry.com/yogi/hazmat/articles/nimby.html

Barney, William L. *The Passage of the Republic: An Interdisciplinary History of Nineteenth-Century America.* Lexington, Mass.: D. C. Heath, 1987.

Barry, John. *Rising Tide.* New York: Simon and Schuster, 1998.

Beilharz, Edwin A., and Carlos U. Lopez, eds. *We Were 49ers!: Chilean Accounts of the California Gold Rush.* Pasadena, Calif.: Ward Ritchie Press, 1976.

Belasco, James. *Americans on the Road.* Cambridge: MIT Press, 1979.

Benton, Thomas Hart. *Thrilling Sketch of the Life of Col. J.C. Fremont.* London: J. Field, 1850.

Berman, Marshall. *All That Is Solid Melts into Air.* New York: Penguin, 1988.

Black, Brian. "Organic Planning: Ecology and Design in the Landscape of TVA." In *Environmentalism in Landscape Architecture,* ed. Michel Conan. 2000.

————. *Petrolia: The Landscape of America's First Oil Boom.* Baltimore, Md.: Johns Hopkins University Press, 2000.

Boli, J., and G. Thomas. *Constructing World Culture: International Nongovernmental Organizations Since 1875.* Stanford, Calif.: Stanford University Press, 1999.

Bormann, F. Herbert, et al. *Redesigning the American Lawn.* New Haven, Conn.: Yale University Press, 1995.

Boyer, Paul. *By The Bomb's Early Light.* Chapel Hill: University of North Carolina Press, 1994.

Bragg, William Harris. *Griswoldville.* Macon, Ga.: Mercer University Press, 2000.

Brehm, V.M. "Environment, Advocacy, and Community Participation: MOPAWI in Honduras." *Development in Practice* 10, no. 1 (2000): 94–98.

Brennan, Timothy J., et al. *A Shock to the System—Restructuring America's Electricity Industry.* Washington, D.C.: Resources for the Future, 1996.

Brinkley, Douglas. *Wheels for the World: Henry Ford, His Company and a Century of Progress.* New York: Viking, 2003.

Broad, William. *The Universe Below.* New York: Simon and Schuster, 1997.

Brooks, H. Allen. *The Prairie School.* New York: W.W. Norton, 1996.

Brower, Michael. *Cool Energy: Renewable Solutions to Environmental Problems,* rev. ed. Cambridge, Mass.: MIT Press, 1992.

Bryant, Bunyan I. *Environmental Justice: Issues, Policies and Solutions.* New York: Island Press, June 1995.

Bryant, Keith L. Jr., ed. *Railroads in the Age of Regulation, 1900–1980.* New York: Facts on File, 1988.

Bryson, J.M. *Strategic Planning for Public and Nonprofit Organizations.* San Francisco: Jossey-Bass Publishers, 1995.

Bullard, Robert, John Lewis, and Benjamin Chavis. *Unequal Protection: Environmental Justice and Communities of Color.* New York: Sierra Club Books, 1994.

Bush letter from June 13, 2001 is available on-line at: http://www.usemb.se/Environment/letter.html

Cagan, Joanna, et al. *Field of Schemes: How the Great Stadium Swindle Turns Public Money into Private Profit.* New York: Common Courage Press, 1998.

Calloway, Colin G. *First Peoples.* Boston: Bedford, 1999.

Calthorpe, Peter. *The Next American Metropolis.* New York: Princeton Architectural Press, 1993.

Cantelon, Philip, and Robert C. Williams. *Crisis Contained: Department of Energy at Three Mile Island.* Carbondale: Southern Illinois University Press, 1982.

Carr, Ethan. *Wilderness by Design.* Lincoln: University of Nebraska Press, 1988.

Carson, Rachel. *Silent Spring.* New York: Mariner Books, 2002.

Carson is available on-line at: http://www.smithsonianmag.si.edu/smithsonian/issues02/sep02/presence.html

Chernow, Ron. *Titan: The Life of John D. Rockefeller, Sr.* New York: Random House, 1998.

Clark, A. M., E. J. Friedman, and K. Hochstetler. "The Sovereign Limits of Global Civil Society: A Comparison of NGO Participation in UN World Conferences on the Environment, Human Rights, and Women." *World Politics*, no. 51 (1998): 1–35.

Clark, Cifford Edward Jr. *The American Family Home.* Chapel Hill: University of North Carolina Press, 1986.

Colignon, Richard A. *Power Plays.* Albany: SUNY Press, 1997

Collin, Richard H. *Theodore Roosevelt's Caribbean: The Panama Canal, The Monroe Doctrine, and the Latin American Context.* Baton Rouge: Louisiana State University Press, 1990.

Colten, Craig. *Transforming New Orleans and Its Environs.* Pittsburgh: University of Pittsburgh Press, 2001.

Columbian Exposition is available on-line at: http://xroads.virginia.edu/~MA96/WCE/title.html

Connolly, James A. *Three Years in the Army of the Cumberland: The Letters and Diary of Major James A. Connolly,* ed. Paul M. Angle, 1928; reprint, Bloomington: Indiana University Press, 1996.

Conzen, Michael, ed. *The Making of the American Landscape.* Boston: Unwin Hyman Publishers, 1990.

Cooper, Gail. *Air-Conditioning America.* Baltimore: Johns Hopkins, 2002.

Cowles is available on-line at: http://memory.loc.gov/ammem/award97/icuhtml/aepsp4.html

Creese, Walter L. *TVA's Public Planning.* Knoxville: University of Tennessee Press, 1990.

Cronon, William. *Nature's Metropolis.* New York: Norton, 1991.

Crosby, Alfred. *America's Forgotten Pandemic: The Influenza of 1918.* New York: Cambridge, 1990.

Cunfer, Geoffrey. *On the Great Plains: Agriculture and the Environment.* College Station: Texas A & M Press, 2005.

Cutright, Paul. *Theodore Roosevelt: The Making of a Conservationist.* Urbana: University of Illinois Press, 1985.

Dana, C. W. *The Great West, or the Garden of the World.* Boston: Wentworth & Co., 1857.

Dangerfield, George. *The Awakening of American Nationalism, 1815–1828.* New York: Harper and Row, 1965.

Darrah, William Culp. *Pithole, the Vanished City.* Gettysburg, Pa., 1964.

Darst, Robert G. *Smokestack Diplomacy: Cooperation and Conflict in East-West Environmental Politics.* Cambridge, Mass.: MIT Press, 2001.

Davis, Susan G. *Spectacular Nature.* Berkeley: University of California Press, 1997.

Demarest, David P. Jr. *"The River Ran Red": Homestead, 1892.* Pittsburgh, Pa.: University of Pittsburgh Press, 1992.

Dilsaver, Lary M., ed. *America's National Park System: The Critical Documents.* New York: Rowman and Littlefield, 1997.

Domer, Dennis, ed. *Lawrence on the Kaw: A Historical and Cultural Anthology.* Lawrence: University of Kansas Press, 2000.

Douglass, Frederick. *My Bondage and My Freedom.* Urbana: University of Illinois Press, 1987.

Doyle, Jack. *Taken for a Ride: Detroit's Big Three and the Politics of Air Pollution.* New York: Four Walls Eight Windows, 2000.

Dunlop, Beth, and Vincent Scully. *Building a Dream: The Art of Disney Architecture.* New York: Harry N. Abrams, 1996.

Edwards, M., and D. Hulme. *Beyond the Magic Bullet: NGO Performance and Accountability in the Post-Cold War World.* West Hartford, Conn.: Kumarian Press, 1996.

Elkington, J., and S. Fennell. "Partners for Sustainability: Business-NGO Relations and Sustainable Development." *Greener Management International,* no. 24 (1998): 48–61.

Erikson, Kai. *A New Species of Trouble—The Human Experience of Modern Disasters.* New York: W.W. Norton, 1994.

Etheridge, Elizabeth W. *Sentinel for Health.* Berkeley: University of California Press, 1992.

Everhart, William C. *The National Park Service.* Boulder, Colo.: Westview Press, 1983.

Feller, Daniel. *The Jacksonian Promise: America, 1815–1840.* Baltimore, Md.: Johns Hopkins University Press, 1995.

Flink, James J. *The Automobile Age.* Cambridge, Mass.: MIT Press, 1990.

Foreman, Dave. *Ecodefense: A Field Guide to Monkeywrenching.* 3rd Edition. Chico, Calif.: Abbzugg Press, 1994.

Foresta, Ronald A. *America's National Parks and Their Keepers.* Washington, D.C.: Resources for the Future, 1985.

Fox, Stephen. *The American Conservation Movement.* Madison: University of Wisconsin Press, 1981.

Fri, R. "The Corporation as Nongovernment Organization." *Columbia Journal of World Business* 27, nos. 3/4 (1992): 90–96.

Garner, John S., ed. *The Midwest in American Architecture.* Chicago: University of Illinois Press, 1991.

Garwin, Richard L., and Georges Charpak. *Megawatts and Megatons: A Turning Point in the Nuclear Age.* New York: Knopf, 2001.

Gatell, Otto, and Paul Goodman. *Democracy and Union: The United States, 1815–1877.* New York: Holt, Rinehart, and Winston, 1972.

Gelbspan, Ross. *The Heat is On: The Climate Crisis.* Reading, Mass.: Perseus Books, 1995.

Geraint, John, and Rod Sheard. *Stadia: A Design and Development Guide.* Boston: Architectural Press, 1997.

Giddens, Paul. *Early Days of Oil.* Gloucester, Mass.: Peter Smith, 1964.

Glatthaar, Joseph T. *The March to the Sea and Beyond: Sherman's Troops in the Savannah and Carolinas Campaign.* New York: New York University Press, 1985.

Glave, Dianne. "A Garden So Brilliant with Colors, So Original in its Design," *Environmental History* 8, no. 3: 395–411.

Gordenker, L., and T.G. Weiss. "Devolving Responsibilities: A Framework for Analyzing NGOs and Services." *Third World Quarterly* 18, no. 3 (1997), 443–56.

Gordon, Robert B. and Patrick M. Malone. *The Texture of Industry.* New York: Oxford University Press, 1994.

Gorman, Hugh. *Redefining Efficiency: Pollution Concerns.* Akron, Oh.: University of Akron Press, 2001.

Gottlieb, Robert. *Forcing the Spring: The Transformation of the American Environmental Movement.* Washington, D.C.: Island Press, 1993.

Graebner, Norman B., ed. *Manifest Destiny.* New York: Bobbs Merrill, 1968.

Graham, Frank. *The Adirondack Park: A Political History.* New York: Random House, 1978.

Groves Report available on-line at: http://www.atomicarchive.com/Docs/Trinity/Groves.shtml

Gura, Philip F., and Joel Myerson, eds. *Critical Essays on American Transcendentalism.* New York, G. K. Hall, 1982.

Gutfreund, Owen D. *20th Century Sprawl: Highways and the Reshaping of the American Landscape.* New York: Oxford University Press, 2005.

Hague, John A., ed. *American Character and Culture.* Greenwood, 1979.

Hampton, Wilborn. *Meltdown: A Race against Nuclear Disaster at Three Mile Island: A Reporter's Story.* Cambridge, Mass.: Candlewick Press, 2001.

Hardin, Garrett. "The *Tragedy* of the Commons." *Science,* 162 (1968):1243–48.

Hargrove, Erwin C. *Prisoners of Myth.* Princeton: Princeton University Press, 1994.

Hargrove, and Paul K. Conkin, eds. *TVA: Fifty Years of Grass-Roots Bureaucracy.* Knoxville: University of Tennessee Press, 1984.

Hart, John Fraser, ed. *Our Changing Cities.* Baltimore, Md.: Johns Hopkins University Press, 1991.

Hartzog, George B. Jr. *Battling for the National Parks.* Mt. Kisco, NY: Moyer Bell, 1988.

Harvey, Mark. *Wilderness Forever: Howard Zahniser And The Path To The Wilderness Act.* Seattle: University of Washington Press, 2005.

Hays, Samuel P. *Conservation and the Gospel of Efficiency.* Pittsburgh: University of Pittsburgh Press, 1999.

———. *Beauty, Health, and Permanence: Environmental Politics in the United States, 1955-85.* New York: Cambridge University Press, 1993.

Health is available on-line at: http://www.nlm.nih.gov/exhibition/phs_history/intro.html

Henderson, Henry L. and David B. Woolner, eds. *FDR and the Environment.* New York: Palgrave, 2004.

Hietala, Thomas Randall. *Anxiety and Aggrandizement: The Origins of American Expansion in the 1840s.* Ann Arbor, Mich.: University Microfilms International, 1981.

Hines, Thomas S. "The Imperial Mall: The City Beautiful Movement and the Washington Plan of 1901–02." In *The Mall in Washington, 1791–1991.* Washington: National Gallery of Art, 1991.

Hirt, Paul W. *A Conspiracy of Optimism: Management of the National Forests since World War Two.* Lincoln: University of Nebraska Press, 1994.

Holliday, J.S. *The World Rushed In.* New York: Simon and Schuster, 1981.

Horowitz, Daniel, *Jimmy Carter and the Energy Crisis of the 1970s.* New York: St. Martin's Press, 2005.

Horsman, Reginald. *Race and Manifest Destiny.* Cambridge: Harvard University Press, 1981.

Hughes, Thomas P. *American Genesis: A Century of Invention and Technological Enthusiasm.* New York: Penguin Books, 1989.

———. *Networks of Power: Electrification in Western Society, 1880–1930.* Baltimore, Md.: Johns Hopkins University Press, 1983.

Hurley, Andrew. *Environmental Inequalities: Class, Race, and Industrial Pollution in Gary, Indiana, 1945–1980.* Chapel Hill: University of North Carolina Press, 1995.

Influenza is available on-line at: http://www.stanford.edu/group/virus/uda/

Irwin, William. *The New Niagara: Tourism, Technology and the Landscape of Niagara Falls, 1776–1917.* University Park, Pa.: Penn State University Press, 1996.

Ise, John. *Our National Park Policy: A Critical History*. Baltimore, Md.: Johns Hopkins University Press, 1961.

Isenberg, Andrew. *The Destruction of the Bison*. New York: Cambridge University Press, 2001.

Jackson, Donald C. *Building the Ultimate Dam*. Lawrence: University of Kansas Press, 1995.

Jackson, Kenneth T. *Crabgrass Frontier*. New York: Oxford University Press, 1985.

Jacobs, Jane. *The Death and Life of Great American Cities*. New York: Vintage Books, 1961.

Jenkins, Virginia Scott. *The Lawn*. Washington, D.C.: Smithsonian Institution Press, 1994.

Jones, Holway R. *John Muir and the Sierra Club: The Battle for Yosemite*. San Francisco: Sierra Club, 1965.

Jordan, Terry, and Matti Kaups. *The American Backwoods Frontier*. Baltimore: Johns Hopkins University Press, 1986.

Josephson, Paul R. *Red Atom: Russia's Nuclear Power Program from Stalin to Today*. New York: W.H. Freeman, 2000.

Kasson, John. *Amusing the Million: Coney Island at the Turn of the Century*. New York: Hill and Wang, 1978.

Kay, Jane Holtz. *Asphalt Nation*. Berkeley: University of California Press, 1997.

Kellogg, Paul U. contained on-line at: http://www.clpgh.org/exhibit/stell30.html

Kennedy, Robert. F. *Crimes Against Nature: How George W. Bush and His Corporate Pals Are Plundering the Country and Hijacking Our Democracy*. New York: Harpercollins, 2004.

Kennett, Lee B. *Marching through Georgia: The Story of Soldiers and Civilians during Sherman's Campaign*. New York: HarperCollins, 1995.

Kern, Stephen. *The Culture of Time and Space, 1880–1918*. Cambridge: Harvard University Press, 1983.

Klobuchar, Amy. *Uncovering the Dome*. New York: Waveland Press, 1986.

Kremen, C., A.M. Merenlender, and D.D. Murphy. "Ecological Monitoring: A Vital Need for Integrated Conservation and Development Programs in the Tropics." *Conservation Biology* 8, no 2 (1994), 388–97.

Kunstler, James H. *The Geography of Nowhere*. New York: Touchstone Books, 1993.

Labaree, Benjamin. *America and the Sea*. Mystic, Conn.: Mystic Seaport, 1999.

Lead is available on-line at: http://www.epa.gov/history/topics/perspect/lead.htm

Lear, Linda. *Rachel Carson: Witness for History*. New York: Owl Books, 1997.

Legler, Dixie, and Christian Korab. *Prairie Style: Houses and Gardens by Frank Lloyd Wright and the Prairie School*. New York: Stewart, Tabori and Chang, 1999.

Lemann, Nicholas. *The Promised Land : The Great Black Migration and How It Changed America*. New York: Vintage, 1992.

Lemlich is available on-line at: http://www.ilr.cornell.edu/trianglefire/texts/stein_ootss/ootss_cl.html?location=Sweatshops+and+Strikes

Leopold, Aldo: *A Sand County Almanac, and Sketches Here and There*. [1948.] New York: Oxford University Press, 1987.

Letts, C. W., W.P. Ryan, and A. Grossman. *High Performance Nonprofit Organizations: Managing Upstream for Greater Impact*. New York: John Wiley and Sons, 1999.

Lewis, Tom. *Divided Highways.* New York: Penguin Books, 1997.

Liebs, Chester H. *Main Street to Miracle Mile.* Baltimore, Md.: Johns Hopkins University Press, 1995.

Limerick, Patricia Nelson. *Legacy of Conquest.* New York: Norton, 1987.

Livernash, R. "The Growing Influence of NGOs in the Developing World." *Environmental Conversation* 34, no. 5 (1992): 12–43.

Love Canal is available on-line at: http://ublib.buffalo.edu/libraries/projects/lovecanal/

Lovins, Amory. *Soft Energy Paths.* New York: Harpercollins, 1979.

Low, Nicholas, and Brendon Gleeson. *Justice, Society and Nature: An Exploration of Political Ecology.* New York: Routledge, 1998.

Lowitt, Richard. *The New Deal and the West* Norman: University of Oklahoma Press, 1984.

Mackintosh, Barry. *The National Parks: Shaping the System.* Washington, D.C.: National Park Service, 1991.

Maher, Neil. "Neil Maher on Shooting the Moon." *Environmental History* 9.3 (2004): 27 Jan. 2006.

Marsh, G. P. *Man and Nature.* Cambridge, Mass.: Harvard University Press, 1965.

Martin, Albro. *Railroads Triumphant: The Growth, Rejection and Rebirth of a Vital* New York: Oxford University Press, 1992.

Marx, Leo. *The Machine in the Garden.* New York: Oxford, 1964.

Matthiessen, Peter. *Arctic National Wildlife Refuge: Seasons of Life and Land.* The Mountaineers Books, 2005.

May, Elaine Tyler. *Homeward Bound.* New York: Basic Books, 1988.

May, Ernest R. *American Cold War Strategy.* Boston: Bedford Books, 1993.

McCullough, David. *Path Between The Seas: The Creation of the Panama Canal, 1870–1914.* New York: Simon and Shuster, 1978.

McGreevy, Patrick V. *Imagining Niagara.* Amherst: University of Massachusetts Press, 1994.

McHarg, Ian. *Design with Nature.* New York: John Wiley and Sons, 1992.

McKinsey, Elizabeth. *Niagara Falls: Icon of the American Sublime.* Cambridge: Cambridge University Press, 1985.

McNeil, John R. *Something New Under the Sun: An Environmental History of the Twentieth-Century World.* New York: Norton, 2001.

McPhee, John. *Assembling California.* New York: Farrar, Strauss, Giroux, 1993.

McShane, Clay. *Down the Asphalt Path.* New York: Columbia University Press, 1994.

Meikle, Jeffrey L. *American Plastic: A Cultural History.* New Brunswick: Rutgers University Press, 1997.

Melosi, Martin V. *Coping with Abundance: Energy and Environment in Industrial America.* New York: Alfred A. Knopf, 1985.

———. *The Sanitary City : Urban Infrastructure in America from Colonial Times to the Present.* Baltimore: Johns Hopkins University Press, 1999.

Merchant, Carolyn. *Major Problems in American Environmental History.* New York: Heath, 2004.

Metlar, George W. *Northern California, Scott and Klamath Rivers, Their Inhabitants and Characteristics. . . Mining Interests.* Yreka, Calif.: Yreka Union Office, 1856.

The Millennium Whole Earth Catalog. San Francisco: Harper, 1998.

Miller, Joaquin. *My Life Amongst the Indians.* Chicago: Morril, Higgins & Co., 1892.

———. *My Life Amongst the Modoc.* Chicago: Morril, Higgins, & Co., 1890.

Miller, Judith. *Germs: Biological Weapons and America's Secret War.* New York: Simon and Schuster, 2001.

Moorhouse, John C., ed. *Electric Power: Deregulation and the Public Interest.* San Francisco: Pacific Research Institute for Public Policy, 1986.

Morris, Edmund. *Theodore Rex.* New York: Random House, 2001.

Morrison, Ernest. *J. Horace McFarland: A Thorn for Beauty.* Harrisburg: PHMC, 1995.

Motavalli, Jim. *Forward Drive: The Race to Build "Clean" Cars for the Future.* San Francisco: Sierra Club Books, 2001.

Muir, John. *The Yosemite.* New York: Century, 1912.

Mumford, Lewis. *Technics and Civilization.* New York: Harcourt, 1963.

Nash, Roderick. *Wilderness and the American Mind.* New Haven, Conn.: Yale University Press, 1986.

Niven, John. *The Coming of the Civil War, 1837–1861.* Arlington Heights, Ill.: Harlan Davidson, 1990.

Norris, Frank. *The Octopus.* New York: Penguin, 1986.

NSC-68 is available on-line at: http://www.fas.org/irp/offdocs/nsc-hst/nsc-68.htm

Nye, David E. *Consuming Power: A Social History of American Energies.* Cambridge, Mass.: MIT Press, 1999.

———. *Electrifying America: Social Meanings of a New Technology.* Cambridge: MIT Press, 1991.

Oliens, Roger M. and Dianna Davids. *Oil and Ideology: The American Oil Industry, 1859–1945.* Chapel Hill: University of North Carolina Press, 1999.

Olmsted, Frederick Law. "Draft of Preliminary Report upon the Yosemite and Big Tree Grove" and "Letter on the Great American Park of the Yosemite." Typed transcriptions, *Frederick Law Olmsted Papers,* Manuscript Division, Library of Congress, Washington, D.C.

———. Letter, *New York Evening Post,* June 18, 1868.

———. *The Papers of Frederick Law Olmsted, Volume Five: The California Years, 1863–1865,* pp. 488–516, ed. Victoria Post Ranney. Baltimore, Md.: Johns Hopkins University Press, 1990.

———. *Civilizing American Cities.* New York: DaCapo Press, 1997.

Opie, John. *Nature's Nation.* New York: Harcourt Brace, 1998.

Oster, S.M. *Strategic Management for Nonprofit Organizations.* New York: Oxford University Press, 1995.

Painter, Nell Irvin. *Exodusters.* New York: Norton, 1992.

Parrington, Vern Louis. *The Romantic Revolution in America, 1800–1860.* Norman: University of Oklahoma Press, 1987.

Peffer, W.A. *The Farmer's Side.* New York, 1891.

Petrikin, Jonathan S. *Environmental Justice,* New York: Greenhaven, 1995.

Pinchot, Gifford. *Breaking New Ground.* New York: Island Press, 1998.

Pollan, Michael. *Second Nature.* New York: Delta, 1992.

Poole, Robert W. Jr., ed. *Unnatural Monopolies: The Case for Deregulating Public Utilities.* Lexington, Mass.: Lexington Books, 1985.

Price, Jenny. *Flight Maps.* New York: Basic Books, 2000.

Price, M. "Ecopolitics and Environmental Nongovernmental Organizations in Latin America." *Geographic Review* 84, no. 1 (1994): 42–59.

Princen, T., and M. Finger. *Environmental NGOs in World Politics*. London: Routledge, 1994.

Pyne, Stephen J. *Fire in America: A Cultural History of Wildland and Rural Fire*. Seattle: University of Washington Press, 1997.

Rabe, Barry. George *Beyond Nimby: Hazardous Waste Siting in Canada and the United States*, Brookings Institute, November 1994.

Raustalia, K. "States, NGOs, and International Environmental Institutions." *International Studies Quarterly* 41 (1997): 719–40.

Reiger, John. *American Sportsmen and the Origins of Conservation*. Norman: University of Oklahoma Press, 1988.

Reisner, Marc. *Cadillac Desert*. New York: Penguin, 1986.

Relph, Edward, *The Modern Urban Landscape*. Baltimore, Md.: Johns Hopkins University Press, 1987.

Rettie, Dwight F. *Our National Park System: Caring for America's Greatest Natural and Historic Treasures*. Urbana: University of Illinois Press, 1995.

Reuss, Martin. *Water Resources Administration in the United States: Policy, Practice, and Emerging Issues*. Ann Arbor: Michigan State University Press, 1993.

Ridenour, James M. *The National Parks Compromised: Pork Barrel Politics and America's Treasures*. Merrillville, Ind.: ICS Books, 1994.

Riegel, Robert E. *Young America, 1830–1840*. Norman: University of Oklahoma Press, 1949.

Riis, Jacob. *How the Other Half Lives*. Available on-line at: http://www.cis.yale.edu/amstud/inforev/riis/title.html

Robbins, William G. *Colony and Empire: The Capitalist Transformation of the American West*. Lawrence: University Press of Kansas, 1995.

Rohrbough, Malcolm J. *Days of Gold: The California Gold Rush and the American Nation*. Berkeley: University of California Press, 1997.

Rome, Adam. *The Bulldozer in the Countryside: Suburban Sprawl and the Rise of American Environmentalism*. New York: Cambridge University Press, 2001.

Roosevelt available online at: http://www.theodore-roosevelt.com/trmdcorollary.html.

Roper, Laura Wood. *FLO: A Biography of Frederick Olmsted*. Baltimore, Md.: The John Hopkins University Press, 1973.

Rosensweig, Roy and Elizabeth Blackmar. *The Park and the People: A History of Central Park*. Ithaca: Cornell University Press, 1998.

Roth, Leland M. *A Concise History of American Architecture*. New York: Harper and Row, 1970.

Rothman, Hal K. *Preserving Different Pasts: The American National Monuments*. Urbana: University of Illinois Press, 1989.

———. *Saving the Planet: The American Response to the Environment in the 20th Century*. Chicago: Ivan R. Dee, 2000.

———. *The Greening of a Nation*. New York: Harcourt, 1998.

Rowley, William D. *U.S. Forest Service Grazing and Rangelands: A History*. Texas A&M University Press, 1985.

Runte, Alfred. *National Parks: The American Experience*, 3d ed. Lincoln: University of Nebraska Press, 1997.

Russell, Edmund and Richard P. Tucker, eds. *Natural Enemy, Natural Ally: Toward an Environmental History of War*. Corvallis: Oregon State University Press, 2005.

Russell, Edmund. *War and Nature : Fighting Humans and Insects with Chemicals from World War I to Silent Spring*. New York: Cambridge University Press, 2001.

Salm, J. "Coping with Globalization: A Profile of the Northern NGO Sector." *Nonprofit and Voluntary Sector Quarterly* 28, no. 4 (1999): 87–103.

Savage, William Sherman. *Blacks in the West*. Westport, Conn.: Greenwood Press, 1976.

Scharff, Virginia. *Taking the Wheel: Women and the Coming of the Motor Age*. New York: Free Press; Toronto: Collier Macmillan Canada, 1991.

Schiffer, Michael B., Tamara C. Butts, and Kimberly K. Grimm. *Taking Charge: The Electric Automobile in America*. Washington, D.C.: Smithsonian Institution Press, 1994.

Schlebecker, John T. *Whereby We Thrive: A History of American Farming, 1607–1972*. Ames: Iowa State University Press, 1975.

Schlossler, Eric. *Fast Food Nation: The Dark Side of the All-American Meal*. New York: Harper, 2001.

Schuyler, David. *Apostle of Taste: Andrew Jackson Downing, 1815–1852*. Baltimore, Md.: Johns Hopkins University Press, 1996.

Sellars, Richard West. *Preserving Nature in the National Parks: A History*. New Haven, Conn.: Yale University Press, 1997.

Shankland, Robert. *Steve Mather of the National Parks*, 3d ed. New York: Alfred A. Knopf, 1976.

Shaw, Ronald E. *Canals for a Nation: The Canal Era in the United States, 1790–1860*. Lexington: University of Kentucky Press, 1990.

Smil, Vaclav. *Energy in World History*. Boulder, Colo.: Westview Press, 1994.

———. *Energy in China's Modernization: Advances and Limitations*. Armonk, N.Y.: M.E. Sharpe, 1988.

Smith, Duane. *Mining America: The Industry and the Environment, 1800–1980*. Lawrence: Kansas University Press, 1987.

Smith, Henry Nash. *Virgin Land: The American West as Symbol and Myth*. Cambridge, Mass.: Harvard University Press, 1978.

Smith, Terry. *Making the Modern*. Chicago: University of Chicago Press, 1993.

Smokey can be found on-line at: http://www.smokeybear.com/vault/wartime_prevention.asp

Sobel, Robert. *Conquest and Conscience: The 1840's*. New York: Crowell, 1971.

Solnit, Rebecca. *Savage Dreams: A Journey into the Hidden Wars of the American West*. San Francisco: Sierra Club Books, 1994.

Spence, Clark. "The Golden Age of Dredging." *Western Historical Quarterly* (October 1980): 403–14.

Spence, Mark D. *Dispossessing the Wilderness : Indian Removal and the Making of the National Parks*. New York: Oxford University Press, 2000.

Steen, Harold K. *The U.S. Forest Service*. Seattle: University of Washington Press, 1976.

Steinberg, Theodore. *Nature Incorporated: Industrialization and the Water of New England*. New York: Cambridge University Press, 1991.

———. *Down to Earth: Nature's Role in American History*. New York: Oxford University Press, 2002.

Stephanson, Anders. *Manifest Destiny: American Expansionism and the Empire of Right,* New York: Hill and Wang, 1995.

Stevens, Joseph E. *Hoover Dam*. Norman: University of Oklahoma Press, 1988.

Stevenson, Elizabeth. *Park Maker: A Life of Frederick Law Olmsted.* New York: Macmillan, 1995.

Stilgoe, John R. *Borderland.* New Haven, Conn.: Yale University Press, 1990.

————. *Metropolitan Corridor: Railroads and the American Scene.* New Haven, Conn.: Yale University Press, 1983.

Stine, Jeffrey K. *Mixing the Waters: Environment, Politics, and the Building of the Tennessee-Tombigbee Waterway.* Akron: University of Akron Press, 1993.

Stradling, David. *Smokestacks and Progressives : Environmentalists, Engineers, and Air Quality in America, 1881–1951.* Baltimore: Johns Hopkins University Press, 1999.

Stratton, David. *Tempest over Teapot Dome: The Story of Albert B. Fall.* Norman: University of Oklahoma Press, 1998.

Sutter, Paul S. *Driven Wild: How the Fight Against Automobiles Launched the Modern Wilderness Movement.* Seattle: University of Washington Press, 2002.

Swain, Donald C. *Wilderness Defender: Horace M. Albright and Conservation.* Chicago: University of Chicago Press, 1970.

Tansley is available on-line at: http://memory.loc.gov/ammem/award97/icuhtml/aepsp6.html

Tarr, Joel. *The Search for the Ultimate Sink.* Akron: University of Akron Press, 1996.

————, ed. *Devastation and Renewal.* Pittsburgh: University of Pittsburgh Press, 2003.

Taylor, B., R. Chait, and T. Holland. "The New Work of the Nonprofit Board." *Harvard Business Review* (1996): 36–46.

Tempest-Williams, Terry. *Refuge.* New York: Vintage, 1992. Excerpt available on-line at: http://www.ratical.org/radiation/inetSeries/TTW_C1-BW.html

Terrie, Phillip. *Forever Wild: A Cultural History of Wilderness in the Adirondacks.* Syracuse, N.Y.: Syracuse University Press, 1994.

Teysott, George, ed. *The American Lawn.* Princeton, N.J.: Princeton Architectural Press, 1999.

Trachtenberg, Alan. *The Incorporation of America: Culture and Society in the Gilded Age.* New York: Hill and Wang, 1982.

Turner, Frederick Jackson. *The United States, 1830–1850.* New York: Henry Holt, 1934.

Twain, Mark. *Roughing It.* London: George Routledge, 1871.

Tyler, Alice Felt. *Freedom's Ferment: Phases of American Social History to 1860.* New York: Harper and Row, 1962.

Valavenes, Panos. *Hysplex.* Berkeley: University of California Press, 1999.

Vergara, R. "NGOs: Help or Hindrance for Community Development in Latin America?" *Community Development Journal* 29, no. 4 (1994): 322–28.

Vieyra, Daniel I. *Fill 'Er Up: An Architectural History of America's Gas Stations.* New York: Macmillan, 1979.

Ward, James A. *Railroads and the Character of America.* Knoxville: University of Tennessee Press, 1986.

Weiner, Douglas R. *Models of Nature: Ecology, Conservation, and Cultural Revolution in Soviet Russia.* Bloomington: Indiana University Press, 1988.

Weiss, T.G., and L. Gordenker. *NGOs, the UN, and Global Governance.* Boulder, Colo.: Lynne Rienner Publishers, 1996.

Wellman, Paul I. *The House Divides: The Age of Jackson and Lincoln.* Garden City, N.Y.: Doubleday, 1966.

West, Elliot. *The Contested Plains: Indians, Goldseekers, and the Rush to Colorado.* Lawrence: University of Kansas Press, 2000.

White, Richard. *"It's Your Misfortune and None of My Own."* Norman: University of Oklahoma Press, 1991.

———. *Organic Machine.* New York: Hill and Wang, 1996.

Williams, Michael. *Americans and Their Forests: A Historical Geography.* New York: Cambridge University Press, 1989.

Wilson, Alexander. *The Culture of Nature.* Cambridge: Blackwell, 1992.

Wirth, Conrad L. *Parks, Politics, and the People.* Norman: University of Oklahoma Press, 1980.

Worster, Donald. *Dust Bowl: The Southern Plains in the 1930s.* New York: Oxford University Press, 1979.

———. *Nature's Economy.* New York: Cambridge University Press, 1994.

———. *A River Running West: The Life of John Wesley Powell.* New York: Oxford University Press, 2000.

Wright, Gwendolyn. *Building the Dream.* Cambridge, Mass.: MIT Press, 1992.

Yergin, Daniel. *The Prize : The Epic Quest for Oil, Money & Power.* New York: Free Press, 1993.

Young, James Harvey. *The Medical Messiahs: A Social History of Health Quackery in Twentieth-Century America.* Princeton, N.J.: Princeton University Press, 1967.

———. *Pure Food: Securing the Federal Food and Drugs Act of 1906.* Princeton, N.J.: Princeton University Press, 1989.

Zimmerman, Michael E., J. Baird Callicott, George Sessions, Karen J. Warren, and John Clark, eds., *Environmental Philosophy: From Animal Rights to Radical Ecology.* Englewood Cliffs, N.J.: Prentice-Hall, 1993.

INDEX

About the Author

BRIAN BLACK is associate professor in the departments of history and environmental studies at Penn State University, Altoona. He is the author of *PETROLIA: The Landscape of America's First Oil Boom*.

The Greenwood Press
Nature and the Environment in Everyday Life Series

Nature and the Environment in Nineteenth-Century American Life
Brian Black